"I THOUGHT POCAHONTAS WAS A MOVIE."*

"I THOUGHT POCAHONTAS WAS A MOVIE."*

Perspectives on Race/Culture Binaries in Education and Service Professions

Edited by Carol Schick and James McNinch

University of Regina

CPRC PRESS

Printed and bound in Canada at Friesens. This book is printed on 100% post-consumer recycled paper.

Cover and text design by Duncan Campbell. Editor for the Press: Donna Grant.

Library and Archives Canada Cataloguing in Publication

"I thought Pocahontas was a movie" : perspectives on race/culture binaries in education and service professions / edited by Carol Schick and James McNinch.

(University of Regina publications, ISSN 1480-000 ; 22) Includes bibliographical references and index. ISBN 978-0-88977-211-3

1. Native peoples—Canada—Social conditions. 2. Native peoples—Education—Canada. 3. Native peoples—Civil rights—Canada. 4. Canada—Race relations. 5. Discrimination in education—Canada. 6. Equality—Canada. I. Schick, Carol II. McNinch, James, 1947– III. Series: University of Regina publications ; 22

E78.C212 2009   305.897'071   C2009-904817-5

Canadian Plains Research Center
University of Regina
Regina, Saskatchewan
Canada, S4S 0A2
TEL: (306) 585-4758
FAX: (306) 585-4699
E-MAIL: canadian.plains@uregina.ca
WEB: www.cprc.uregina.ca
www.cprcpress.com

We acknowledge the financial support of the Government of Canada through the Book Publishing Industry Development Program (BPIDP) for our publishing activities. We also acknowledge the support of the Canada Council for the Arts for our publishing program.

 Canadian Heritage / Patrimoine canadien   Canada Council for the Arts / Conseil des Arts du Canada

Mixed Sources
Cert no. SW-COC-001271
© 1996 FSC
FSC

CONTENTS

ACKNOWLEDGEMENTS

From concept to cover, publishing a book is a collective endeavour, but it is especially so when it has its genesis in a conference. This book was conceived at the sixth annual Canadian Critical Race Conference of the Researchers and Academics of Colour for Equality (RACE) held in Regina, Saskatchewan, in 2006. The editors and authors would like to thank the organizers and sponsors of that conference, which proved to be a fertile seedbed for the growth and development of this collection of essays. In turn, we would like to thank each author for his or her patience and persistence through the often-laborious peer review and editing processes to produce this substantive and provocative volume. Two papers that arose out of the conference and which were selected for inclusion in this volume have been previously published elsewhere. Because their arguments are germane to the overall tenor and thesis of this collection, we are grateful to the publishers for their permission to reprint them here.

We appreciate the sponsorship of the conference and subsequent financial support provided by the Centre for Social Justice and Anti-Oppressive Education located in the Faculty of Education at the University of Regina.

We are indebted to the Canadian Plains Research Center and, in the first instance, Brian Mlazgar, CPRC Publications Manager, for believing in the worth and quality of this project. Duncan Campbell, CPRC Art Co-ordinator, thank you for your arresting cover design and your suggestion for a provocative title. We would particularly like to thank Donna Grant, CPRC Senior Editor, firstly for positioning herself as a most careful and attentive reader and, as a result, helping us to provide coherence and consistency across the chapters and helping us to avoid academic jargon and shorthand. Secondly, Donna navigated us through the many steps to publication including copy-editing, design, layout, final proofs, production and marketing. Thank you, Donna, for your astute guidance on this journey.

We would like to acknowledge the work of Dr. Lisa Comeau, former research associate of the Centre for Social Justice and Anti-Oppressive Education. Lisa started this project as one of our co-editors and initiated the first contacts with conference participants to solicit manuscripts and then began the peer review and editing process. Lisa had to let this work go when she moved to Ottawa to become a senior researcher with Human Resources and Skills Development Canada. We miss her good judgement, scholarly opinion and sense of humour. Lisa knows many of these articles well and we hope, as our friend and colleague, that she is as pleased with the final product as we are.

Finally, we appreciate the tried and untiring support of Dan Coggins and Michael Hamann and the encouragement and kindness of friends. Thank you.

Carol Schick and James McNinch

A NOTE ABOUT THE TITLE . . .

The title of this collection is taken from the title of Chapter 10 by James McNinch. McNinch applies discourse analysis to an infamous sexual assault trial involving three white prairie "boys" in their twenties and a 12-year-old First Nations girl. "I thought Pocahontas was a movie" was a comment one of these men made to/about the girl, essentially his "pickup line." McNinch argues that, in context, the comment may well have been intended as a compliment, and even received by the girl as such; nonetheless, it stereotypes racial difference and defines power relationships. This pickup line, then—just six words—can be seen to symbolize a flawed white masculinity that is nevertheless dominant and excused, no matter how it is performed. Further, the sexual assault trial that provides the context for this symbolic line has itself become a tragic metaphor of the contemporary power relations between First Nations people and white settler descendants. As such, those six words— "I thought Pocahontas was a movie"—capture the essence of the race/culture divide and provide an apt title for this book, through which we seek not to avoid that divide, but to acknowledge it and deliberately to engage ourselves and our readers in this country's continuing struggle with its colonial past.

INTRODUCTION

This collection follows from a conference held at the University of Regina on the topic of how inequality based on racial and/or cultural identifications can be addressed in practical and theoretical terms within and across professions such as education—including both public school-based and higher education—the law and helping professions. Even though professions have their own codes of conduct, there are fruitful overlaps that can be shared in conceptualizing and troubling the responses of professionals to assumptions of racial, cultural and ethnic differences—including their own.

Public professionals and service providers are authorized by a waiting public to deliver up healthcare, education, economic welfare and civil society to those who are seen to lack these qualities, to those who will be more useful to a civil society if they are healthy, educated and economically secure. Although the conduct of individual professionals may at times be criticized, the role of professions themselves in providing a "public good" largely goes unquestioned. The interest of professional societies in their own ethical standards and moral behaviour is certainly not new, of course; what has changed, however, is that the relational inequality between professionals and those with whom they engage is no longer simply assumed or taken for granted. Rather, the social positioning and divers power relations between professional and client has become something to be investigated because, at a minimum, the effects of unequal relations may be a barrier to effective service.

Questions concerning effective and ethical practice for all professions increasingly take into account the social and historic positions and identities of both practitioners and the people they engage as their various publics, clients and stakeholders. The one in need of professional services has been positioned in the past as a petitioner, a learner, or someone who lacks what the professional has to offer. More recently, he or she might be seen as client, agent and perhaps even employer. Despite this shift in positioning, the majority of interactions in the service professions are not typically characterized by mutuality and empowerment, and more often than not, the relationships between practitioners and their clients continue to reflect differences in social, political and economic power.

The discourses of cultural sensitivity and diversity training describe familiar tropes in the shaping of public attitudes, perhaps the most popular trope being multicultural displays reflecting ethno-cultural differences. One of the purposes of "cultural sensitivity training" is to familiarize one group of people about the "other" by disseminating information that the dominant group is assumed not to know about the cultural traits of "minorities." Depending on the profession, educational training has consisted of particular sets of "cultural competencies" that attend to client diversity in curricula, communication patterns and demonstrations of respect, as well as knowledge of a group's social and cultural history.

One of the purposes of this anthology is to consider whether and to what extent professionals understand that cultural competence, as well intended as this may be, does not adequately address the social, economic and historical politics of the working environment among people who are assumed to be "different" in their encounter with public and service professionals. The anthology stands on the assumption that social difference is constructed on racial, historic, economic and other types of inequalities that will not be remedied simply by a practitioner's cultural awareness.

Why does the notion of "cultural difference" continue to fuel educational perspectives and professional interactions between service providers and racialized others? An answer found within this volume offers that, with culture as an explanation for difference, the basis for inequality can be explored in endless ways that mainly avoid the unequal social, material and ideological conditions that prefigure the client/professional encounter. Although racialized groups are no longer widely portrayed as *biologically* inferior (as a cruder version of racism would have it), the dominant discourses, such as those found in professions, nonetheless perceive subordinate groups as *culturally* inferior, that is, as possessing cultures that are, for instance, overly patriarchal and not reasonable or modern. With dominant white culture as the normative referent, the culture of minorities has been identified as the marker of difference and the "reason" for inequality (O'Connor, Lewis, & Mueller, 2007). Under the thin disguise of culture—aided by elaborate discourses of "culture talk"—unarticulated assumptions of innate racial or biological difference continue to confound the cause and effect of inequality. The effects of racism are often held up as deliberate choices or attributes of cultural practices, as if First Nations peoples, for example, would *choose* poverty as a way of life. "Culture talk" discursively eliminates racialization and the effects of racism as a variable of difference from "proper" professional dialogue. Attributing inequality to cultural differences is not only unproductive, but also actively misleading. Discourses for examining the effects of structural and "commonsense racism" are less readily available for examining how race has constructed experiences of otherness from colonial times. "Cultural difference" as an explanation for inequality does not begin to account for discrepant outcomes of professional interventions in healthcare, education or social services.

Furthermore, when "culture" is used in an essentialist way, cultural practices stand outside of critical analysis. Deference that places cultural practices beyond scrutiny fixes culture as if it were a bounded, definitional, unchanging quality. When culture trumps critique because "culture is destiny," it parallels the previously dismissed idea of "race as biology" as a force for shaping social relations in deterministic ways. The outcome limits the discourses open to discussion, as if one's culture encompassed all identities. What can't be talked about are inequalities and hierarchies of class, gender, sexual orientation and other distinctions within group formation. St. Denis (2007) explains that marginalized women are accused of being disloyal to their communities when they talk about inequality or violence between male and female group members. The particular identifications of a marginalized woman or a racial minority gay man who are cautioned not to open their group to public scrutiny are glossed under cultural determinism. When professionals are ready to accept simplistic notions of others, there is little nuance for identifications outside of culture.

In spite of considerable critique of cultural training, most professional education typically sets out to do the following: develop sensitivity towards, appreciation for, understanding of and knowledge about "the other." The assumption is that this information and heightened awareness will promote a familiarity with and a good feeling towards others; awareness of likes and customs; acknowledgement of past differences and a reduction in hostility—and that all of these will take place if professionals know more about people who are assumed to be unlike them. Yet, a cultural competence method of managing diversity for the purpose of improving professional practice is problematic on many levels, not the least of which is the transmission style of imparting information that renders the knowledge about others available for taking or leaving. This is not unlike the delivery of other types of knowledge that will ostensibly improve one's life, such as knowing how to stay on a diet, keep to a budget, exercise regularly, stop smoking, stop speeding on the highway or change any other long-standing practices that persist in spite of knowledge to the contrary. The optimistic dream of public education is that information delivery will save us: if only we can learn enough about a topic, we will think more clearly and make better choices. The information provided in cultural training, then, is served up as a lack of knowledge that, if it could be overcome, would accomplish a change of heart, mind and behaviour on the part of the professional towards those in need who are said to be diverse. The purpose of diversity training is to promote prejudice management; it is not equipped to deliver a critical social analysis or to educate professionals about their own complicity in reproducing unequal systems.

Perhaps the most important limitation of diversity training that describes the preferences and cultural details of others, also called "education *about* the other" (Kumashiro, 2000), is that difference is assumed to reside *in the other*. This orientation persists in the assumption that the practitioners themselves are fine the way they are, that contagion and difference, indeed otherness itself, must be managed, confined and regulated if it cannot be entirely eliminated.

"Overcoming" ethnic/cultural/racial difference has been a force behind the education of public professionals during their pre-service and in-service education and apprenticeship programs. Despite the fact that cultural display as mentioned above, and its promotion of mutual familiarity, is often recognized as a cliché, the tenacity of this assumption is not easily dislodged. Its persistence in higher education and various professional education programs is fuelled in part by the multicultural narratives of modernity and citizenship at the heart of North American nation building. In performing their roles of managing difference, professions are publicly authorized to participate in "civilizing" and improving the "other." Professional practice serves to define social reality and participate in the project of state regulation. In the national narrative, where hegemonic inequalities are part of the social fabric, raising the topic of fundamental social inequality is taken as a sign of overreacting, and is further evidence of not understanding how "things are done." The persistence of a cultural cure is grounded, therefore, in the assumption that professionals don't need to change because difference (the problem) resides in the other.

To state that all peoples have "culture" is to state the obvious. Nonetheless, white people often struggle to name or describe their culture, as if it were a separate part of how their lives are lived. Many people of European descent otherwise default to a particular ethno-cultural group or identify as middle class or "average" or "normal" or "mainstream." The largely unnamed presence of dominating cultural norms, such as whiteness, is more visible to those who are outside of a particular version of its "normative" cultural identities and practices, examples of which include masculinity, whiteness, heteronormativity, able-bodiedness, or being middle class, Christian or English-speaking. It is a hegemonic assumption that dominant cultural practices are neutral or natural, that any departures from "mainstream" are worthy of note and that "difference" resides *outside* of dominance. Hegemonic cultures that reside in professional practices—such as in education, the law and other helping professions—are steeped in dominant cultural norms and unequal power relations that go largely unacknowledged as the constructed cultural productions that they are. Practices of domination embedded in normative systems render it easy to overlook or ignore inequality and to explain differences as individual group preferences and idiosyncrasies. Therefore, deconstructing the hegemonies of dominant cultures is an example of how the focus on culture can be used to advance equitable professional practices. In this respect, however, culture is not neutral, but is affixed to power relations and productive of social and material practices that construct differences in everyday ways. Zeus Leonardo (2004) offers a method of showcasing cultural dominance in a way that does not reify it, but rather illustrates the deliberate construction of inequality that passes for routine, commonplace social practice. Sense of place and cultural context, including hegemonic power relations, is inevitably what allows dominant groups to feel at home in North American culture, to the extent that white culture is difficult to see from the inside.

When we ignore the effects of unnamed dominance that operate as white supremacy, that dominance is unassailable as well as unavailable for discussion. Without a post-colonial critique of unequal power relations, "difference" in the professional encounter is marked by the persistent otherness of the client that must be addressed by cultural knowledge. A cultural explanation of "difference" in the encounter, however, undermines the ability of non-dominant groups to name serious and legitimate issues of discrimination on the basis of race. Instead, the culture of the other *is* the problem to be overcome; and racial and cultural minorities must rely on well-meaning and empathetic professionals who see them as "other." It must be said, however, that even if cultural awareness of racial and minority peoples is ineffective as a way of promoting just social relations, knowledge of one's *own* cultural history, background, ethos and customs has been important for many racialized and dominated groups in claiming their dignity and voice. Increasingly, the performance of culture is a political stand and a reminder of the rights and claims of minority people, especially for indigenous Canadians. Appreciating one's own culture and demonstrating it for others are ways of solidifying group identity and laying claim to dignity and due respect.

Examining cultural assumptions and teaching critically through particular cultural lenses can be helpful for addressing inequality. A social/critical perspective is especially useful because it recognizes that culture is an organic, fluid process that constructs and describes the economic, social and historic milieu of individuals or a people at any one moment. Thus, a social/critical perspective sees indigenous knowledge as a living process and not merely an icon of the past. The best exploration of indigenous knowledge also includes the ability to critique it, rather than treating knowledge and the cultures it represents as closed systems of meaning and interpretation. The work of Paulo Freire (1970) and a recent volume by Jeffrey Duncan-Andrade and Ernest Morrell (2008) exemplify the long-standing practices of using social and cultural analysis to deconstruct inequality critically. The field of critical race theory takes as its central concern the critical examination of daily racism; it is one example of how the taken-for-grantedness of racial inequality can become the starting point of social analysis and experience.

In a number of different ways, the chapters of this book take up the challenges and complexities inherent in addressing inequality based on cultural and racial identifications. The first chapter, "Language as an agent of division in Saskatchewan schools," draws on research conducted by author **ANDREA STERZUK** in a community school in a small city in east-central Saskatchewan where the author herself grew up as a descendant of white settlers. Sterzuk writes, "My time in this particular school left me with the impression that First Nations and Métis students are perceived by many white settler educators as arriving at school with limited language abilities. Further, the students' lack of experience with written language use is seen as a deficit rather than as a difference." Sterzuk's research draws on the work of Purcell-Gates (2002); in this article, Sterzuk documents how a deficit model affects the teachers' expectations of a student's abilities. She argues that narrow views of what constitutes literacy, coupled with well-intentioned but misguided "cultural remedies," not only reflect the biases and belief systems of white settler teachers but also contribute to institutional racism and systemic inequality. Sterzuk concludes: "If settler schools in Saskatchewan wish to move towards creating equitable outcomes for all students, the white settler gaze will need to turn away from perceived deficits in indigenous homes and look towards the deficits in current literacy practices in settler elementary classrooms in Saskatchewan."

Chapter 2, "Lost in translation: Anti-racism and the perils of knowledge" by **JENNIFER NELSON**, trolls in the gulf between theory and practice and between race and culture in hospital-based research and healthcare. Nelson situates herself struggling in these lived dichotomies and asks salient questions: what counts as research? what counts as knowledge? how do we seek thoughtful reflection and long-term understandings in light of the pressure to have "fast demonstrable solutions to what are framed as problems of 'cultural difference'"? Nelson is concerned with interrogating the relationship between what funding agencies and institutions call "knowledge translation," on the one hand, and the supposedly commonsense ideas surrounding "cultural competence" on the other. Both approaches, she contends, preclude a "necessarily complex consideration of racism" in professional practice. The urge for "objective science" to find "quick answers" to complex issues in the healthcare field is only one of the problems Nelson discusses. She explains how culturalist approaches to knowledge entrench the notion that culture can be generalized, understood and accommodated, and that "diversity" can be managed through better practice and policy. "Culture is employed not only as an explanation for health disparities and inequalities in service provision, but for deflecting attention from racism itself." Reflecting on many of the issues, Nelson concludes that continued, complex conversations are crucial and will need to be "very much grounded in concrete problems and sites.... if problematizing knowledge has no bearing on the 'real world,' we have far greater chasms than translation can bridge."

FRÉDÉRIC DUPRÉ is the author of "From racism to critical dialogue in the academy: Challenges of national minorities at the University of Regina." This third chapter examines the University of Regina and its relationships with the post-secondary institutions of three Canadian founding peoples in a minority setting: the First Nations, the Métis and the Fransaskois. Dupré contends that "the presence of the First Nations University of Canada, the Gabriel Dumont Institute, and the *Institut Français* on the University of Regina campus has shaped the history ... and the identity of this university." Dupré argues that because this reality has not been recognized as a relationship amongst equals, minorities are still oppressed, for while the university celebrates "cultural diversity," it does so on its own terms. As a result, minority status difference "is still a factor of exclusion and separation, a new commodity in the market economy." The challenge for these minorities is in operating and managing their own institutions within a partnership with the institution that once excluded them, while maintaining a strong link with their own peoples. Outlining the history of the relationship of each of these institutions with the University of Regina, Dupré, following Bourdieu (2001), sees examples of the commodification of diversity that has led to the reproduction of social discrimination. "[B]y selecting which cultural heritages it privileges, the university community segregates cultural minorities and maintains specific power relations embedded in social institutions." Dupré calls for constructive dialogue amongst all the parties and concludes that it is time to "reinvent the academy in positive ways and contribute to liberating its knowledge of racist residues."

Chapter 4 focuses this discussion of minorities in a particular academic discipline. "A circle is more than a straight line curved: Mis(sed)understanding about First Nations science" by **ALISON SAMMEL** shows how exclusion and marginalization occurs within the discipline of Western science. She contends that Western science is a highly privileged social construction rather than being a neutral finder, indicator and communicator of truth. "Far from being objective, science and science education reflect a particular paradigm founded upon a political, economic and classist colonial legacy.... [and] have served certain peoples to the detriment or exclusion of others." Sammel understands, too, how she is implicated in this process as a white female science educator, but "I believe science education needs to illustrate how the current relationships between rationality, nature, culture and science are not 'naturally' linked but are constructed within the boundaries and influences of a certain historical period." Sammel discusses the qualitative research she did with three distinct groups of science education students—First Nations students, Métis students, and descendants of white settlers. Her research shows that the inclusion of First Nations science content in the academy can be seen as "rooted in culturalist and revivalist discourses and therefore embodies a deficit approach." Sammel calls for a critique of Western science as well as what passes as First Nations science, and, citing Cajete (2000), she makes the case for a non-Western or "Native or First Nations science" that is ontologically different from Western science.

In Chapter 5, "Encountering strangers: Teaching difference in the social work classroom," **DONNA JEFFERY** extends this discussion from the perspective of someone teaching in a professional school. Like Sammel, Jeffery asked students to reflect on their educational experiences. As a professor of social work, she is concerned with how to dismantle the certainty of the caregiver subject as expert and the client as a fragmented, needy stranger. She asks, "What pedagogical strategies might be best deployed in this education for recreating a subject who is less compelled towards certainty?" What are the interconnections between "experience, empathy and judgement" in the classroom and the way these play out as students anticipate, "with some anxiety, the encounter between themselves and the mythical (un)knowable 'client' other." Too often in the classroom, the dominant culture is unnamed and unproblematized, as if only racialized persons possess cultures. In such a construct, the culture of the other becomes a "problem" defined against white, Western standards. Similarly, Jeffery helps to expose the limitations of experience and empathy in anti-oppressive practice. It is not the experience itself but how we think about it and tend to privilege it that is important. Students who call for a "gentler classroom" are struggling with the tension and complexity of "pedagogies that implicate us in social practices of marginalization." Jeffery offers critical autobiography as a pedagogical method that can help students to reflect on their experiences and at the same time, and even more importantly, show how experience is not just something that happens to a person because in itself it is a discursive form of social production.

More radically than Dupré or Sammel, **ANDREA SMITH** in Chapter 6, "Native studies beyond the academic-industrial complex," continues the interrogation of the commodified positions that race and culture take in the academy. She finds that the assumption of a split between "activism and academic knowledge speaks to the problematic way Native American studies in particular, and ethnic studies in general, have been articulated." Smith argues that an emphasis on epistemological ways of knowing difference, rather than on the performativity of the lived lives of Native peoples, essentializes knowledge as static content. "To understand fully, to 'know' Native peoples, is the manner in which the dominant society gains a sense of mastery and control over them." Thus, while Native studies implies and calls for an essential difference, which Native peoples are supposed to represent within the academy, it is not, however, "expected to challenge the manner in which the academy is itself based fundamentally on the structures of white supremacy and colonialism." Asking if the academy can be decolonized, Smith proposes that community activism, rather than social elitism, should animate academic work, moving beyond anti-racist work to movement building, using models found outside America and outside academia. Smith suggests that "Native studies and ethnic studies are marginalized within the academy because they are not tied to mass movements for social change," and she concludes with the thoughts of Beth Richie, who offers that the goal of Native studies is not about diversity or inclusion: "it is about liberation."

In Chapter 7, "The more things change... The endurance of 'culturalism' in social work and healthcare," **DONNA JEFFERY** and **JENNIFER NELSON** explore critical questions relating to the role of "culture" in the delivery of service to marginalized groups. "Culture itself, as a social category, has been highly contested due in part to a fundamental lack of clarity over its various meanings and deployments." They ask what the ongoing appeal is of culture-based approaches to understanding problems and providing services when we know that focusing on culture often fails to acknowledge race and poverty as real barriers for the marginalized.

"Cultural competence" in the helping professions has often "failed to consider how contemporary racism is expressed through a language of culture." Jeffery and Nelson are quick to acknowledge that cultural revitalization, for some indigenous populations, has provided a "powerful response to the institutional and structural devastation of colonialism" and should not be dismissed without careful scrutiny. They also believe it is important to resist the demand that all teaching or research in the professions translate into a skill or "outcome." "Centrally, we think it is important to resist the notion that mere critical thinking is somehow antithetical to change." They argue that it is possible to develop skills for professional practice while also employing critical and post-colonial theories "that have new things to teach us about culture and race." Like Lather (2001), the authors conclude that we must "unveil and contest the implicit essentialist categories in the knowledge we produce, while also working to connect theory to lived experience and to account for people's identities in specific historical contexts."

Chapter 8, "Well-intentioned pedagogies that forestall change" by **CAROL SCHICK**, is concerned with how identities are produced and performed. She starts by explaining how and why her students in the field of teacher education are invited "to explore the fluid nature ... and ... impossible fictions of their own identifications and subjectivities." In this context, Schick proceeds to investigate both culturalist and anti-racist discourses and to ask how these two discursive approaches "promote or detract from the goal of socially just teaching." Schick contends that it is necessary to understand the particular context of such discourses to appreciate how both culturalist and anti-racist approaches to pedagogy and curriculum may have "unintended consequences that are counterproductive to the process of decolonizing schooling practices." We can move forward if we understand that "in its embodied form, the identity of teacher" is learned and performed and assessed through normative expectations. Schick quotes Fuss (1995)—"identification has a history—a colonial history"—to emphasize that there are benefits as well as limitations to learning "for and about the other," as Kumashiro (2000) says. Part of the problem is that students who take up culturalist or anti-racist approaches are then in a position to perform as "good citizen" and "good teacher"—"in their care to 'do the right thing,' they also become better at being white." One of Schick's conclusions is that white teachers, including herself, "in this historic and geographic location, ... are socially positioned as settler colonizers because and in spite of our social histories and chosen means of identifications." Schick concludes that we must continually ask ourselves, "Who do you think you are?" and forever problematize the answers.

JOYCE GREEN, in Chapter 9, takes us outside the academy to interrogate racism in the "real world." "From *Stonechild* to social cohesion: Anti-racist challenges for Saskatchewan" challenges the context of Aboriginal-settler relations in Saskatchewan by studying the judicial inquiry into the death by freezing, in Saskatoon, of an Aboriginal man, Neil Stonechild. Illustrating clearly how the personal tragedy of one marginalized individual has become a political agenda for all of us, Green argues that Neil Stonechild's death and the subsequent revelations, denials, obfuscations and deliberations surrounding the suspect circumstances of his death are exemplars of the racism inherent in our colonial heritage. In the final report of the inquiry Green sees examples of structural, institutional and individual racism and notes that "cultural differences" have become a code for a neutral façade of a "less explicit racism." Green goes on to argue, in light of "the demographic trajectory, which indicates a majority Aboriginal population in the near future" in Saskatchewan, that a "failure to deal with white racism will guarantee social stresses between Aboriginal and non-Aboriginal populations." Ominously, Green argues that the criminal activities of Aboriginal gangs, including prostitution and drugs, "have fused identity and resistance with the sordid side of gang life to create a form of loyalty against the oppressor." Green concludes that a systemic process of decolonization is a "necessary political project to eradicate the kinds of systemic practices that arguably killed Neil Stonechild" and others.

JAMES MCNINCH, in the final chapter, "'I thought Pocahontas was a movie': Using critical discourse analysis to understand race and sex as social constructs," moves us out of the classroom and through the courtroom into contemporary social reality. McNinch examines testimony given in the criminal trials resulting from the sexual assault in 2001 of a 12-year-old Aboriginal girl by three men of Saskatchewan white settler stock. He suggests that a "cross-cultural" sexual assault case allows us to question the illusion of objectivity embedded in legal culture and to interrogate coercive functions of law. The transcripts provide opportunities to see "how gender, race, sex and class are linguistically and textually mediated processes rather than pre-discursive identities." McNinch argues that by using critical discourse analysis, we might better understand how white privilege, as a racialized construct, is normalized in the everyday. Critical race theorists Crenshaw and Peller (1993) write that "at stake at each axis of conflict is a contest over whose narrative structure will prevail in the interpretation of events in the social world" (p. 283). McNinch first asks how, in this particular axis of conflict, these three men and this one girl embodied and then related and transcribed the experience. He then asks how the lawyers, judge and jury vicariously experienced the "incident." Finally, he asks how all of the players, both first and second hand, "made sense of" and constructed the events of the evening of the sexual assault. For McNinch, this case reveals that there are at least four "frames" for better understanding white privilege: "(1) the history of colonization and immigration in this country, (2) the homosociality of male heterosexuality, (3) embodied and vicarious linguistic interpretations of 'reality,' and (4) the social and cultural practice of the law itself."

Our goal in this volume is not to pit discourses of anti-racist/anti-oppressive pedagogies against discourses of cultural familiarity and relevance as if they were binaries and opposites. While they are distinct approaches, clearly both are useful, and both have limitations. What emerges from these discussions is an understanding that there is no neutral space in what or how we teach or practice. Professional education, in its practices and in its discourses, has already been shaped through colonialism, immigration and other relations of empire, and the assumptions that accompany these existing structures tend to impede our attempts to promote justice and equality for all members of our society. The possibility of justice can only be realized by first exposing and critiquing these assumptions and structures and disrupting our accustomed ways of understanding ourselves and our society. To that end, this volume is an attempt to disrupt our own professional practices and those of our students, and thus to come a little closer to the justice and equality we seek.

REFERENCES

Bourdieu, P. (2001). *Masculine domination.* (R. Nice, Trans.). Stanford CA: Stanford University Press.

Cajete, G. (2000). *Native science: Natural laws of interdependence.* Santa Fe, NM: Clear Light Publishers.

Crenshaw, K., & Peller, G. (1993). Reel time/Real justice. In R. Gooding-Williams (Ed.), *Reading Rodney King, reading urban uprising* (pp. 56-70). New York: Routledge.

Duncan-Andrade, J., & Morrell, E. (2008). *The art of critical pedagogy: Possibilities for moving from theory to practice in urban schools.* New York: Peter Lang.

Freire, P. (1970). *Pedagogy of the oppressed.* New York: Herder and Herder.

Fuss, D. (1995). *Identification papers.* New York: Routledge.

Kumashiro, K. (2000). Toward a theory of anti-oppressive education. *Review of Educational Research, 70*(7), 25-53.

Lather, P. (2001). Postbook: Working the ruins of feminist ethnography. *Signs, 27*(1) 199-227.

Leonardo, Z. (2004). The color of supremacy: Beyond the discourse of white privilege. In Z. Leonardo (Ed.), *Critical pedagogy and race* (pp. 37-52). Malden, MA: Blackwell.

O'Connor, C., Lewis, A., & Mueller, J. (2007). Researching "black" educational experiences and outcomes: Theoretical and methodological considerations. *Educational Researcher, 36*(9), 541–552.

Purcell-Gates, V. (2002). "...As soon as she opened her mouth!" In L. Delpit and J. K. Dowdy (Eds.), *The skin that we speak: Thoughts on language and culture in the classroom* (pp. 121-142). New York: New Press.

Smith, J. (2005). Indigenous performance and aporetic texts. *Union Seminary Quarterly Review, 59*(1,2) 114-124.

St. Denis, V. (2007). Feminism is for everybody: Aboriginal women, feminism and diversity. In J. Green (Ed.), *Making space for indigenous feminism* (pp. 33-52). Black Point, NS: Fernwood Publishing.

CHAPTER 1
LANGUAGE AS AN AGENT OF DIVISION IN SASKATCHEWAN SCHOOLS

Andrea Sterzuk

The western Canadian province of Saskatchewan is sandwiched between the provinces of Alberta and Manitoba and lies north of the American states of Montana and North Dakota. In terms of geographical features, no real obstacles such as mountain ranges or large bodies of water divide this prairie region. Saskatchewan's borders, created by colonial powers, are straight lines that form the shape of an A-line skirt, a fact I appreciated as a small child when I had to draw maps of my province. Yet, despite the smooth lines of its borders, a very real divide exists between the settlers and the indigenous peoples who inhabit this space. This division is created and maintained through practices and policies of social institutions in Saskatchewan, including those practices found in public schooling. In this chapter, I describe some of the ways that educator beliefs and institutional practices regarding language variation and literacy development help to perpetuate inequity between settlers and indigenous peoples in the social institution of Saskatchewan schools.

Saskatchewan is a province of indigenous peoples and settlers, the latter including both families who have lived here for generations and those who are relative newcomers. Results from the Statistics Canada 2001 census (Statistics Canada, 2003) indicate that 84 percent of people living in Saskatchewan self-identify as being of *European origin* (white settler). The next largest group is made up of those who identify as *North American Indian, Métis,* or *Inuit* (indigenous peoples); these three groups make up 14 percent of the Saskatchewan population. Saskatchewan residents who self-identify as belonging to *other visible minority groups* constitute 2 percent of the population. While these statistics help us to understand who lives on the Saskatchewan post-colonial landscape, they tell us little of what these lives are like. Let me paint part of that picture with some broad brush strokes, by summarizing three documents that address the issue of discrimination in Canada.

A 2002 press release issued by the United Nations Committee on the Elimination of Racial Discrimination (CERD) indicates that Canada's problems related to racial discrimination include: deaths among indigenous peoples in custody, unresolved indigenous land title claims, high rates of black and indigenous peoples as prisoners, high poverty rates among recent immigrants, "mass" deportation of the Jamaican diaspora and the high number of indigenous peoples who are homeless in urban areas (CERD, 2002). The second document is an Amnesty International Canada (AIC) report indicating that four groups in Canada experience the effects of discrimination: indigenous peoples, refugees, migrant workers and communities targeted by hate crimes. The report further describes a number of human rights violations including: discriminatory attitudes and practices of police, arbitrary application of law, stereotyping of refugees and closing of borders, lack of access to legal services, migrant women in the sex trade, holocaust denial and prosecution of hate criminals (AIC, 2002). The third document is a report specific to the experiences of indigenous peoples. Compiled by a group of community-based indigenous peoples and Canadian human rights organizations, it addresses Canada's violations of the *International Convention on the Elimination of All Forms of Racial Discrimination*. Indigenous peoples in Canada are now often described as "Fourth World" peoples, that is, nations without a state, and this report links their economic, social and cultural experiences to oppressive treatment by Canadian institutions (CERD Report Ad Hoc National Network, 2002). Let's examine now one of these institutions— public schooling—and ask this important question: What role do schools have in creating and maintaining inequity in opportunities for settler and indigenous peoples in Saskatchewan?

Institutional racism, school literacy practices and inequity in Saskatchewan schools

Schools are locations where children are socialized into behaviours and beliefs that are carried with them into adult life. In my research, I describe some of the ways that educator beliefs and institutional practices regarding language variation and literacy development help to perpetuate and maintain the race divide in Saskatchewan schools. Many language researchers and theorists have documented the relationship between language and power (Heath, 1986; Kouritzin, 1999; Miller, 1999; Norton Peirce, 1995; Pavlenko, 2002). In order to explain the links between language and literacy practices in schools and the race divide in the Saskatchewan context, I link examples from my research to the existing body of literature concerning language and power. In this section, I illustrate how the ways in which education professionals engage with issues of race, culture, language and power in Saskatchewan schools contribute to an unequal division of opportunities between white settler and indigenous peoples.

Second language education researcher Jim Cummins defines institutional racism as "ideologies and structures which are systematically used to legitimize unequal division of power and resources between groups which are defined on the basis of race" (2000, p. 131). The examples in this chapter are taken from a qualitative classroom study I conducted in an urban Saskatchewan school. Through this discussion, I will make visible some of the institutional practices that serve to create and maintain the race divide in Saskatchewan.

The First Nations students involved in my research speak a variety of English called Indigenous English. The term *language variety* is more neutral than the more commonly used term *dialect* (Wardhaugh, 2002). While both terms are used to show differences between varieties of a language, the term *dialect* carries pejorative meaning in that it indicates that one variety is superordinate or standard, while other varieties of the language are subordinate or non-standard. As a linguistic system, Indigenous English differs from English varieties spoken by settlers (Dubois, 1978; Heit & Blair, 1993; Leap, 1993; Olson Flanigan, 1987; Schilling-Estes, 2000; Sterzuk, 2003, 2007; Wolfram, 1984). In the post-structuralist view of language, language use is thought to be fluid, with speakers crossing between languages, language varieties and social registers seamlessly. So it would be a mistake to claim that all indigenous peoples are unilingual speakers of Indigenous English. Some might be fluent in Indigenous English and a settler variety of English (bidialectal), others may be speakers of an English variety often associated with settlers, and others may speak an indigenous language, Indigenous English and an English variety typically spoken by settlers. Any and all of these combinations are possible. It is also important to note that Indigenous English is best thought of as a spectrum of English varieties that reflects community influences of indigenous languages or French, among other factors.

Robust educational research links teacher expectations of minority language students to student performance (Cecil, 1988; Chambers et al., 2004; Crago, 1992; Eller, 1989; Ford, 1984; Ghosh, 2002; Tollefson, 2002; Wolfram et al., 1999). A child's language and behaviour in the classroom influences a teacher's perceptions of the student's potential. Teacher expectations of a student, in turn, influence the performance of the child. Awareness of the link between educator perceptions of minority language students and student performance is what prompted me to interview educators regarding their awareness of Indigenous English. An earlier paper by Mary Heit and Heather Blair (1993) describes the stigmatization of indigenous students in Saskatchewan because of the way they use the English language. My area of study investigates the assumption—held by the majority population—that the language variety of minority students is a deviant form of English.

This research into educational practices involving language and literacy development was conducted in a school community where I spent three months as a researcher and classroom volunteer. The school neighbourhood consists of mainly low-income families: white settler, Métis and First Nations. There is some gentrification occurring in one area of the neighbourhood, but not within walking distance of the school. As you drive along the streets, hints of how decades of oppression affect marginalized peoples can be glimpsed in the dilapidated state of houses and the absence of any commercial enterprise; the closest thing to a store is the Salvation Army thrift shop. Urban planning websites indicate that average family incomes for homes in the three neighbourhoods in which the school's students live range from $26,753 to $32,690, while the average family income for the city is $62,451. The school lies at the centre of this neighbourhood and provides education from pre-kindergarten through to grade 8. Each classroom has roughly 20–23 students. In terms of the student population, 67 percent self-identify as First Nations or Métis.

I spent most of my time in a grade 3/4 classroom. The teacher was a First Nations woman named Deborah Desjarlais,[1] with over ten years of teaching experience, herself a bidialectal speaker of Indigenous English and an English variety typically spoken by settlers. She is also fluent in her native Saulteaux language. Student participants in this classroom included First Nations, Métis and white settler children, eight to ten years old. The total number of students in the classroom throughout the three months that I was present was 25. This number, however, fluctuated, as four students arrived later in the study and two students also left before the study was complete.

During the three months that I spent in the classroom, I maintained an observational logbook in which I focused on classroom language, language behaviour, student-to-student interactions, student-to-teacher interactions and literacy practices. In addition to keeping observational logbooks, I conducted interviews with ten educators: four indigenous and six white settler educators. Semi-structured interviews using questions adapted from Gary Plank (1994) were conducted with these educators in an effort to discern attitudes and perceptions of language. The tapes of the interviews were transcribed in order to facilitate the analysis of reoccurring patterns in educator responses to my questions. A number of themes emerged from the analysis of interview transcripts and observational logbooks; this chapter offers examples related to educator expectations and beliefs around First Nations students' literacy development and educator awareness of Indigenous English.

Being a speaker of an English variety that is not the English variety valued by a school system can affect the literacy development of students in a number of ways (Roy, 1987; Wolfram et al., 1999). Children who speak language varieties such as Indigenous English or African American English do not automatically become fluent in the language variety valued by an educational system simply upon entering school (Roy, 1987). Many linguists and educational researchers

---

1.   Pseudonyms are used for all participants in my study.

argue that fluency of this kind can be achieved only through formal instruction (Delpit, 1988; Wolfram et al., 1999). Lack of fluency in a school-valued language variety may cause interruptions and delays in a student's mastery of literacy skills and, subsequently, subject matter. The white settler, First Nations and Métis educators involved in this study are all aware that many First Nations and Métis students at their school speak a variety of English that differs from the English spoken by white settlers. While awareness of linguistic and discourse differences is apparent, this consciousness does not necessarily extend to an understanding of Indigenous English as a language variety or to appropriate interpretations of language and literacy development.

Rebecca Eller (1989) claims that the view of a particular language variety as substandard is evidence of educator bias and suggests that the tendency to label children as verbally inept is a result of the majority's need for these children to conform to the majority linguistic models. The perpetuation of the language deficit theory among educators is germane to this chapter. None of the educators with whom I spoke in the school had any awareness of the existence of multiple English language varieties or that differences between language varieties were rule-governed and not simply evidence of "bad English." I found educators who openly discussed the "deficit" in First Nations and Métis students' language, as if it were a fact. Alternately, I also found educators who, while not familiar with the idea of language varieties, were open to my explanations of Indigenous English and very surprised that they had never been provided with a copy of Saskatchewan Learning's curricular document, *Language Arts for Indian and Métis students: A guide for adapting English Language Arts* (Saskatchewan Learning, 1994).

The following educator comments came from interviews with two white settler educators, Anita and Lisa. In the first utterance, Anita's statement regarding language was in response to my question about possible factors contributing to higher rates of *retention,* that is, holding a child back from advancing to the next grade, among indigenous students than among white settler children in the school. Anita explained this pattern in the following way:

> ANITA: I think that, again, [this] is because of difference in level of language skills because they do present very different levels. In the past, here, we don't usually retain kids anymore. They, um, I probably have it somewhere if you want, the research done, retaining does not improve anything.

Anita's statement reveals a belief in the prevalence of lower language skills among indigenous students. While it is possible that some students may have delays, I do not think it is fair to describe this as a characteristic common to all indigenous students. Instead, it is more likely that language assessments and teaching methods used are not appropriate for students who do not speak the English language variety valued by schools or who have limited experience with written language use outside school (Purcell-Gates, 2002). Also interesting is Anita's statement regarding the non-retention of students. She was not the only educator to inform me of this school policy, yet I learned of many cases of student retention in conversations with children and educators.

The following response, made by Lisa, whose class, with one exception, is made up of indigenous students, is similar to Anita's in that it attributes limited language skills to First Nations and Métis students.

> ANDREA: Okay, is there anything that you'd like to add that we haven't already talked about or anything that you just want to mention?

> LISA: I, just uh, the importance of the early language because we're feeling the deficits when they get up to grade 2 or 3. They just can't write a proper sentence because they can't speak. They don't speak with complete sentences or they don't, we can't anticipate what word would come next because they don't really use proper grammar necessarily and uh, how do you spell 'gonna,' well it's 'going to,' how do you spell 'grewed,' 'growed.' Well, so it's just a lot, I'm all for the full-time kindergarten for the children that need it, not everybody, but those kids that aren't getting enough language. So starting sooner and keeping the play in the day as well though, so just, all about language development in as many different ways as we can.

Lisa's description of her students' use of language indicates that she attributes their literacy development difficulties to language deficits or delays.

The following comment presents ideas that differ from the above descriptions of Indigenous English as evidence of a language deficit. This comment is taken from an interview with Tom, who is a Métis educator at the school:

> TOM: So if we're trying to encourage these children to speak but every time, you know, they're saying something improperly because it doesn't flow with that certain type of sentence structure that we're expecting. You're closing that bridge um and you're not going to have that language development with that child. You're just going to see deficit every time you sit them down for testing.

I heard similar comments from other First Nations educators at the school. While they did not use the linguistic term *language variety* or describe Indigenous English as rule-governed, they did talk about it as simply the way people speak in their communities. That is not to say that attention is not paid to literacy development by indigenous educators in this school. Rather, *not speaking properly* is not seen by indigenous educators as the largest stumbling block to an indigenous child's progress in school.

In examining reading and literacy education in schools, it is important to question power relations, discourses and the construction of student identities in light of the larger goal of challenging inequality. Misconceptions regarding linguistic equality—when held by educational policy makers, administrators and educators—can affect the literacy, academic and social development of speakers of less valued language varieties. James Berlin (1987) explains that when we teach writing—and I would add reading—we are teaching a version of the world and the student's place in it. With this argument in mind, understanding educator perceptions of literacy development becomes all the more urgent.

My principal source of information regarding how literacy and reading programs are structured in the school was Deborah, the classroom teacher with whom I worked. From my time with her, I was able to see how she worked with the children and gained insight into their past literacy experiences in previous grades. I discovered that, of the approximately 25 students in her class, three had been retained in earlier grades, and these three were all indigenous students. Additionally, regarding speech and language assessment, seven children had been referred for assessment in earlier grades and only one of these children was white settler. These findings are similar to reports I received from other classroom teachers. Based on my interviews, conversations and observations with children and adults, I concluded that First Nations and Métis children experience retentions or speech and language referrals more frequently than white settler children. Deborah, who has been teaching in the school for almost ten years, as well as other educators, confirmed this conclusion.

Children in this school have their reading tested through the use of two standardized tests: Benchmark and Dolch. These tests are used to discern whether a child is at grade level in reading and to uncover which areas of reading are most difficult for a particular child. Children who score below grade level early in the year are tested again in the winter months to ascertain whether or not improvement has been made. What I found particularly interesting during my time in Deborah's class was being able to observe this second series of testing. Interestingly, on the first test, almost all the First Nations and Métis children were one to two years below grade level in their reading abilities. While one or two white settler students had some reading struggles, none of them were a full grade level behind where they were expected to score.

At the time of the second series of testing, conducted by Deborah and the resource room teacher, all the First Nations and Métis children had made huge improvements in their reading abilities such that some were at grade level and others were considered to be only a half year behind. These remarkable test results were what prompted me to focus on literacy development. It became apparent to me that Deborah was doing something differently from the other primary teachers who had taught these children and that her approach was working.

I discussed the test results with Deborah and asked if she could pinpoint one area where First Nations and Métis children seem generally to experience difficulty. All the children had lower scores in the area of reading comprehension. Word recognition and oral reading were not challenges to them, but when it came time to retell stories or answer comprehension questions, the children struggled. The children had the ability to decode language but had not been taught strategies to achieve comprehension. What this tells me is that previous teachers most likely focused on reading attack skills—sounding words out, memorizing words, teaching phonetics—which, when not combined with the teaching of comprehension strategies, result in students who can read but who cannot make sense of what they are reading.

In addition to these reading attack skills, Deborah, in contrast, explicitly teaches her students comprehension strategies that they can use to understand a text. She teaches them to pay attention to titles, to examine pictures; she reminds them of previous experiences they might have had with their families that are similar to what they are reading about; she interrupts a reading to do comprehension checks; and she leads the children in a discussion of the text topic before, during and after reading. In short, she uses all possible means to "front-load" the story and to trigger previous schemas in an effort to enable comprehension by modeling and explaining comprehension strategies to her students. Most important, she believes that all her students, regardless of race or home experiences, have the ability to learn to read and write (Purcell-Gates, 2002).

I asked Deborah about the ideas and goals behind the strategies she uses. She explained that many of the texts her students are expected to read are not culturally appropriate. Whenever possible, she chooses texts that are related to the lived experiences of her students. However, Deborah is also keenly aware that her students will not always be provided with culturally relevant material, and so, she wants them to have the skills to tackle any new reading material.

In large part, I attribute her students' improvements to her intense focus on teaching reading strategies and her positive expectations of them. Additionally, Deborah seems to be aware that her students need to be able to recognize differences between Indigenous English and the English language variety valued by the school. Interestingly, Deborah makes use of many explicit feedback moves described in second language research (Lyster, 2004). On a number of occasions, I witnessed Deborah drawing students' attention to their utterances through the repetition of their words in a questioning tone of voice. Sometimes, the children were able to reproduce the utterance as it would be said in an English variety spoken by settlers; at other times they needed her explicit instruction. In some instances, I heard her explicitly indicate that a word was not used in standard written English by asking a student a question. For example, I heard her ask Crystal: "Do we say *et?*" At this point, Crystal was able to erase *et* from her text and replace it with the settler English equivalent, *ate*.

My impression of Deborah's classroom was that rich learning was taking place in the area of Language Arts. I wondered what was happening in the earlier grades that could help to explain the children's first Benchmark and Dolch scores. It was clear to me from my conversations and interviews with educators that they were not familiar with the Saskatchewan Learning document *Language Arts for Indian and Métis students: A guide for adapting English Language Arts.* This well-crafted document acknowledges the legitimacy of Indigenous English and provides guidelines and sample lesson plans that could positively contribute to developing literacy in Indigenous English-speaking children. To understand better what was happening in other classrooms, I chose to enter into discussions regarding beliefs and practices related to literacy development in my interviews with educators. The following excerpt is from an interview with white settler educator Lisa, whose grade 2 class consisted of 18 First Nations students and 1 white settler student:

ANDREA: And have any of these children repeated kindergarten or grade 1?

LISA : Let me, I always have to go through the class, one, two, three, four, five, five off the top of my head, this one is going to repeat this year, six, without checking their files I would say 6 out of 19 have repeated already.

ANDREA : And you say that that's mostly due to literacy development?

LISA: Yeah, yeah, they come in, they have significant delays in all literacy areas, in speech patterns, articulation, vocabulary, um, listening skills, if you read a story, they just don't get it, they don't have the kind of background.

ANDREA: Hm-hmm, what kind of stories do you use?

LISA: A lot of the early, who do I like, I like Dr. Seuss for all the rhyming. I like Robert Munsch for the repetition, and they usually find his are funny. They most often can grasp that situation. Anything more imaginative is tough, anything slightly removed from their world, which I find has been quite narrow, is tough. I'll read some Aboriginal stories and it's fun to see their eyes light up at something familiar, or we've made bannock or something like that, you can really see there's a link. But I find a lot of times, there aren't.

Lisa's description of the literacy skills of her students seems to indicate lowered expectations of their literacy and language abilities and little understanding of their language as rule-governed. Additionally, it would seem that her students could benefit from learning strategies that could help them to make sense of unfamiliar texts.

In my interview with Deborah, I asked her about how white settler educators perceived the literacy skills of indigenous students. The following comments are her response to my question:

DEBORAH: (sigh) it's always like, "They don't understand, the comprehension's not there, the vocabulary's not there." And it's always, "The understanding's not there, they're not quick enough for recall, their attention . . .," there's always . . .

My sense is that Deborah's description is accurate as it mirrors much of what Lisa described in the excerpt taken from my interview with her. My time in this particular school left me with the impression that First Nations and Métis students are perceived by many white settler educators as arriving at school with limited language abilities. Further, the students' lack of experience with written language use is seen as a deficit rather than as a difference. Victoria Purcell-Gates (2002) argues that it is important for educators to understand limited experience with written language as a *difference* and not as a *deficit,* as this distinction affects teacher expectations of learning. In the school described in this study, these children typically are not expected to do well in developing literacy skills and, often, the blame is placed on the home environment. In contrast, Deborah made efforts to increase students' experiences with written language, and the test results indicate a marked improvement in their literacy skills.

Many of the First Nations students in Deborah's class began the school year below grade level in reading. Throughout the course of the year, Deborah was able to help them improve their literacy skills through her unwavering attention to good reading instruction. In Saskatchewan schools, much attention is paid to including "Aboriginal content" as a means of decolonizing settler schools and making schools welcoming spaces for indigenous and settler students. Unfortunately, such cultural remedies have little effect on the cultural and language biases of white settler teachers. The real barrier to literacy development for indigenous students is not the lack of a cultural elixir but, rather, the biased belief systems of their white settler educators.

Discussion

Schools reflect the culture and beliefs of mainstream society. Children who are not members of dominant racial or ethnic groups routinely experience educational challenges that are not faced by mainstream society members (Ogbu, 1992). Because the challenges experienced by minority children are often invisible to members of the dominant society, mainstream educators have traditionally relied on deficit theories to explain the academic difficulties experienced by minority children. As outlined by Donna Deyhle and Karen Swisher (1997), deficit theories have been used to imply both biological and home environmental inadequacies in minority children, conveniently avoiding the examination of any role that schools themselves might have in indigenous students' academic difficulties. Cornel Pewewardy (2002) explains that "the conventional deficit syndrome as an educational ethos and practice has been used to address the needs of American Indian/Alaska Native students despite evidence suggesting that American Indians/Alaska Native students have definite cultural values and traits that affect learning and academic achievement" (p. 25).

Deficit theories do not offer any real explanation of the challenges faced by indigenous students. Instead, such arguments allow the systemic barriers to remain invisible and place the responsibility for the challenges faced by this student population firmly on the shoulders of the oppressed community. Mainstream educators and administrators tend to view problems experienced by indigenous students as "imbedded in the individual, though they are more likely derived from structural and social conditions in the environment" (Wilson, 1991, p. 379). The comments of white settler educators involved in my study revealed issues of language bias and lowered expectations of literacy development in indigenous students. Their perception of Indigenous English as evidence of a *lack of language* creates lowered expectations of their indigenous students that, in turn, leads to lower levels of performance in indigenous students.

In the early years of primary school in North America, classroom activities are primarily organized with the goals of providing students with the opportunity to gain literacy skills. Successful acquisition of these skills is often a determining factor in assessing whether a student is performing at grade level. Furthermore, in order to gain access to subject matter in social studies or science, a student must possess adequate literacy skills. Once a student falls behind in literacy development, these difficulties extend to other areas of formal education. In turn, these difficulties, if not resolved, are carried through to secondary and post-secondary classrooms. Unequal opportunities in literacy development in primary years can affect students long after they leave their grade two or three classrooms.

The First Nations children in my study did not have equitable opportunities for literacy development. These unequal opportunities are, in part, linked to white settler educator expectations of and teaching practices in language and literacy development. If settler schools in Saskatchewan wish to move towards creating equitable outcomes for all students, the white settler gaze will need to turn away from perceived deficits in indigenous homes and look towards the deficits in current literacy practices in settler elementary classrooms in Saskatchewan.

REFERENCES

AIC (Amnesty International Canada). (2002, July). *Without discrimination: The fundamental right of all Canadians to human rights protection.* Retrieved May 25, 2005, from www.amnesty.ca/canada/un_cerd.pdf

Anderson, D. (2006, May). Narrative revolt on the prairie landscape of colonial Saskatchewan. Paper presented at the annual meeting of the Canadian Critical Race Conference, Regina, Saskatchewan.

Berlin, J. A. (1987). *Rhetoric and reality: Writing instruction in American colleges, 1900–1985.* Carbondale, IL: SIU Press.

Cecil, N. (1988). Black dialect and academic success: A study of teacher expectations. *Reading Improvement, 25,* 34–38.

CERD (Committee on the Elimination of Racial Discrimination) (2002, August 6). *Anti-discrimination committee concludes consideration of Canada's reports on compliance with international convention.* Retrieved May 25, 2005, from http://www.unhchr.ch/huricane/huricane.nsf/0/F706CB862AAC5B66C1256C0E00461E95?opendocument

CERD Report Ad Hoc National Network (2002, July 30). *Report on racial discrimination against indigenous peoples in Canada: Summary.* Retrieved August 6, 2009, from www.turtleisland.org/news/cerd.pdf

Chambers, J. K., Schilling-Estes, N., & Trudgill, P. (Eds.). (2004). *The handbook of language variation and change.* Malden, MA: Blackwell.

Crago, M. (1992). Communicative interaction and second language acquisition: An Inuit example. *TESOL Quarterly, 26,* 489–505.

Cummins, J. (2000). *Language, power, and pedagogy: Bilingual children in the crossfire.* Clevedon, England: Multilingual Matters.

Delpit, L. D. (1988). The silenced dialogue: Power and pedagogy in educating other people's children. *Harvard Educational Review, 58,* 280–298.

Deyhle, D., & Swisher, K. (1997). Research in American Indian and Alaska Native education: From assimilation to self-determination. *Review of Research in Education, 22,* 113–194.

Dubois, B. (1978). A case study of Native American child bidialectalism in English: Phonological, morphological, and syntactic evidence. *Journal of English Linguistics, 20*(2), 181–199.

Eller, R. (1989). Johnny can't talk, either: The perpetuation of the deficit theory in classrooms. *Reading Teacher, 42,* 670–674.

Ford, C. E. (1984). The influence of speech variety on teachers' evaluation of students with comparable academic ability. *TESOL Quarterly, 18,* 25–40.

Ghosh, R. (2002). *Redefining multicultural education* (2nd ed.). Scarborough: Nelson.

Heath, S. (1986). What no bedtime story means: Narrative skills at home and school. In B. B. Schieffelin & E. Ochs (Eds.), *Language socialization across cultures* (pp. 97–124). Cambridge: University Press.

Heit, M., & Blair, H. (1993). Language needs and characteristics of Saskatchewan Indian and Metis students: Implications for educators. In S. Morris, K. McLeod, & M. Danesi (Eds.), *Aboriginal languages and education: The Canadian experience* (pp. 103–128). Oakville: Mosaic.

Kouritzin, S. (1999). *Face[t]s of first language loss.* Mahwah, NJ: Lawrence Erlbaum Associates.

Leap, W. L. (1993). *American Indian English.* Salt Lake City: University of Utah Press.

Lyster, R. (2004). Differential effects of prompts and recasts in form-focused instruction. *Studies in Second Language Acquisition, 26,* 399–432.

Miller, J. (1999). Becoming audible: Social identity and social language use. *Journal of Intercultural Studies, 20,* 149–165.

Mulholland, V. (2006). Conscious of my fictions: A postcolonial reading of the autobiography of a Saskatchewan English teacher. Unpublished doctoral dissertation, University of Regina, Regina, Saskatchewan, Canada.

Norton Peirce, B. (1995). Social identity, investment, and language learning. TESOL *Quarterly, 29,* 9–31.

Ogbu, J. (1992). Understanding cultural diversity and learning. *Educational Researcher, 21*(8), 355–383.

Olson Flanigan, B. (1987). Language variation among Native Americans: Observations on Lakota English. *Journal of English Linguistics, 20,* 181–199.

Pavlenko, A. (2002). Poststructuralist approaches to the study of social factors in second language learning and use. In V. Cook (Ed.), *Portraits of the L2 User* (pp. 277–302). Toronto: Multilingual Matters.

Pewewardy, C. (2002). Learning styles of American Indian/Alaska Native students: A review of the literature and implications for practice. *Journal of American Indian Education, 41*(3), 22–56.

Plank, G. (1994). What silence means for educators of American Indian children. *Journal of American Indian Education, 34*(1), 3–19.

Purcell-Gates, V. (2002). " . . . As soon as she opened her mouth!": Issues of language, literacy, and power. In L. Delpit & J. K. Dowdy (Eds.), *The skin that we speak: Thoughts on language and culture in the classroom* (pp. 121–142). New York: New Press.

Razack, S. (Ed.). (2002). *Race, space and the law: Unmapping a white settler society.* Toronto: Between the Lines.

Roy, J. (1987). The linguistic and sociolinguistic position of Black English and the issue of bidialectism in education. In P. Homel, M. Palif & D. Aaronson (Eds.), *Childhood bilingualism: Aspects of linguistic, cognitive, and social development* (pp. 231–242). Hillsdale, NJ: Erlbaum.

Saskatchewan Learning (1994, February). *Language Arts for Indian and Métis students: A guide for adapting English Language Arts.* Retrieved March 17, 2005, from http://www.sasklearning.gov.sk.ca/docs/indlang/adapt/index.html

Schilling-Estes, N. (2000). Investigating intra-ethnic differentiation: /ay/ in Lumbee Native American English. *Language Variation and Change, 12,* 141–176.

Statistics Canada (2003, June). *2001 Census Aboriginal population profiles.* Retrieved April 13, 2005 from http://www12.statcan.ca/english/profil01/AP01/Details/Page.cfm?Lang=E&Geo1=PR&Code1=47&Geo2=PR&Code2=01&Data=Count&SearchText=Saskatchewan&SearchType=Begins&SearchPR=01&B1=All&GeoLevel=&GeoCode=47

Statistics Canada (2003, June). *2001 Census Data.* Retrieved April 13, 2005 from http://www12.statcan.ca/english/census01/Products/standard/themes/

Sterzuk, A. (2003). *A study of Indigenous English speakers in the Standard English classroom.* Unpublished master's thesis, McGill University, Montreal, Quebec, Canada.

Sterzuk, A. (2007). *Dialect speakers, academic achievement, and power: First Nations and Métis children in Standard English classrooms in Saskatchewan.* Unpublished doctoral dissertation, McGill University, Montreal, Quebec, Canada.

Tollefson, J. (Ed.). (2002). *Language policies in education: Critical issues.* Mahwah, NJ: Erlbaum.

Wardhaugh, R. (2002). *An introduction to sociolinguistics* (4th ed.). Oxford: Blackwell.

Wilson, P. (1991). Trauma of Sioux Indian high school students. *Anthropology & Education Quarterly, 22*(4), 367–383.

Wolfram, W., Temple Adger, C., & Christian, D. (1999). *Dialects in schools and communities.* Mahweh, NJ: Erlbaum.

Wolfram, W. (1984). Unmarked tense in American Indian English. *American Speech, 59,* 31–50.

CHAPTER 2

LOST IN TRANSLATION: ANTI-RACISM AND THE PERILS OF KNOWLEDGE

Jennifer J. Nelson

Introduction

Most researchers hope to generate new knowledge and ideas that are more than simply interesting. We hope our work will contribute to a broader goal or some form of improvement in people's lives. This is true in a particular way if our work is concerned with systems of domination, marginality and struggles for social justice. But what happens when critical research on racism encounters the demand for fast, demonstrable solutions to what are framed as problems of "cultural difference"?

In exploring this dilemma, this chapter is concerned with two bodies of work and thought that have become prominent in research and professional practice contexts across various disciplines. One is "knowledge translation," a relatively recent term for how the knowledge generated by research gets employed in practice, policy and decision making. The other, which is not so new but is still common in some settings, is "cultural competence," a pedagogical and practice approach in which professionals, presumably from the dominant racial/cultural group, learn to work inoffensively with people from "other" cultural and racial communities. Of course, there is much more to each term than these quick descriptions convey, and I will enter these terrains shortly. But what may be less apparent is the connection between them.

This chapter argues that the discourse of knowledge translation demands that knowledge be organized and marketed in particular ways, which, I suggest, precludes a complex, systemic consideration of racism. Cultural competence as a practice strategy seems a logical "answer" to the demand that knowledge be distilled, generalized and employed to generate observable outcomes. As such, cultural competence exemplifies the risks of knowledge translation that precludes a necessarily complex consideration of racism.

This conceptual discussion is not the result of any systematic attempt to measure the relationship between knowledge translation and culture-based solutions to difference. It is informed by my observations and reflections from an academic position, shared between a cancer centre and a university, which bridges healthcare and critical sociological work on race. It is a discussion of the profound paradigmatic tension, as I see it, emerging from the need to demonstrate research "outcomes" or tangible institutional changes while just beginning to embark on some much-needed conceptual and theoretical shifts in thinking about race in health disciplines.

My research over the last several years has focused on bringing an analysis of systemic racism to bear on the healthcare context in which racialized women undergo treatment and seek supportive services for breast cancer. In healthcare, I have found that "culturalist" approaches remain the dominant framework through which practitioners and researchers conceptualize racial and ethnic difference,[1] and some forthcoming examples should make clearer what this looks like. At the same time, my hospital-based research unit has been required to engage with knowledge translation theory and strategies in some depth, as a way of demonstrating the applicability and effectiveness of our work to healthcare practice. This means, for instance, finding dissemination strategies to ensure the "uptake" of research results, tracking instances in which results have been put into practice in some program or service and evaluating the effectiveness of communication and outreach strategies in light of the need to make changes in practice as quickly as possible.

In what follows, I elaborate both a definition and a critical perspective of knowledge translation. I also discuss the research context in which I work, and explain the prominence and function of the "culturalist" knowledge to which I've referred. Since I see these concepts as interdependent in the discussion, the text weaves back and forth between them, interspersed throughout with examples (in italics) from my work. I conclude with some reflections on ways in which the two phenomena are mutually supportive, and the perils this might pose for a critical analysis of racism and for subsequent action to address inequality, rather than just "difference."

Translating knowledge

What I have referred to as a trend towards knowledge translation encompasses a spectrum of terms and meanings. The Canadian Institutes of Health Research (CIHR, 2004) defines knowledge translation as "the exchange, synthesis and ethically-sound application of knowledge—within a complex system of inter-

---

1.   See Chapter 7, "The more things change . . . : The endurance of "culturalism" in social work and healthcare," in this volume.

actions among researchers and users—to accelerate the capture of the benefits of research for Canadians through improved health, more effective services and products, and a strengthened health care system." Similar definitions follow alternate terms like "knowledge exchange,"[2] knowledge transfer, knowledge brokering or even knowledge "management" (Balas & Boren, 2000; Gabbay & le May, 2004). This focus speaks to heightened requirements for funding bodies to rationalize the resources directed to research (Nutley et al., 2004), as well as for health professionals to justify their interventions with research knowledge.[3]

While these requirements have some particular applications in healthcare, they also inflect social science work in similar ways. In her work on the complexities and methodological tensions around doing race research in health, Yasmin Gunaratnam (2003) notes that "trends in the funding of research, for example, stress the need for social science research to be seen as 'relevant' and 'useful' for addressing 'everyday' concerns—with 'usefulness' being interpreted in relation to the need to build and support policy and practice" (p. 18). The Social Sciences and Humanities Research Council of Canada (SSHRC) has recently refocused its mandate to reflect a concern with research knowledge transfer, through strategic grant initiatives defined in terms such as "mobilizing knowledge" and "facilitating uptake" (SSHRC, 2006; Tetroe, 2007). Both SSHRC and CIHR make frequent reference in their funding guidelines to "knowledge users," emphasizing a consumer orientation to knowledge that seems significant in light of the focus on "impact" (CIHR, 2009; SSHRC, 2006).

Knowledge translation itself is becoming an academic subfield, with its own stratum of experts and its own cadre of theories which, although in their infancy, offer insight about the best relationships to foster through "social network analysis" (Chan & Liebowitz, 2006; West et al., 1999) and the most effective strategies for creating impact from research knowledge (Graham & Logan, 2004; Grunfeld et al., 2004; Lavis et al., 2003; Lomas, 2000). Moreover, evaluative research has developed around the need to quantify the impact or end results from new knowledge. There is increasing discussion of the need for "knowledge brokers"—a whole new category of professionals who specialize in marketing research and fostering its uptake in practice and policy settings.

Research that counts
In health, and increasingly in social science generally, knowledge translation has become an axiomatic prerequisite for any research project, program or

---

2.   Knowledge Exchange has been defined as "collaborative problem-solving between researchers and decision makers that happens through linkage and exchange. Effective knowledge exchange involves interaction between decision makers and researchers and results in mutual learning through the process of planning, producing, disseminating, and applying existing or new research in decision-making" (CHSRF, 2006).

3.   For critical work on evidence-based practice, see for example, Holmes, Perron & O'Byrne, 2006; Holmes, Murray, Perron, & Rail, 2006; Mykhalovskiy & Weir, 2004; Traynor, 1999.

agency worth its salt. Researchers are often called on to have a knowledge dissemination plan at the proposal phase—significantly (and obviously) well before they know what the research results will be—and to indicate how the research is likely to change policy, practice or society at some level.

Notwithstanding the chronological problem this poses, some researchers have begun to wonder how this might affect exploratory forms of research—both qualitative work and basic laboratory science (Sinding et al., 2006). Will the demand for demonstrable impact serve to curb more creative lines of inquiry in favour of "translatable" projects—namely, studies promising the right kind of impact? Further, knowledge translation discourse is concerned not simply with the utilization of research, but with the more expedient application of knowledge to practice. How might this influence both research questions and funding decisions? Texts like the following are offered as personal reflective data collected in response to these questions that I have been considering over a period of time.

> *2005: A funding representative recently told our director that our research group is a "hard sell": he received a call from a cancer patient's brother wondering why things had been so difficult financially for his sister following her diagnosis when our group had done a study two years ago on the problems of lower-income women with breast cancer. It seemed that the research was not actually making any difference, so why was money being spent on it?*

While it might seem obvious that this caller was uninformed about the practicalities of "making change" on a widespread basis from the funding of one pilot research project (and also that he probably spoke in a moment of emotional crisis), the funding representative did take it seriously as an example of how difficult it is to "market" qualitative, psychosocial research. When deciding what to feature in their research portfolio, and perhaps what to fund, such an example mattered. Moreover, the remark was passed on to the researchers, implying that tangible "results," at such a level, were necessary for the research to be considered viable.

The power of knowing

The explosion of interest in knowledge translation and the necessity of demonstrating one's commitment to it in order to obtain research funds makes it difficult, at best, to question its positivist underpinnings. This may partially explain what feels like the impermeability of the discourse—namely, there is almost no criticism of it. My search for insurgent voices has come up nearly empty time and again, save for some critical questions in a recent essay by some colleagues (Sinding et al., 2006) and a compelling oral presentation in a workshop, in which the speaker also noted that she had found no dissenting sources.

To be clear, I am not questioning the value of thinking through better ways to apply research knowledge. I do not dismiss the need for good communication between researchers and practitioners, nor the need for research to extend beyond the academic setting in positive, transformative ways. Knowledge translation theorists and proponents are rightly concerned with finding ethical and effective ways to see that research does not simply sit on the shelf or remain in elite academic circles. Further, I am not suggesting that there is no dialogue or evolution within the field of knowledge translation itself. There is much discussion of new strategies and approaches, and there is critical reflection on what is not working (Best, 2006; Graham & Tetroe, 2007; Mitton et al., 2007). However, such debates seem to take place within a wholly positivist landscape, with the unstated assumption that knowledge itself is something verifiable and unproblematic.

For my purposes, it is important to consider this in light of healthcare research contexts and the particular situation of psychosocial work. Here, the positivist underpinnings of "knowledge" are so pervasive that social scientists and qualitative researchers, some of whom one might expect to argue for the "situatedness" of both researcher and researched, are often swept along by the need to offer what is seen as "truth," or "real" evidence, in order to compete in a context that recognizes and respects little beyond "hard science." This is particularly true in healthcare settings, where qualitative work and attention to the patient experience or perspective is still considered quite novel by its proponents and quite trivial by the scientists. There is an urge to develop psychosocial research according to the standards of traditional "objective" science, in order that it gain ground in health contexts. It is extremely difficult to insinuate notions of subjectivity, power and inequality in a field that is already silent about its own conceptual and theoretical situation.

The purported "newness" of knowledge translation is itself rather suspect (exemplified, for instance, in seminars where people present their research and the audience asks questions, which are now termed "knowledge exchange events"). I think it is important to question what seems to be the pervasive adoption of knowledge translation as an innovative, new, and axiomatically positive idea. Has knowledge—about people, groups, cultures and social phenomena—not already been applied in particular ways "in practice," for instance, in colonial conquest, in prisons, in psychiatric wards, in schools, in holocausts (and in ways deemed academic, empirical, justified in their time and place)? When we think of knowledge translation this way—as an act of employing knowledge—its alleged newness seems ridiculous. But more importantly, the missing link in the knowledge-to-practice equation becomes apparent: Where is power? How do we ask critical questions about how knowledge is produced, whose knowledge is being employed and who is deciding how it will be used? Who is able to make change, and to what ends? Who makes change on behalf of others, in what are deemed their best interests? What conditions make it possible for knowledge to be accessed, applied, utilized by some people and not others?

These questions are far from mine alone, and they are far from new. They are exemplified in the work of Michel Foucault, who saw knowledge and power as so intricately bound that he coined the term "power/knowledge" (Foucault,

1982; Gordon, 1980) to describe how knowledge is always shaped and mediated by social forces—the power to dictate meaning, the assumptions (conscious or not) of the author, the social and political conditions in which it is produced and the goals to which it might be applied. Many feminist theorists, too, have been concerned with the nature of knowledge, asking critical questions about objectivity and truth, and under what conditions they are determined (Flax, 1990; Haraway, 1991). Social positionality, standpoint theory (Harding, 1991; Stoetzler & Yuval-Davis, 2002), situated knowing (Haraway, 1991), and "sociology of knowledge" (Smith, 1990) are just a few examples of theories from a wide body of social thought that has incited many researchers to analyze and articulate the problems of location, subjectivity and power with regard to knowledge production.

No matter where one stands on such questions, it seems surprising that healthcare research, particularly that claiming to be qualitative or psychosocial, remains generally untouched by critical dialogues on knowledge itself. For example, there is a continued focus on "authentically" reproducing patient or research participant voices, and a prevailing (but unnamed) assumption that through good research practice we can come to understand and represent others' experiences, taking their meaning at face value. David Allen and Kristin Cloyes (2005) provide an excellent critical discussion of the focus on "experience" in nursing research, noting that "the way first person accounts are treated . . . reveals a lingering positivism: they are taken to be uncontestable *facts*" (p. 99).

In this form of research, data are simply "reported" as "the findings," much the way it might be possible to do in a laboratory experiment. There is some acknowledgment that it is more difficult to uncover the meanings of people's actions and thoughts, and that social factors have an influence, but the focus then becomes how best to control for "bias," with the underlying assumption that a "true" or at least a close meaning (to the best of one's abilities) can be ascertained. The sense of a researcher without identity, history or location remains, as does the notion of a "knowable" interviewee, whose words offer a window into his or her "true" thoughts and mind. There is rarely any discussion of the theoretical or conceptual frameworks through which a researcher is "reading" the data, and discussion of "methods" is limited to the mechanics of research, i.e., participant recruitment, data collection and the process of unearthing "themes." Methodology (as a set of theoretically informed reading practices) is largely absent. As Allen and Cloyes write of experience-focused health studies,

> the conditions under which the statements were produced (the interview) and their management (analysis) disappear, positioning the researcher as an impartial ventriloquist, a scientist. The subjects speak through the researcher to the reader. This is also a political move, one that protects the status and position of the researcher relative to the research/ed (Mishler, 1986). Making the experience of subjects sacrosanct, and eliminating any

legitimate role of the researcher as interpreter and judge, puts
search/er firmly in the camp of knowledge revelation, as opposed
ative production. A researcher merely uses acquired, scientific
let the data, and the subjects, 'speak for themselves.' (2005, p. 99)

As such, issues of narration, authority, subjectivity and power seldom enter the
health terrain as considerations for ethical research practice. I have found that
there is little response or interest when they are raised, perhaps because they
are simply seen as theoretical, with little bearing on the "real" work of change.
For example, when expressing my misgivings about knowledge translation discourse I am asked, "If you don't like it, what do you propose instead; what
should we *do*?" It is hard to engage in such conversations without being positioned as somehow "against" change. By slowing things down, one is seen as
regressing to the way things used to be before the entrée of knowledge translation, talking only about ideas (which are not seen to have impact), or not caring
about making things better for the subjects of the research.

Culture and knowing

For the purposes of this discussion, I want to highlight the vein of knowledge
production most pertinent to my argument and to the themes of this book. As
I noted earlier, and despite increasing criticism, culturalist discourses remain
central in cancer contexts (Altman, 1996; Galambos, 2003; Jackson et al., 2000;
Leigh, 1998) and in healthcare literature generally (Betancourt et al., 2003;
McKennis, 1999; Mir & Tovey, 2002; Shen, 2004). Such work tends to focus
on different "help-seeking," screening and other health behaviours, or on the
level of knowledge of various groups, including the "myths" they believe about
health and cancer (Bourjolly et al., 2003; Guidry et al., 2003; Kinney et al., 2002;
Phillips et al., 2001). There is some growing awareness that oncology support
services and information unfairly reflect a dominant, white, middle-class patient,
and efforts to overcome these problems typically follow a "cultural competence"
approach. This involves the development of skills, knowledge and attitudes
(Daley & Wong, 1994; Faulkner et al., 1994; Jackson et al., 2000; McKennis,
1999; Purnell, 2002) to address what is often termed "the challenge of diversity."
As the following excerpt from my research notes suggests, my observations of
psychosocial cancer research bear out this emphasis.

> *2003. At an American breast cancer conference: I am witnessing a plethora of
> psychosocial work on different cultural groups. Presenter after presenter gets up
> to educate the audience about culture after culture. Hispanics, we learn, are afraid
> to touch their breasts because their culture forbids it—this is a "barrier" specific to
> them. They also display "cultural" fears of losing their husbands following mas-
> tectomy. Various groups believe in "cancer myths," rely on religious belief or folk
> remedies and do not trust the healthcare system; their "barriers" are mainly due*

to ignorance. Culturalized Others are seen to require "cultural competence" on the part of healthcare workers, to re-educate them about breast health as well as to respond appropriately to things like different diet, lifestyle and family structures. There is sometimes mention of socio-economic circumstances, but the "gaps" in healthcare are mainly attributed to cultural beliefs and traditions, none of which are identified for white, middle-class women. I write in my conference notes on Day 3: No one's mentioned racism yet.

Shortly after this conference, I began to read breast cancer stories from mainstream literature for survivors. Here, racially unmarked women continually expressed concerns that were almost identical to those mentioned in the presentations about "culture," especially around body image—fears of losing a breast, concerns about being less attractive to their husbands, and spiritual issues—but none of these behaviours or beliefs was ever attributed to the "culture" of these women. I realized that "culture" was frequently employed to delineate non-white groups and bodies only, and to describe and explain problems that were deemed specific to them.

Although there has been much criticism of culture-based approaches to difference (Burman et al., 2004; Gunaratnam, 1997; Nairn et al., 2004; Razack, 1995, 1998; St Denis, 2002, 2004), culturalism remains the central paradigm by which dominant subjects both understand racial "Others" and strategize how to serve their health needs. As many theorists have pointed out, unequal access and treatment in health and social services are often attributed to cultural differences, rather than social, economic or political causes that are part and parcel of systemic inequality (Abrums & Leppa, 2001; Browne & Smye, 2002; Culley, 1996; Fassin, 2001; Yee & Dumbrill, 2003). Similarly, as Jennifer Malat notes, "ethnicity theories," also common in health research, "conceive of divisions between racial groups as being born of cultural differences" (2006, p. 308). Employing "ethnicity," then, proffers a culturalist focus on customs and beliefs, which "distracts attention from the structures and practices that create inequality" (Malat, 2006, p. 308).

Further, culture and its attributed meanings have come to offer a contemporary framework through which racism can be expressed. As Philomena Essed notes, more blatant expressions of biological racism have been "replaced by a much more subtle ideology, built on the bedrock of cultural inferiority" (1991, p. 13). Commitments to "multiculturalism" can promote the notion that people are simply "different but equal"; in this sense, culture discourse seems to express liberal good intent, but masks real systemic inequities. Dominant society continues to rest on hierarchies, even as it purports to appreciate and include the diverse qualities of different cultures.

Didier Fassin (2001) provides an effective analysis, with clear case examples, of how cultural explanations serve to overshadow more likely socio-political reasons for poor access to healthcare. In his research, health professionals and researchers attributed Indian Equadorean women's distrust of healthcare systems and failure to seek obstetric care to their cultural beliefs. Fassin's work revealed the women's long, arduous journey to the hospital site, their meager financial resources, their lack of childcare at home and their undignified treatment in the hospitals, when they did attend, by professionals who regarded them with racist aversion. His analysis shifts the focus from the culture of the racial Other to both an examination of subjects' socio-economic and political life circumstances and a critique of the institutional context in which they are treated. As he notes, it is crucial to understand the forms of knowledge at work in explanatory frameworks, as these knowledges determine the actions taken to address problems.

Malat has written similarly about the tendency of health disparities research to ignore social inequality, focusing on factors like access, patient preferences (often assumed to be culturally driven), and "physician bias," which is treated as a conscious and observable feature. None of these approaches offers a satisfactory, in-depth or comprehensive explanation for inequality in treatment. Malat argues that research on disparities in healthcare is an area "starved of theory" and proposes that *race critical theories* (Essed & Goldberg, 2002) offer researchers the conceptual tools to "explicitly describe how race operates as a social category," while simultaneously attending to the effects of other social locations (Malat, 2006, p. 308).

The dis/solution of race critique

2004: At a psychosocial oncology conference: I am talking about the institutional and social barriers faced by women of colour when they are dealing with breast cancer. I have some examples that point to the socio-historical context in which women of colour negotiate the cancer care system and white social service agencies. I thought I was talking about racism. As it turns out, I am expected to talk about culture—about cultural "barriers" to healthcare and "disparities" in health, and the different "help-seeking behaviours" of various groups. By including "women of colour" in my title, I have implicitly designated myself a scientist who scopes out and explains "culture" in the service of devising better ways to help others.

Moreover, I am a white woman in a sea of whiteness; I am not speaking from either of the two perspectives that would be acceptable here: the white anthropologist bringing "culture" for the dominant group's consumption, or the "native informant" whose experience is romanticized and consumed by the dominant audience. Both my claims and my motives are suspect: How did I get them to talk to me? What are the strategies that other white researchers could use to gain entry into these communities? But more to the point—How did I confirm the truth of what the women said about racism? Did I lead them to a discussion of racism? Do I think this knowledge is generalizable? What about their culture? The problem has to be with their traditions, their beliefs, their misconceptions—because we can do something about that. . . . What, then, are my recommendations?

No one is happy to hear that white practitioners may need to examine critically the knowledge about women of colour on which they draw when deciding how to "treat" them. I am not particularly happy myself. I cannot offer a solution. It is not enough to say that I am, at this stage, merely pointing out some new critical directions, or initiating a conversation about racism. It seems trite just to say that my work is in its early stages and "more research is needed"—that is what everyone says about everything. It seems arrogant to suggest I'm the only one concerned with this angle, but in this setting, it does feel like that.

The experience of this conference reinforced the prominence of cultural explanations for inequities in healthcare, while also revealing what seemed to be an underlying assumption that research must initiate some kind of action, in a direct and immediate sense. The request for recommendations resulting from any project or idea is a common one. My own sense that an individual project or paper was merely a stepping stone or a strand in the web of a much larger, long-term body of work was problematic. It meant that I was only raising problems, being critical, but not offering anything new in place of the phenomena I didn't like. If one is to complain, it seems, one better have a new solution in hand and be ready to argue for its efficacy.

The constant demand for solutions and recommendations also reinforces the notion of the researcher as "expert." To fail or decline to solve problems is to diminish that status, which calls into question the validity of the work. To insist on an in-depth analysis of the problem is to prolong that problem, to avoid the "real" need for a solution or "deliverable" by indulging oneself in a theoretical discussion that is perhaps interesting, but not practical. The traditional white anthropologist or the proper native informant would offer cultural knowledge that could be translated into action: If they eat something different, we can provide it; if they have certain religious rituals, we will know to ask about them.

Whitewashing racism

2005: I am sitting in a focus group to which I have been invited to give my views on the information needs of breast cancer patients. When I briefly introduce my research on discrimination against immigrant women of colour in cancer care, the white woman next to me responds: "I think the real problem is the ethnic doctors." She explains that any ethnic doctor she's had has been terrible and that women of colour "always" tell her that they prefer to go to white doctors over "their own" because they are treated so much better. The subtext is that these are sexist male doctors from misogynist cultures. The two other white women present nod in agreement, and one notes that she has had two doctors, both "ethnic," and neither was good. The facilitator asks if she thinks this was because of their ethnicity and she confirms that it was.

I find myself making an essentialist assumption that this facilitator, a young South Asian woman, will be offended by the remarks. Instead, she asks if maybe it could be that these doctors were trained in other cultures, as those trained in Canada would likely be more progressive. The white women agree; my attempts at intervention go nowhere. The facilitator sums up the discussion by saying that it seems that the problems "work both ways"—i.e., things aren't any easier for white women. The note taker records this. I know it will be "reported" as "the data."

As noted earlier, the common emphasis on experience dictates that we treat participants as "experts" on their own situations, offering a slippery slope towards essentializing research subjects' words as "truth." This tendency is often particularly strong if the participants come from a marginalized group (in this case, they are women and cancer survivors), since to question their stories would position the researcher as elitist and insensitive (Allen & Cloyes, 2005). Thus, at the conference described through the lens of the above scenario, several things were produced. One was knowledge about the problems of the healthcare system, directly from the patient/victim/cancer survivor: male doctors of colour are sexist; if allowed to exist at all, they need to be trained in Canada, where cultural standards of gender equality and enlightened male behaviour are superior; women of colour generally agree with this. Two, a situation developed in which the white women's perspectives were not seen as racist; they merely described a problem of cultural difference, which might be remedied by better training and skills in a more advanced cultural context. Three, the absent women of colour were spoken for, assumed to be complicit in this view. They were not actually needed in order to understand the problems with culture, because all women are its victims. Consequently, sexism was narrated through racism under the guise of culture; the racism against women of colour was erased.

The conflation of knowledge and experience has particular implications when the knowledge generated reinforces racism. What might a "knowledge translation strategy" based on the above "knowledge" (ethnic doctors are the problem) look like? Or, if we are to conclude that all women suffer similarly from sexism, but that racism does not exist, how will that be translated into practice or policy? As Fassin (2001) entreats us to consider, if we accept culturalist explanations for what are the results of institutionalized racism, what solutions might follow?

The sea of bullets: further translational "points"
To treat knowledge in a utilitarian manner requires some particular techniques for "getting it out." Thus, knowledge translation technologies do not simply communicate information; they organize knowledge in particular ways.

2006. Lately, I have attended several knowledge translation workshops in which researchers are instructed, for example, to use catchy "tag lines" to market the ideas, simplify the language and, above all, use lots *of bullet points. We are told that listeners cannot be expected to take in any but the most basic and general facts, and that they will be unlikely to remember more than two or three things in any case. To that end, we are to list the most important two or three things, so as to define just what it is that they take away. We are guided to expect that people will be unable and unwilling to engage in depth with research material, and that busy professionals and policy-makers cannot be expected to take any time to listen. One workshop gave the example of the "thirty second elevator conversation," for which one should always be prepared. This means having one's research tag lines and two or three most significant highlights clearly in hand for when we happen to encounter that important policy-maker between the seventh and tenth floors.*

I keep hearing that researchers aren't good communicators, that we only talk to each other and that we use jargon that is inaccessible to anyone outside our fields. (Knowledge translation has set out to remedy this problem.) I think a few things about this: 1) Yes, this is often true, but sometimes "jargon" is used to dismiss any complex ideas or big words that people don't want to be bothered to learn; 2) Hasn't knowledge translation itself brought us a whole new collection of jargon, especially that which pointlessly relabels the acts of talking, learning and asking questions? 3) Whenever our researchers try to explain our knowledge translation agenda, no one understands what we are talking about.

Our research unit was recently advised to "consolidate our findings across projects." After some further discussion, this appeared to mean that we should draw out themes that applied to all our work (potentially 28 research studies over five years, many in vastly different areas of inquiry) and present the "general idea" as a way to sum up and present a sort of polished, finalized research "package." It seems almost too obvious to point out the difficulties of doing something like this. However, it is in fact "successful" in knowledge translation terms—after generalizing that much about any twenty-eight (or two or three) research projects, one is bound to come up with no more than two or three bullet points.

What is particularly interesting to me about such knowledge "marketing" is the presumption that research *can* be presented in these formats. The organization of knowledge in lists, themes, findings or point form ideas precludes arguments that follow a particular train of thought, building upon ideas as they go. It also precludes an argument or theory that is not linear, as it is difficult to depict something simply and visually that involves interdependent themes or incorporates several bodies of thought. It is particularly difficult, not to mention undesirable, to attempt to depict an argument about interlocking factors or systems of oppression in a few bullet points. Research questions and projects more often take the shape of a puzzle or knot than a line or list. "What to do" often takes the form of a paradigm shift, a need to rethink critically what one is doing on a systemic problem; theory is not an end in itself, but a tool to help us think differently, to turn ideas on their heads and to posit new approaches.

2006: The workshops and the reading I have done about knowledge translation are instructive. For my work to be marketable, I would have to follow the acceptable language and format. For instance, I know that the "analysis of systemic racism in the healthcare system" or "histories of colonialism influencing healthcare encounters" will, at best, produce a few blank nods, as people wait for the part about "what to do." What is really wanted is the following:

> *Women of colour report:*
> * *Not seeing their cultures reflected in the literature*
> * *Fear of encountering discrimination*
> * *Lack of openness about cancer in their communities*

> *Recommendations:*
> * *Resources translated into different languages*
> * *More culturally/ethnically diverse images on pamphlets*
> * *Cultural Competence training for healthcare staff*

Here, we cannot ask, nor do we need to ask, why things are not "equal" in the first place. We do not need to think about the reasons why so many women of colour feel unable to attend a support group. We are not able to attend to the participant whose doctor asks her "who let you into Canada?" We don't make it anywhere near the two participants who offer explanations of the community's fear and isolation that are grounded in colonialism and slavery. (Besides, two is not the majority, and thus they cannot be said to espouse "general themes.")

Then again, it's not as if there is no middle ground. I do make recommendations, attempting to shape them in language that doesn't reproduce the same old culturalist tropes or encourages people to ask more questions; I contextualize data in particular ways; I attempt to problematize and situate my narration of "knowledge," as well as the sources from which it comes. I am becoming adept at providing rather expedient thematic "reports" of my data, and saving the analysis for the published paper when there is more time or an interested audience. But I am far from having mastered the dance of effectively resisting "knowledge translation" as a phenomenon while still demonstrating the "usefulness" of critical work.

Discussion: directions for a critical dialogue

The marriage of culturalism and knowledge translation is not an inadequate means of solving particular kinds of problems, but quite the opposite—it offers a very effective set of solutions. It provides ways for professionals to engage with racial difference that do not require a systematic rethinking of institutionalized racism. It gestures towards the accommodation of different marginalized groups in mainstream institutions, while not disturbing existing hierarchies. It offers techniques for satisfying funding demands for "outcomes" and measurable changes in practice resulting from research. It satisfies the sense that research should be more accessible to those outside its fields, and that others need not engage with it in any depth; rather, knowledge is made simple, manageable, relevant, effective and available to everyone, rather than mystical, inaccessible, difficult and elitist. These are persuasive and alluring selling points.

What I have posited here is that knowledge translation, as it is currently developing and proliferating, is fundamentally a positivist project. Like any approach to problem solving, it rests on a scaffold of conceptual apparatuses and methods. However, these assumptions and processes are largely invisible and unarticulated. And by this I do not mean to posit a kind of hidden agenda; rather, I believe that any project seemingly founded upon the notion that knowledge is transparent and verifiable calls for caution and skepticism. (And, if it is *not* founded upon such thought, knowledge translation theorists need to make this clear and explain their epistemological assumptions.) Further, any set of practices that has set out to position itself as mandatory and impermeable across research disciplines demands critical consideration. The very parameters that seem to have risen around engagement with knowledge translation—that is, particular strategies can be debated, but the underlying value of the discourse is not disrupted—raise important questions about the ways in which knowledge production might be shaped, managed and constrained.

In some very similar ways, knowledge production and its related implications in healthcare practice are founded on a series of unstated assumptions: that knowledge is something to be gleaned simply by asking or observing, that a "true" glimpse into another's thoughts and experiences is possible and that the researcher functions merely as conduit between the unknown and the known, as well as between the research and its application. In particular, culturalist approaches to knowledge entrench the notion that culture can be generalized, understood and accommodated, and that "diversity" can be managed through better practice and policy. Again, the researcher can gather, translate and transmit cultural information, and then work with its "users" to formulate better ways to apply it to those who "have cultures." Culture is employed not only as an explanation for health disparities and inequalities in service provision, but for deflecting attention from racism itself.

I have attempted to point to two "streams" of critique: one involves the particular modes of culturalist knowledge production and translation that are prevalent in my own work context. The other could be seen as a more general need to be vigilant about knowledge translation: culturalist knowledge is one example of a discourse that presents particular problems in its service to overly simplified and positivist knowledge translation strategies, but many forms of knowledge making, from many fields and disciplines of inquiry, are surely beginning to raise further questions and to spark some compelling dialogues.

At the conclusion of a paper, there is always a perceived need to provide the recommendations—one imagines the reviewers and audience asking, "so, where do we go from here?" Somewhat ironically, I have struggled with this point despite my central intention to critique the demand for fast solutions and expedited "resolutions" to research work. I have resisted the pressure to "answer" the questions this discussion has broached, and have hoped simply to contribute to the opening of a new dialogue and to suggest that we must keep it open. This does not preclude looking for ways in which aspects of our research can have more immediate effects or applications where appropriate; it need not stall the goals of social change. It does call for space to consider ideas thoughtfully, creatively and critically, to preserve and extend conversations and debates about knowledge and the problems of its application. And it suggests that many of these conversations are, and will continue to be, very much grounded in concrete problems and sites. For if problematizing knowledge has no bearing on the "real world," we have far greater chasms than translation can bridge.

REFERENCES

Abrums, M. E., & Leppa, C. (2001). Beyond cultural competence: Teaching about race, gender, class, and sexual orientation. *Journal of Nursing Education, 40*(6), 270–276.

Allen, D., & Cloyes, K. (2005). The language of "experience" in nursing research. *Nursing Inquiry, 12*(2), 98–105.

Altman, R. (1996). *Waking up/fighting back: The politics of breast cancer* (Hardcover ed.). Boston: Little, Brown & Co.

Balas, E. A., & Boren, S. A. (2000). Managing clinical knowledge for health care improvement. *Yearbook of Medical Informatics 2000,* 65–70.

Best, A. (2006, February). Integrating knowledge strategies: New models for more effective action. Paper presented at OBCCRI Workshop on Knowledge Exchange, Toronto.

Betancourt, J. R., Green, A. R., Carrillo, J. E., & Ananeh-Firempong, O. (2003). Defining cultural competence: A practical framework for addressing racial/ethnic disparities in health and health care. *Public Health Reports, 118*(4), 293.

Bourjolly, J. N., Barg, F. K., & Hirschman, K. B. (2003). African-American and white women's appraisal of their breast cancer. *Journal of Psychosocial Oncology, 21*(3), 43–61.

Browne, A., & Smye, V. (2002). A post-colonial analysis of healthcare discourses addressing Aboriginal women. *Nurse Research, 9*(3), 28–41.

Burman, E., Smailes, S. L., & Chantler, K. (2004). 'Culture' as a barrier to service provision and delivery: Domestic violence services for minoritized women. *Critical Social Policy, 24*(3), 332–357.

CHSRF (Canadian Health Services Research Foundation). (2006). Glossary. Retrieved January 30, 2006, from http://www.chsrf.ca/keys/glossary_e.php

CIHR (Canadian Institutes of Health Research). (2009). About Knowledge Translation. Retrieved from http://www.cihr-irsc.gc.ca/e/29418.html

CIHR (Canadian Institutes of Health Research). (2004). CIHR Innovation and action: Knowledge translation strategy 2004–2009. http://www.cihr-irsc.gc.ca/e/30162.html

Chan, K., & Liebowitz, J. (2006). The synergy of social network analysis and knowledge mapping: A case study. *Management and Decision Making, 7*(1), 19–34.

Culley, L. (1996). A critique of multiculturalism in health care: The challenge for nurse education. *Journal of Advance Nursing, 23*, 564–570.

Daley, J., & Wong, P. (1994). Community development with emerging ethnic communities. In A. Faulkner, M. Roberts-DeGennaro, & M. Weil (Eds.), *Diversity and development in community practice* (pp. 9–24). New York: The Haworth Press, Inc.

Essed, P. (1991). *Understanding everyday racism: An interdisciplinary theory.* Newbury Park, NJ: Sage.

Essed, P., & Goldberg, D. (2002). *Race critical theories: Text and context.* Malden: Blackwell Publishers.

Fassin, D. (2001). Culturalism as ideology. In C. M. Obermeyer (Ed.), *Cultural perspectives on reproductive health* (pp. 300–317). Oxford: Oxford University Press.

Faulkner, A., Roberts-DeGennaro, M., & Weil, M. (Eds.). (1994). *Diversity and development in community practice.* New York: The Haworth Press, Inc.

Foucault, M. (1982). The subject and power. *Critical Inquiry, 8*, 777–795.

Flax, J. (1990). *Psychoanalysis, feminism and postmodernism in the contemporary west.* Berkeley: University of California Press.

Gabbay, J., & le May, A. (2004). Evidence-based guidelines or collectively constructed "mind-lines?": Ethnographic study of knowledge management in primary care. *British Medical Journal, 329*(7473), 1013–1019.

Galambos, C. M. (2003). Moving cultural diversity toward cultural competence in health care. *Health & Social Work, 28*(1), 3–22.

Gordon, C. (Ed.). (1980). *Power/knowledge: Selected interviews & other writings, 1972–1977 by Michel Foucault.* New York: Pantheon Books.

Graham, I. D., & Tetroe, J. (2007). CIHR Research: How to translate health research knowledge into effective healthcare action. *Healthcare Quarterly, 10*(3), 20–22.

Graham, I., & Logan, J. (2004). Innovations in knowledge transfer and continuity of care. *Canadian Journal of Nursing Research, 36*(2), 89–103.

Grunfeld, E., Zitzelsberger, L., Evans, W., Cameron, R., Hayter, C., Berman, N., & Stern, H. (2004). Better knowledge translation for effective cancer control: A priority for action. *Cancer Causes and Control, 15*, 503–510.

Guidry, J. J., Matthews-Juarez, P., & Copeland, V. A. (2003). Barriers to breast cancer control for African-American women: The interdependence of culture and psychosocial issues. *Cancer, 97*(S1), 318–323.

Gunaratnam, Y. (1997). Culture is not enough: A critique of multi-culturalism in palliative care. In D. Field, J. Hockey & N. Small (Eds.), *Death, gender and ethnicity* (pp. 166–186). London: Routledge.

Gunaratnam, Y. (2003). *Researching race and ethnicity: Methods, knowledge and power.* London: Sage Publications.

Haraway, D. (1991). *Simians, cyborgs and women: The reinvention of women.* London: Free Associated Books.

Harding, S. (1991). *Whose science, whose knowledge?* London: Open University Press.

Holmes, D., Perron, A., & O'Byrne, P. (2006). Evidence, virulence, and the disappearance of nursing knowledge: A critique of the evidence-based dogma. *Worldviews on Evidence-Based Nursing 3*(3), 95–102.

Holmes, D., Murray, S. J., Perron, A., & Rail, G. (2006). Deconstructing the evidence-based discourse in health sciences: Truth, power and fascism. *International Journal of Evidence-Based Healthcare, 4*(3), 180–186.

Jackson, J. C., Taylor, V. M., Chitnarong, K., Mahloch, J., Fischer, M., Sam, R., & Seng, P. (2000). Development of a cervical cancer control intervention program for Cambodian American women. *Journal of Community Health, 25*(5), 359–375.

Kinney, A. Y., Emery, G., Dudley, W., & Croyle, R. (2002). Screening behaviors among African American women at high risk of breast cancer: Do beliefs about God matter? *Oncology Nursing Forum, 29*(5), 835–843.

Lavis, J., Robertson, D., Woodside, J., McLeod, C., & Abelson, J. (2003). How can organizations more effectively transfer research knowledge to decision makers? *The Milbank Quarterly, 81*(2), 221–248.

Leigh, J. W. (1998). *Communicating for cultural competence.* Toronto: Allyn and Beacon.

Lomas, J. (2000). Using "linkage and exchange" to move research into policy at a Canadian foundation. *Health Affairs, 19*(3), 236–240.

Malat, J. (2006). Expanding research on the racial disparity in medical treatment with ideas from sociology. *Health: An Interdisciplinary Journal for the Social Study of Health, Illness and Medicine, 10*(3), 303–321.

McKennis, A. T. (1999). Caring for the Islamic patient. *Association of Operating Room Nurses, 69*(6), 1185–1206.

Mir, G., & Tovey, P. (2002). Cultural competency: Professional action and South Asian carers. *Journal of Management in Medicine, 16*, 7–19.

Mishler, E. G. (1986). *Research interviewing: Context and narrative.* Cambridge, MA: Harvard University Press.

Mitton, C., Adair, C. E., McKenzie, E., Patten, S. B., & Waye Perry, B. (2007). Knowledge transfer and exchange: Review and synthesis of the literature. *The Milbank Quarterly, 85*(4), 729–768.

Mykhalovskiy, E., & Weir, L. (2004). The problem of evidence-based medicine: Directions for social science. *Social Science and Medicine, 59*(5), 1059–1069.

Nairn, S., Hardy, C., Parumal, L., & Williams, G. A. (2004). Multicultural or anti-racist teaching in nurse education: A critical appraisal. *Nurse Education Today, 24*(3), 188–195.

Nutley, S., Davies, H., Walter, I., & Wilkinson, J. (2004). Developing projects to assess research impact. Unpublished report from seminar: Research Unit for Research Utilization, University of St. Andrews.

Phillips, J. M., Cohen, M. Z., & Tarzian, A. J. (2001). African American women's experiences with breast cancer screening. *Journal of Nursing Scholarship, 33*(2), 135–140.

Purnell, L. (2002). The Purnell model for cultural competence. *Journal of Transcultural Nursing, 13*(3), 193–196.

Razack, S. (1995). The perils of talking about culture: Schooling research on South and East Asian students. *Race, Gender & Class, 2*(3), 67–82.

Razack, S. (1998). *Looking white people in the eye: Gender, race, and culture in courtrooms and class-rooms.* Toronto: University of Toronto Press.

Shen, M. Z. (2004). Cultural competence models in nursing: A selected annotated bibliography. *Journal of Transcultural Nursing, 15*(4), 317–322.

Sinding, C., Gould, J., & Gray, R. (2009). Making a difference with research. In J. Nelson, J. Gould, & S. Keller-Olaman (Eds.), *Cancer on the margins: Method and meaning in participatory research.* Toronto: University of Toronto Press.

Smith, D. (1990). *The conceptual practices of power: A feminist sociology of knowledge.* Boston: Northeastern University Press.

sshrc (Social Sciences and Humanities Research Council of Canada). (2006). Framing our Direction. Retrieved from http://www.sshrc.ca/site/about-crsh/publications/framing_our_direction_e.pdf

Stoetzler, M., & Yuval-Davis, N. (2002). Standpoint theory, situated knowledge and the situated imagination. *Feminist Theory, 3*(3), 315–333.

St. Denis, V. (2002). *Exploring the socio-cultural production of Aboriginal identities: Implications for education.* Unpublished doctoral dissertation.

St. Denis, V. (2004). Real Indians: Cultural revitalization and fundamentalism in Aboriginal education. In C. Schick, J. Jaffe, & A. Watkinson (Eds.), *Contesting fundamentalisms* (pp. 35–47). Halifax: Fernwood Publishing.

Traynor, M. (1999). The problem of dissemination: Evidence and ideology. *Nursing Inquiry, 6,* 187–197.

Tetroe, J. (2007). *Knowledge translation at the Canadian Institutes of Health Research: A primer.* The National Centre for the Dissemination for Disability Research. Focus Technical Brief, 18, 1–8.

West, E., Barron, D., Dowsett, J., & Newton, J. (1999). Hierarchies and cliques in the social networks of health care professionals: Implications for the design of dissemination strategies. *Social Science and Medicine, 48,* 633–646.

Yee, J., & Dumbrill, G. (2003). Whiteout: Looking for race in Canadian social work practice. In A. Al-Krenawi & J. Graham (Eds.), *Multicultural social work in Canada: Working with diverse ethno-racial communities* (pp. 98–121). Don Mills: Oxford University Press.

CHAPTER 3

FROM RACISM TO CRITICAL DIALOGUE IN THE ACADEMY: CHALLENGES OF NATIONAL MINORITIES AT THE UNIVERSITY OF REGINA

Frédéric Dupré

Racism was part of the Canadian ideology of nation building. This racist landscape in a settler economy caused suffering in many different ways for the First Nations, Métis and Francophone populations in western Canada; it also forged the spirit of many public institutions—educational institutions among them—that were established during the period of nation building at the beginning of the twentieth century (Dei et al., 2004; Ettner, 2004; Eudaily, 2004). Education, therefore, was one of the public tools which was intended to create a strong and cohesive national identity, but which also reproduced racial and cultural hierarchies in Canadian society (Cummins & Danesi, 1990; Friesen, 1983; Morrow & Torres, 1998). During the first decades of the twentieth century, national legislation forced residential schooling on Aboriginal people, and a ban on teaching languages other than English in public schools was implemented to assimilate racially and culturally diverse peoples into the white, Christian Anglo-hegemony that wove the fabric of an early Canadian nation. As founding peoples in a minority situation, First Nations, Métis and Francophones experienced various prejudices and assimilation policies that endangered their way of life and their survival as nations within a nation (Denis, 2006; Heber, 2004; Littlejohn, 2006). Throughout their struggle for recognition of their treaty rights and rights as national minorities,[1] they used

---

1.   The term "national minority" is understood here as Will Kymlicka (2003) defines it: " . . . a group that sees itself as a 'nation' inside Canada and that throughout its history has searched to obtain some sort of political autonomy to achieve the conservation of its cultural distinctiveness inside the State that includes it" (personal translation) (p. 15).

specific strategies to increase access to and achieve control of their own education in both secondary schooling and higher education. This long-standing fight for control of education has now reached the level of formal access to and control of their higher education. Currently, the challenge is one of operating and managing their own institutions within a partnership with the institutions that once excluded them while maintaining a strong link with their own people.

Racial exclusion and elitist approaches regarding higher education are still haunting these institutions at the pinnacle of education, namely, the university. Important initiatives have been implemented since the mid-1970s to increase access by national minorities to higher education; however, old institutional trends based on ethnocentric ideology, as shown by many studies in Canada and the United States, are not totally absent from the core of the practices and discourses of universities (Battiste, 2000; Calliste, 2000; Dei et al., 2004; Hale, 2004; Popkewitz, 1998). Still, First Nations, Métis and Francophone peoples have succeeded in establishing partnerships with some universities to achieve their goals of gaining control of their post-secondary education. These successes are fairly rare in Canada; thus, the ones that do exist constitute interesting case studies for better understanding the challenges and opportunities inherent in the attempt to unlock old power relations. In responding to the challenges of furthering institutional diversity in regard to Canadian founding peoples, these cases represent unique examples of strategies of resistance and critical approaches. The purpose of this chapter is to explore one of these unique sites of intercultural dialogue and partnership in higher education in Canada.

The University of Regina has one great, and largely underrated, distinction in the Canadian post-secondary landscape. Located in the heart of Saskatchewan's prairies, this university is home to the post-secondary institutions of three Canadian founding peoples in a minority setting: the First Nations, the Métis and the Fransaskois. The University of Regina has established unprecedented agreements with each of these national minorities, agreements that have served as models in other countries and provinces (Barnhardt, 1991; Stonechild, 2006). Although the agreements differ in their specifics, they have the same goals. By its particular agreement, each national minority seeks to establish an autonomous institution on campus through which to offer university programs to its youth. Besides offering training programs, these institutions, more importantly, provide a space in which to strengthen their nation's culture and language, to teach their specific histories and to train future leadership.

The presence of the First Nations University of Canada, the Gabriel Dumont Institute and the *Institut Français* on the University of Regina campus has shaped the history, and in some respect the identity, of this university. This specific history of the University of Regina is something that is not appropriately recognized. I wish here to claim that this non-recognition is a form of oppression and, as Charles Taylor (1994) states, "it can imprison people in a false, distorted and reduced mode of being" (p. 25). While a unique university identity has been accomplished by implementing these partnerships, has this long-standing relationship truly transformed both parties? Could we highlight the effects of this dialogue, or is it more *monological* instead? Are all parties still re-producing old power relations in new forms? In this paper I wish to explore this specific issue by, first, presenting some critical perspectives on how cultural diversity has taken form in the institutional landscape of higher education, and, second, giving brief histories of each of these four distinct institutions located on the University of Regina campus in the province of Saskatchewan.

In the more diverse and multilingual world in which we all live, we should be asking whether cultural diversity remains a factor of exclusion and separation, whether it has been transformed into just another commodity in the market economy or whether, instead, it has the potential to serve as an effective source of institutional renewal. These theoretical and contextual elements are helpful in situating the effect of the power inequities towards Canadian national mi-norities reproduced by the dominant ideologies of the past (Eudaily, 2004). Moreover, these elements may help us to understand whether the opportunity is present at the University of Regina to create a campus where national mi-norities can take part in the evolution of Canadian higher education even though racial, cultural and linguistic marginalization persists in many ways.

From exclusion to commodification of diversity in the academy

Modern universities, through their mandate of delivering/preserving/producing knowledge, tend to reproduce hierarchical, stratified structures and cultural se-lection in society. According to Pierre Bourdieu (1982), "the university field re-produces in its structure the field of power which its own action of selection and inculcation contributes to reproduce its structure . . ." (p. 63). By owning and disseminating knowledge as cultural capital within society, the university contributes to the reproduction of social discrimination. Therefore, by selecting which cultural heritages it privileges, the university community segregates cul-tural minorities and maintains specific power relations embedded in social in-stitutions. Historically, the main purpose of the modern university was to produce and maintain an elite that would propagate the values and ideology of the dominant culture in society (Bourdieu & Wacquant, 1992; Freitag, 2002; Giroux, 2006). In her study of the foundations of the eighteenth-century English university, Reba Soffer (1994) claims that "higher education in England, directly and indirectly, provided a complete and enveloping educational envi-ronment which created durable patterns of behavior and permanent habits of thought" (p. 11). Higher education in modern society has been crucial in main-taining and building a strong and distinct national identity—at the expense, in many ways, of the diversity present within a nation's own boundaries.

Although much of the clerical, elitist and nationalist aspect of the university of the seventeenth to twentieth centuries is past, the overt integration of cultural diversity in universities remains an ongoing strategic issue in the context of the rise of the economy of knowledge in higher education (Laidler, 2002). Moreover, the university's tradition of pursuing excellence in research and education is now under additional pressure as universities must also face: 1) the challenges associated with the post-colonial era (Said, 1978); 2) the new imperatives of late modernity (Giddens, 1984); and 3) the complexities of the new information world (Castells, 2000). In the pluralistic societies of today, population mobility has increased, more fluid interrelations are present, information exchanges are instantaneous and cultural contacts are intensified; all of these factors have significant implications for university development. Universities are encouraged now, more than ever before, to value and integrate diversity as a commodity in the market economy of knowledge (Kirwan, 2004). In that particular capitalistic perspective, universities need to be a competitive actor in this emerging market in which cultural diversity can represent an important added value.

These new social and economic trends have brought to the surface the challenging issue of creating a better campus climate for cultural diversity. As Mayhew, Grunwald and Dey (2006) explain, universities can " . . . measure a campus's climate for diversity [by] ensuring that multiple perspectives from the campus are represented, including individuals who play different roles on campus (faculty, students, staff) as well as multiple campus communities that may be based on race, gender, disability, or field of study" (p. 64). The capacity of universities to integrate more cultural minorities into their administration, staff and faculty is certainly as important as enhancing the general climate for diversity on the campus by supporting specific institutions for cultural minorities. More important, but probably more difficult to achieve, is the decolonization of knowledge itself. As Michael Marker (2004) highlights, " . . . the comfortable patterns of university life and knowledge production not only alienate Indigenous people, they impede healthy institutional change" (p. 111). Enhancing diversity in the academy is linked to reflexive, critical thinking about the concept of "culture," because knowledge itself constitutes a tool for structural change and is a powerful instrument of cognitive imperialism that disclaims other knowledge bases and values (Battiste, 2000).

Diversity and universalism can be seen as among the most important attributes of liberal education associated with the modern university. Frank Hale, Jr. (2004), discussing American universities, states that "it is an illusion to believe that diversity in its genuine sense is alive and well in the academy. . . . We need to face the stark fact of institutional hypocrisy on the issue of diversity" (p. 13). The concept of diversity, taken in the academic and anthropological sense, is an act of resistance to dogmatism, which several scholars argue should be at the heart of the university's mission. Both Alain Giroux (2006) and Bill Readings (1999) define the university as a community of independent thinkers that interrogates reality, where "thought can only do justice to heterogeneity if it does not aim at consensus" (Readings, 1999, p. 187). Thinking critically and questioning consensus are particularly essential in the present state of the institution;

however, these have been disregarded (Good, 2001) by national elitist ideologies, ethnocentric perspectives and, more recently, by the imperatives of the dominant capitalistic market ideology invading the ivory tower.

As Readings presents in his book *The University in Ruins,* the university should become one place, among others, to consider "the social bond without recourse to a unifying idea, whether of Culture or of the State" (1999: 191). A main purpose of the modern university was to link the social service of knowledge production and dissemination to the goal of nation building. This historical mandate has been transformed to respond to the new authority of the market economy of knowledge. Today, the university, like the business world, is guided by indicators of performance that dictate the new arithmetic of academic quality (Giroux, 2006). Quality becomes a synonym for productivity. This new perspective has to be taken into account in order to study the position of national minority institutions within the global context of higher education administration.

From this perspective, cultural diversity is seen less as a source of diversity of knowledge and experience than as a commodity to be exchanged, and from which the institution can gain access to new markets. In this regard, Canada has repositioned itself in the global market, focusing less on the political rights of the people than on the economic benefits offered by plurilingual abilities (Heller, 1998). The present dynamic within a globalized and neo-liberal economy places these institutions in new social settings that make diversity a more critical issue for the future. Increased diversity now seems crucial in adapting more rapidly to global changes. Commenting on this challenging and crucial issue, William Kirwan (2004), president of Ohio State University from 1998 to 2002 and of the University of Maryland from 1989 to 1998, states, "our challenge is not just to prepare enough minority students for success in this new environment. The challenge is to prepare students from *all* races and backgrounds to work effectively in a decidedly more diverse work place" (p. *xxxiii*). Cultural minorities have now become valuable social actors who must deal with the challenges that are bound to a more diverse, multilingual and market-oriented global world. This instrumental perspective on cultural diversity is increasingly valued as a response to the new imperatives of the corporate-oriented university. The democratization of the institution has been subverted; it has subordinated knowledge and research to the direct instrumentality of the economy.

As critiqued by various authors (Freitag, 2002; Giroux, 2006; Good, 2001), the market ideology is now shaping the academic and administrative discourse in higher education institutions by creating a new kind of control over diversity on the campus. "Excellence" has become the buzzword in research and teaching in the new ideology of social service within today's universities. As Readings (1999) states: "Excellence draws only one boundary: the boundary that protects the unrestricted power of the bureaucracy" (p. 33). That boundary "is a problem intimately linked to that of race" (p. 49). There is no cultural content to the notion of excellence; bureaucracies tend to opt for colour-blind policies that favour instrumental action to attain *excellence* in a market perspective. Knowledge and culture have become merchandise to be exchanged in the market economy. This reality, which the university has to manage in order to be more competitive in this market, creates an obstacle in facilitating and promoting the development of critical thought for social change, where national minorities could take part in the renewal of the university. Their specific histories and situation in the university structure also constitute an important aspect of the ability of national minorities to act upon the institution and to keep alive their distinct values and knowledges.

Brief institutional journeys

The University of Regina

Regina College, established by the Methodist Church in 1911, became a satellite campus of the University of Saskatchewan in 1959. It was only in 1974 that the University of Regina was founded by the legislature of the Province of Saskatchewan. The Regina campus took shape in a time of social change, in the '60s, when the drive for social justice and equality spread throughout Canada by various impulses, such as the Quiet Revolution in Quebec, claims to Aboriginal treaty rights and indigenous rights to self-government and the women's liberation movement. These social movements shaped this young university that was deeply rooted in the tradition of liberal education. The mission statement defining the liberal education for the Regina campus gave an emphasis to critical thinking, the pursuit of truth and the desire for societal transformation, while reaffirming its traditional role of "preserving, transmitting and increasing the intellectual heritage of man" (Pitsula, 2006, p. 161). The University of Regina, while adopting liberal education values of equality and pluralism, has embraced a higher educational ideology of an individual meritocratic perspective.

The Fransaskois community

Access to French education for the Francophones of Saskatchewan was almost non-existent for most of the twentieth century (Denis, 2006; Behiels, 2004). Through judicial contestation and Charter rights, Fransaskois did receive funding and the full management of their schools in 1997 after many court procedures. Post-secondary education for Francophones outside Quebec was not included in their constitutional rights. However, since 1968, the French language has had an important legislative status under the federal *Official Languages Act* and through the national policy of bilingualism, both of which have facilitated the presence of the French language at the university, even though French-speaking people represented no more than 5 percent of the provincial population in the 1960s.

At Regina College, French was first a subject of study offered by the Department of Modern Languages. The idea of a bilingual college and French cultural institution was discussed at the Regina campus as early as 1964. Four years later, the *Centre d'Études Bilingues* was created, offering cultural activities and bilingual B.A. and B.ED. programs. In 1971, a French Department was created, separating French from Germanic and Slavic Studies. By 1982, a teacher education program in French (*Baccalauréat en Éducation Française*) was launched through the Faculty of Education. Almost 10 years later, the federal and provincial governments financed the construction of the Language Institute building to house the *Institut de Formation Linguistique,* which was intended to offer more programs in French for Fransaskois youth and which would replace the *Centre d'Études Bilingues.* This new institute did not respond totally to the aspirations of the Fransaskois community, being mainly oriented to the teaching of French language and, later on, international languages. The community pledged, after an internal review of the *Institut* by the university in 2002, to create a new institution which would receive a broader mandate—to support through educational programs and research activities the development of French language and culture in the province of Saskatchewan. At the time of writing, the *Institut Français* is in its sixth year of existence. In the Fall of 2007, in partnership with various faculties on campus and with universities in Québec and New Brunswick, it offered its first original B.A. program (*Baccalauréat en études francophones*). The *Institut Français* is fairly well-recognized by the Fransaskois community as an important tool for research and French post-secondary programming for its youth.

The First Nations

Saskatchewan has the highest provincial population per capita of First Nations in the country. Through treaty rights, elementary and secondary education of First Nations youth is the responsibility of the federal government through the Department of Indian Affairs. Higher education is not formally recognized as a right for First Nations people, who have struggled to access post-secondary education since the mid-1960s, and who are still working to remove the obstacles blocking this goal. In that regard, the partnership initiated in 1976 between First Nations people of Saskatchewan and the University of Regina can offer some light on this particular challenge as it has evolved over the past thirty years.

Saskatchewan's First Nations people accepted the federated college model proposed by the newly appointed university president, Dr. Lloyd Barber, in 1976. Dr. Barber had strong liberal values (Pitsula, 2006), and he had completed a term as the federally appointed Indian Land Commissioner. The Saskatchewan Indian Federated College (SIFC) was then created and incorporated under the Federation of Saskatchewan Indian (FSI) legislation. Many observers regarded the agreement between the University of Regina and the SIFC as a novel experiment, unique in Canada. The FSI's Chief Ahenakew stated that this college was "a major breakthrough and a significant step forward for Indian education in North America. This is the only place, to the best of our knowledge, where Indians have succeeded in establishing a formalized, equal partnership with a university" (as cited in Stonechild, 2006, p. 93).

The agreement gave important administrative autonomy to SIFC to employ professors and to offer multiple programs for First Nations students. These programs were required to be presented to academic committees for accreditation by the university. SIFC struggled with financial issues. While the number of student credit hours rose, funding by Indian Affairs became a fixed, annual operating cost. SIFC taught more classes than the two other federated colleges, Campion and Luther, but received only a quarter of their provincial grants (Stonechild, 2006, p. 109). In this difficult, but promising, situation, Dr. Eber Hampton, president of SIFC from 1991 to 2005, pushed towards the objective of a fully independent First Nations university. In 2002, the First Nations University of Canada (FNUC) was founded and located east of the main campus in a new building designed by Douglas Cardinal to reflect and symbolize an Aboriginal world view.

In 2005, FNUC had internal problems when a political appointee, board chairman Morley Watson, one of the vice-chiefs of the Federation of Saskatchewan Indian Nations, intervened in the management of the university, which led to the resignation of the highly respected FNUC president, Dr. Eber Hampton. This political intrusion into the academic realm brought the credibility of the FNUC to its lowest point, putting its accreditation by the Association of Canadian Colleges and Universities in peril. As Blair Stonechild (2006) affirms, "creating, operating, and maintaining an Aboriginal post-secondary institution within a colonialist environment that produces more failures than successes is a daunting challenge" (p. 135). The internal difficulties at FNUC are not yet resolved, and the University of Regina seems to be powerless in the matter.

The Métis

The federated college agreement with First Nations people led the way, in 1986, for the affiliation of the Métis teacher-training program, SUNTEP,[2] instigated by the newly created (in 1980) Gabriel Dumont Institute (GDI). The GDI was established as the educational arm of the Association of Métis and Non-Status Indians of Saskatchewan (representing Native people of mixed ancestry) with the following mission: " . . . to promote the renewal and development of Native culture through appropriate research activities, material development, collection and distribution of educational materials, and by the design, development and delivery of specific educational and cultural programs and services. Sufficient Métis and Non-Status Indian people will be trained in the required skills, commitment and confidence to make the goal of self-government a reality" (GDI, 1987). This new partnership did not develop into a federated college model, but into an "affiliation" that gave to the GDI's SUNTEP program academic accreditation and, therefore, specific provincial funding. Spaces for teaching and for administration of the program were rented from the University of Regina. This

2.   Saskatchewan Urban Native Teacher Education Program.

partnership allows the program to benefit from the infrastructure of the university while maintaining its independence from the university administration.

Policies of recognition in higher education

During the 1960s and 1970s, North America witnessed the rise of social movements for human rights, social justice and the establishment of a "politics of recognition" for minority populations. In Canada, a multicultural policy was proposed and adopted by the federal government to negotiate cultural conflicts emerging in the '60s and '70s. The policy of multiculturalism is an ideal of a democratic, pluralistic society, advocating empathy for minorities on the basis of a common humanity. The multiculturalism discourse is imbued throughout Canadian public institutions as an ideology that negotiates cultural conflicts and is a mechanism to redress inequity through education-sharing and the exchange of ideas. Still, as George Dei and Agnes Calliste argue, it " . . . works with the notion of our basic humanness and downplays inequities of difference by accentuating shared commonalities" (2000, p. 144). Because a multicultural ideology advocates that we all start from a relatively level "playing field," it hides the historical legacies and racial imageries of the past that can perpetuate cultural domination in educational institutions. Social inequity cannot be resolved by only empathy and humanness; critical action must also be undertaken by institutions to highlight and discontinue persistent inequities and power imbalances. Critical perspectives, such as the anti-racist theory proposed by Dei and Calliste (2000), have a primary task to "identify, challenge and change values, structures and behavior that perpetuate systemic racism" (p. 21). They represent an essential approach to redressing the issues of racism through fundamental structural/societal change. However, national minorities refuse, with reason, to be integrated in a Canadian cultural mosaic where they would have the same political status as newly arrived immigrants. As founding people, national minorities argue that they have specific rights over land and language, for example, that newer immigrants should not have.

This kind of national policy is supposedly based on a "neutral set of difference-blind principles of the politics of equal dignity but is in fact a reflection of one hegemonic culture" (Taylor, 1994, p. 43). This form of policies-of-equal-respect has a tendency to implement programs to ensure more dignity for a segregated population by insisting on uniform rules that define those rights without exception. For members of distinct collectivities such as national minorities, however, these policies could be most discriminatory in many ways because, once again, the policies do not recognize their specific collective rights. The main challenge is to find ways to remain receptive to collective goals while operating within a policy-of-equal-respect. In that sense, the creation of a specific higher education institution with a largely autonomous status could better respond to these collective aspirations. In the United States, black colleges and universities were founded to respond better to the specific needs of their communities (Hale,

2004). Support groups and counselling services were also implemented in some of these unique universities. Such mainstream policies have been useful; however, as Glen Jones (1997) has stated, it is simply not enough. Universities also need to develop a university-wide approach, whose ultimate goal would be to increase the retention and graduation rates of students of multiple cultural backgrounds.

The adoption of the *Canadian Charter of Rights and Freedoms* in 1982 responded in many ways to the Francophone community's demands to control their own education. However, in Canada, education has always been a provincial responsibility. Even though national policies defended Francophone rights, communities still had to establish agreements with provincial governments, for example, through court settlements in the 1990s. The Charter did not include any rights regarding higher education. The Francophone presence at the University of Regina was not the result of any specific legislation, but mainly the result of the "open mind" of the university administration, which recognized the value of bilingualism in Canada and the benefits of having a French presence on campus.

In the 1990s, the Conservative government led by Grant Devine was fighting in the courts against the right of the Fransaskois community to obtain school management. Paradoxically, the Devine government agreed to the federal government investment in the construction of the Language Institute building at the university, still the landmark of the Fransaskois presence on campus. In 2002, it was again because of funding from the federal government and agreements with provincial agencies and the university that the Francophone community continued its presence on the campus. However, without sufficient demographics or political weight, Francophones were unable to negotiate a federated agreement. They had to integrate into the university structure under the appellation of *institute,* which greatly limited their academic and administrative autonomy because of its non-academic status, lack of space control and unstable status inside the university.

First Nations are still managed under the 1876 *Canadian Indian Act* and, therefore, are under the management of the federal Department of Indian Affairs, which administers funding for all their educational institutions. This situation constitutes a heavy burden, as jurisdiction over First Nations post-secondary education is still controversial and partly imbued with an unwillingness to change. Stonechild states that the " . . . federal government's current policy is to limit First Nations aspirations by delivering such education as a social program only in order to bring First Nations participation rates to a level comparable to the rest of society." (2006, p. 138). However, education being a provincial responsibility, First Nations had to establish a formal agreement with a provincial institution in order to achieve their aspirations in higher education. While First Nations University of Canada is touted as the only First Nations-controlled university in Canada, having pushed through federal legislation to take the title "university" and directly receive regular federal funds, it is still under the umbrella of University of Regina programs and the "goodwill" of

Indian Affairs to fund it. This situation maintains a state of dependency, reproducing old power relations of colonial status for First Nations people of Canada.

For their part, Métis people are not recognized as status Indians under the *Indian Act* or by the constitution; therefore, they have had to rely mainly on the goodwill of the provincial government to fund their institutions. Although federal funds are set aside for post-secondary indigenous education, these funds are primarily for the use of First Nations and Inuit peoples, with little or no specific support for Métis education (Jenkins, 2005, p. 12). The distribution of these funds was based on agreements between the federal government and provincial or territorial education service providers. The Gabriel Dumont Institute has an affiliation agreement with both Saskatchewan universities (the University of Regina and the University of Saskatchewan), an agreement that opens the access to funding by both the provincial and the federal governments.

Ongoing challenges: partnerships for dialogue in the academy

The University of Regina is a unique campus in Canada, characterized by the presence of three institutions that represent the founding peoples of the country—First Nations University of Canada, Gabriel Dumont Institute and the more recent *Institut Français*—although the University of Regina is still within the context of a dominant Anglophone institution in a settler society. Unique agreements have been signed with each of these communities that allow some sort of administrative autonomy, program development and capacity to maintain their cultural specificities. However, the university as a whole has not implemented any specific policies or programs to "identify, challenge and change values, structures and behavior that perpetuate systemic racism" (Dei & Calliste, 2000, p. 21). For example, there are no university-wide programs that would: first, recognize the national minorities as unique and significant constituent parts of the university's identity; second, acknowledge the added value of cultural diversity for students and faculty on campus; third, facilitate dialogue and awareness about racist histories regarding national minorities; and, finally, promote administrative practices that would enhance the general climate for diversity on campus by ensuring a diversity in staff, faculty and students. While there are specific policies regarding equity and harassment in employment, this is not enough to enhance the climate for diversity and bring forward a critical policy promoted by the highest level in the university administration so that the First Nations, Métis and Francophone populations can be an integrated part of the transformation of the whole institution. It could represent a powerful *communicative action* strategy, as Jürgen Habermas (2003; 1984) has developed it, to create spaces for dialogue between the principal actors of diversity on this unique Canadian campus. However, to be able to create these spaces, all actors have to be open to constructive dialogue with the other and share common knowledge of the issues at hand. Such a context can be facilitated by the hosting university, but cannot succeed without the full commitment of all other parties.

In this regard, important challenges have to be taken into account, namely, the internall difficulties that must be dealt with by these three institutions in minority settings. Sufficient funding must be secured to allow long-term planning and development. Blair Stonechild affirms this regarding FNUC: " . . . federal and provincial governments . . . underfunded the institution, making it impossible to achieve its ambitious mission" (2006, p. 134). The funding issues are crucial, especially considering the high demands these three institutions have to meet in a short period. They have to resolve the social consequences of decades of exclusion from higher education, which include a persistent lack of education of their population, lack of management experience in higher education institutions and the psychological consequences of racism. The trauma of colonialism, assimilation and social exclusion is characteristic, at various levels, of these three higher education institutions, trauma which can cause internal collapse or the emergence of conflicts with partners.

The 2005 crisis at FNUC, where political appointees of the Federation of Saskatchewan Indian Nations intervened in the university administration, profoundly disrupted the academic credibility and the sustainable future of the institution. The intertwined relations between the FNUC and the community political bodies constitute a strong foundation for their development; however, it can, paradoxically, also constitute a significant political obstacle to any possible intercultural dialogue on campus, especially where an ethnic form of governance is present. This type of ethnic governing approach tends to exclude any partners that are not ethnically identical (Breton, 1991). In that sense, strong and formal partnerships with the university were extremely difficult for First Nations and Métis people, because obtaining their autonomy in higher education constituted the broad strategy for these institutions to ensure their own development. It is a strategy that is likely to reproduce some forms of exclusion and poor dialogical partnerships with the University of Regina. In contrast, the Francophones, with an integrated status, had to maintain a strong dialogue with the university's administration to ensure the attainment of their objectives.

The history of higher education for national minorities in Canada in general and, more specifically, in Saskatchewan is very brief. The University of Regina scenario is more promising than other institutions in Canada in regards to establishing partnerships with independent institutions for national minorities. The University of Regina could assume a national leadership role in promoting and exposing the benefits of a more diverse campus. However, this legacy cannot be taken for granted; anti-racist university-wide policies need to be implemented in partnership with Métis, Francophones and First Nations, policies that would recognize national minorities at the core of the university's identity and therefore become a priority in its institutional planning and development.

Policies and action should be taken that definitively affirm that differences are a strength and that diversity can be the essence of excellence in the academy. Again, a policy is not enough; communicative action strategies and spaces of dialogue are essential to breaking the chains of old racist and discriminatory legacies that are ingrained in the relationship between the historically dominant group and national minorities. Trust and confidence have to be fully restored between these groups through constructive dialogue that could, in some respects, reinvent the academy in positive ways and contribute to liberating its knowledge of racist residues. These new foundations for partnership would also contribute to making cultural diversity a powerful tool of social transformation in the university as well as in the communities. This perspective could also fracture the knowledge-economy theory of institutional commodity of diversity. A diverse and inclusive campus constitutes a clear advantage for student recruitment, but it certainly can mean more than an increase in numbers. Higher education in general, and the University of Regina specifically, should assume that the issues of *diversity* and social inclusiveness are an important contemporary challenge and that they have a responsibility to ensure that these ideas do not remain only abstract concepts of the ivory tower, but, rather, values for change.

REFERENCES

Battiste, M. (2000). Maintaining aboriginal identity, language, and culture in modern society. In M. Battiste (Ed.), *Reclaiming indigenous voice and vision* (pp. 192–208). Vancouver: ubc Press.

Barnhardt, R. (1991). Higher education in the Fourth World: Indigenous people take control. *Canadian Journal of Native Education, 18*(2), 199–231.

Behiels, M. D. (2004). *Canada's francophone minority communities: Constitutional renewal and the winning of school governance.* Montreal: McGill-Queen's University Press.

Bourdieu, P. (1982). *Langage et pouvoir symbolique.* Paris: Fayard.

Bourdieu, P., & Wacquant, L. (1992). *An invitation to reflexive sociology.* Chicago: University of Chicago Press.

Breton, R. (1991). *The governance of ethnic communities: Political structures and processes in Canada.* New York: Greenwood Press.

Calliste, A. (2000). Anti-racist organizing and resistance in academia. In G. J. S. Dei and A. Calliste (Eds.), *Power, knowledge and anti-racism education: A critical reader* (pp. 141–164). Halifax: Fernwood Publishing.

Castells, M. (2000). *The information age: Economy, society and culture* (Vols. 1–3). Oxford: Blackwell.

Cummins, J., & Danesi, M. (1990). *Heritage languages: The development and denial of Canada's linguistic resources.* Toronto: Our Schools/Our Selves Education Foundation: Garamond Press.

Dei, G.J.S., & Calliste, A. (Eds.). (2000). *Power, knowledge and anti-racism education: A critical reader.* Halifax: Fernwood Publishing.

Dei, G. J. S., Karumanchery, L., & Karumanchery-Luik, N. (2004). *Playing the race card: Exposing white power and privilege.* New York: Peter Lang.

Denis, W. B. (2006). Francophone education in Saskatchewan: Resisting anglo-hegemony. In B. Nooman, D. Hallman & M. Scharf (Eds.), *A History of Education in Saskatchewan* (pp. 87–108). Regina: Canadian Plains Research Center.

Ettner, C. (2004). Lessons in assimilation and resistance: A cross-cultural perspective on aboriginal/minority education. In R. W. Heber (Ed.), *Issues in aboriginal/minority education: Canada, China, Taiwan* (pp. 41–51). Regina: First Nations University of Canada, Indigenous Studies Research Centre.

Eudaily, S. P. (2004). *The present politics of the past: Indigenous legal activism and resistance to (neo) liberal governmentality.* New York: Routledge.

Friesen, J. W. (1983). *Schools with a purpose.* Calgary: Detselig Enterprises.

Freitag, M. (1999). L'université aujourd'hui: Les enjeux du maintien de sa mission institutionnelle d'orientation de la société. In G. Gagné (Ed.), *Main basse sur l'éducation* (pp. 237–294). Québec: Éditions Nota bene.

GDI (Gabriel Dumont Institute). (1987). *Gabriel Dumont Institute of Native Studies and Applied Research brochure.* Regina: Gabriel Dumont Institute of Native Studies and Applied Research.

Giddens, A. (1984). *The constitution of society: Introduction of the theory of structuration.* Berkeley: University of California Press.

Giroux, A. (2006). *Le pacte faustien de l'université.* Montréal: Liber.

Good, G. (2001). *Humanism betrayed: Theory, ideology, and culture in the contemporary university.* Montreal: McGill-Queen's University Press.

Habermas, J. (2003). *L'éthique de la discussion et la question de la vérité.* Paris: Grasset.

Hale, F. W. (Ed.). (2004). *What makes racial diversity work in higher education: Academic leaders present successful policies and strategies.* Sterling: Stylus.

Heber, R. W. (Ed.). (2004). *Issues in aboriginal/minority education: Canada, China, Taiwan.* Regina: First Nations University of Canada, Indigenous Studies Research Centre.

Heller, M. (1998). *Linguistic minorities and modernity: A sociolinguistic ethnography.* New York: Longman.

Jenkins, A. L. (2007). Indigenous post-secondary institutions in Canada and the U.S. *Higher Education Perspectives, 3*(1), 1–27.

Jones, G. A. (1997). *Higher education in Canada: Different systems, different perspectives.* New York: Garland Publishing.

Kirwan, W. E. (2004). Diversity in higher education—why it matters. In F. W. Hale (Ed.), *What makes racial diversity work in higher education* (pp. xxi-xxiv). Sterling: Stylus.

Kymlicka, W. (2003) *La voie canadienne: Repenser le multiculturalisme.* Montréal: Boréal.

Laidler, D. (Ed.). (2002). *Renovating the ivory tower: Canadian universities and the knowledge economy.* Toronto: C. D. Howe Institute.

Littlejohn, C. (2006). The schooling of First Nations and Metis children in Saskatchewan schools to 1960. In B. Nooman, D. Hallman & M. Scharf (Eds.), *A history of education in Saskatchewan* (pp. 63–86). Regina: Canadian Plains Research Center.

Marker, M. (2004). Theories and disciplines as sites of struggle: The reproduction of colonial dominance through the controlling of knowledge in the academy. *Canadian Journal of Native Education, 28*(1–2), 102–110.

Mayhew, M., Grunwald, H., & Dey, E. (2006). Breaking the silence: Achieving a positive campus climate for diversity from the staff perspective. *Research in Higher Education, 47*(1), 63–88.

Morrow, R. A., & Torres, C. A. (1998). Education and the reproduction of class, gender, and race: Responding to the postmodern challenge. In C. A. Torres & T. R. Mitchell (Eds.), *Sociology of education: emerging perspectives* (pp. 19–46). Albany: State University of New York Press.

Pitsula, J. M. (2006). *As one who serves: The making of the University of Regina.* Montreal: McGill-Queen's University Press.

Popkewitz, T. S. (1998). The sociology of knowledge and the sociology of education: Michel Foucault and critical traditions. In C. A. Torres & T. R. Mitchell (Eds.), *Sociology of education: Emerging perspectives* (pp. 47–90). Albany: State University of New York Press.

Readings, B. (1996). *The university in ruins.* Cambridge, Harvard University Press.

Said, E. (1978). *Orientalism.* New York, Pantheon Books.

Soffer, R. N. (1994). *Discipline and power: The university, history, and the making of an English elite, 1870–1930.* Stanford: Stanford University Press.

Stonechild, B. (2006). *The new buffalo: The struggle for aboriginal post-secondary education in Canada.* Winnipeg: University of Manitoba Press.

Taylor, C. (1994) *Multiculturalism.* Princeton: Princeton University Press.

CHAPTER 4

A CIRCLE IS MORE THAN A STRAIGHT LINE CURVED: MIS(SED)UNDERSTANDING ABOUT FIRST NATIONS SCIENCE

Alison Sammel

The notion that science education is politically neutral is in itself highly political, and should be recognized as such. Further, the purposes served by this myth of neutrality need to be clearly illuminated. (Gill & Levidow, 1987, p. 4)

In this chapter I explore examples of how Western science, and science education[1], is a highly privileged social construction rather than being a neutral finder, indicator and communicator of truth. Far from being objective, science and science education reflect a particular paradigm founded upon a political, economic and classist colonial legacy. Through the research questions science privileges, one can see the legacy of colonialism and how scientific outcomes and processes have served certain peoples to the detriment and exclusion of others. The economic and political interests of what is investigated in the name of science, and what is ignored, are seldom discussed in science education. Further, science education has tended to ignore classism, racism, sexism, heterosexism, ageism and speciesism. For two decades, post-colonial science scholars such as Anne Fausto-Sterling (1991), Sandra Harding (1994), and Maralee Mayberry and Leigh Welling (2000) have been suggesting a critical examination of science's relationship to structures of power in modern and postmodern societies in order to generate social

---

1. Unless stated otherwise, references to "science" and "science education" will imply Western science and Western science education, as it is being argued that the ideological frames are reflective of this paradigm.

action and cultural transformation. As a middle-class, white woman working in science teacher education, I have embraced this challenge: my research seeks to explore how racial concepts are normalized within pre-service science education. Rather than starting with the *a priori* of objectivity or "naturalness," I believe science education needs to illustrate how the current relationships between rationality, nature, culture and science are not "naturally" linked, but are constructed within the boundaries and influences of a certain historical period. My pedagogic goal is for science teachers to appreciate how Western scientific knowledge is constituted in culture, and how it, in turn, manufactures the relationship between nature and culture. More research is needed in this area to explore how white privilege and other forms of dominance impact the learning and teaching of science. I suggest there is a great need for academic discussions around what is taught in the name of science education. It is hoped that these discussions might lead to changes in the ideological foundations, pedagogic implementations, curriculum development and assessment strategies of traditional science pedagogy.

In 2005 I conducted a study that explored how science teacher candidates in Regina, Saskatchewan,[2] made sense of their thoughts and beliefs about the relationship between science education and First Nations science. The participants discussed issues directly relating to science and culture, and their narratives provide important pedagogic information for praxis. This chapter discusses some of the findings of this study in order to investigate the larger picture of the social and educational indoctrination of what is privileged and excluded in the contemporary teaching and learning of science at these institutions.

Goal and method of the study

The background of this study is situated in science education research literature that proposes science teachers' instructional practices are more closely aligned with, and influenced by, general beliefs about teaching and learning than by understandings of the nature of science teaching (Abell & Smith, 1994; Aguirre et al., 1990; Laplante, 1997; Lederman, 1992; Yerrick et al., 1998). A review of science education research showed that much of the research into science pedagogy has focused on analysing the content and strategies of science education, rather than on investigating the beliefs science teachers have about the nature and role of education, or how these understandings affect what they teach, or how they believe science is most effectively taught (Lederman, 1992; Southerland et al., 2003). This study, then, proposed to clarify the relationship between science educators' generic understandings of the teaching and learning of science and their beliefs and actions regarding First Nations science education. This study is particularly important because of the systemic and individual

---

2.   Students were enrolled at the University of Regina, the First Nations University of Canada and in the Saskatchewan Urban Native Teacher Education Program.

transformations that are a necessary part of learning First Nations science ideologies within the teaching and learning of Western orientations of science (Cajete, 2000).

This research used grounded theory to unravel the nature and meaning of an educational experience for a group of people in a particular setting. The researcher identified the main themes found in the data and formatted the themes into summaries and hypotheses as this "story" unfolded. Statistical analysis helped to contextualize further these findings. The aim was to construct an integrated story specific to the narratives of the people participating in this research. Data were collected through an online questionnaire given during the Winter 2005 semester to 91 pre-service science students. Most questions were "open-ended"—such as, "What would successful science education look like?"—and participants were given as much space to respond as they wanted (as it was online).

Of the 91 pre-service students who participated in this study, 13 percent indicated they were of First Nations or Métis ancestry, while 87 percent indicated they were not. The fact that the majority of students taking pre-service science education that semester identified their ethnicity as white is reflective of the teaching demographic in Saskatchewan.

Understanding assumptions of Western science education

A racist society will give you a racist science. (Young, 1987)

There should be no need to state that First Nations peoples of Canada have distinct beliefs, principles and cultures that are inherently valuable, and that infrastructures must be established and resourced to enable them to flourish. However, the majority of science education policies, curricula and teaching processes would indicate that what is taught as science is still tethered to Western understandings of the world. Feminist or "post" studies critique this Western ideology for its flawed façade of objectivity and neutrality and for its belief in a quest towards the "truth" (Calabrese Barton, 1998; Gill & Levidow, 1987; Harding, 1991, 1994; Kumashiro, 2001; Lee, 1999; Letts, 1999; Sammel, 2006; Sammel & Zandvliet, 2003). Such work criticizes science education for normalizing Western ideologies, beliefs and agendas by choosing to ignore the following: underlying political or economic priorities of science; science's appropriation of other cultures' science knowledge; the way science theory has been or is currently used to justify the oppression of peoples for political gain; the central role science and technology play in the defensive, economic and political agendas of nations and multinational corporations; its historical and contemporary roles in rationalizing an exploitative ideological perspective towards the more-than-human world and the natural environment; and, finally, the alienating effect this subject has on students when used as a ranking and sorting mechanism by educational systems (Gill & Levidow, 1987). Despite such examinations, or its own avowed purpose to provide a means for arriving at a truth, much of science education seems resistant to engaging in critical thinking about itself. Subsequently, belief in its epistemology is accepted as a matter of faith and enacted accordingly.

In this era, most science education still reflects the social power base of the hegemonic white, privileged agenda and, through the discourse of meritocracy, proclaims the false promise that all students can succeed. Consequently, dominant science education becomes colour-blind by not seeing "colour" and all related political, social, infrastructural, historical and power agendas and their effects. The diversity of ways of understanding the world within First Nations cultures are rendered invisible and invalid by science and science education, as there is little or no recognition of different cultural understandings or values in science education curricula. The goal of hegemonic Western science education is to increase scientific literacy, and that implies knowledge of contemporary (hegemonic Western) science. Thankfully, there are science educators who speak back to this agenda, and a contemporary literature review produces many examples of anti-racist pedagogy.[3] Frequently, however, it is assumed that science education will help First Nations peoples join the modern world by providing access to jobs in the sciences or other "highly skilled" career fields that require science education as a prerequisite. These jobs are presumed to develop workers' neo-liberal sensibilities and responsibilities as citizens, as they produce patents, products and spendable paycheques, all benefiting Canada's gross domestic product. In this way, science education and the knowledge therein could be described as knowledge constituted within a discourse heavily invested in an ideology that Michael Peters (1996) calls *Homo economicus,* or a form of economic rationalism. Within this discourse, it is advantageous, both for national conformity and for economic success, that every student—whether white, black or brindle—be assimilated into the world of science education through the "white" lens.

To understand the world through another ideology, such as the many frames of North America's First Nations communities, would imply exploring other systems, principles and tenets of cultures that have developed over many centuries within specific geographic locations. A common principle among First Nations is the assumption that in nature everything is in a constant process of change (Kyle, 2001). After long-term observations, one might begin to see regular patterns, but these, too, are subject to change. The only thing that is constant is change. The only truth is change, along with the resulting need to balance oneself and one's society in a constantly living and changing world. This is in opposition to the historical principles of Western science, where certain patterns are thought to remain the same. These are called laws and their "truths" can be "found." Here

3.   See, for example, the work of Angela Calabrese Barton and the journal *Cultural Studies of Science Education,* which "examines science education as a cultural, cross-age, cross-class, and cross-disciplinary phenomenon" (http://www.springer.com/education/journal/11422).

the belief is that all that can be known is waiting "out there" to be discovered by humans. Once found, these laws are perceived as secure and unchanging.

The term "Native science" is used by indigenous researchers such as Gregory Cajete (2000) to articulate how First Nations science is conceptually different from Western science and has the potential to transform student thinking about Western science. In fact, the term "Native science" is a metaphor, as there is no word in native languages for science. Native science describes coming to know what has evolved through human experience with the natural world. Native science is born of a lived and storied participation with the natural landscape. To gain a sense of Native science one must participate with the natural world. To understand the foundations of Native science one must become open to the roles of sensations, perception, imagination, emotion, symbols and spirit, as well as those of concept, logic, and rational empiricism (Cajete, p. 2). From this perspective, First Nations science presents a different ideological frame from that of Western science. Post-colonial education scholars such as Anne Fausto-Sterling (1991) advocate that different cultural positioning is the reason that First Nations or Native science has been deliberately underdeveloped since colonization. She states: "We must talk about how European science and technology helped to kill off non-European science and engineering, and how our seemingly wondrous technological expansion happened at the expense of the rest of the world. We must start to think in terms of European and American over-development as a complement to African underdevelopment" (p. 9). The term "Native science" is used in this chapter, then, not to conjure up dualistic thinking, but in order to highlight a complex, historical, interconnected relationship that is rarely spoken of within science education. By analyzing this complex relationship using words and the meanings pre-service students give to these words, I am seeking to use language as a tool to "trouble," or critique, knowledge (re)production, as described by Elizabeth Ellsworth (1997) and Kevin Kumashiro (2001).

Responses of students

This section explores the narratives of the participants in order to make visible the often-concealed images, storylines, metaphors and concepts of the dominant ideology. By identifying what is normalized within the entanglements of society and the teaching and learning of science, we can engage in the more directed task of re-envisioning science education in such a way as to disrupt Western privilege. It is *this*—its potential for decolonizing scientific knowledge and process, breaking oppressive power relations and creating spaces for new ways of teaching—that I believe science education must seriously begin to address.

Participants' thoughts on science education

At the primary, secondary or tertiary level, science education is predominantly marketed as student-centered and hands-on to help promote understanding of and engagement with Western scientific concepts (Abd-Khalick & Lederman, 2000; Bianchini & Solomon, 2003; Schwartz & Lederman, 2002). Thus, pre-service science education emphasizes making science fun and relevant to students. The assumption is that if students are "experiencing science" through hands-on approaches they will understand rather than memorize the science concepts being taught. It is hoped that through relevant and entertaining activities students will have greater engagement with science concepts and thus increase their scientific literacy. Scientific literacy, in its most common usage in contemporary science education, implies providing students with a useful understanding of science so they can apply this knowledge to a plethora of experiences in their multi-faceted lives (Bybee, 1997; Fensham, 2002; Murcia, 2005).

In this study the participants were asked to complete the open-ended statement, "When I think of science education, I think of. . . ." They could write a few concepts in their responses, and the majority included the following:

- Western science content (46%)
- Laboratory experiments and/or demonstrations (44%)
- Lecturing and note-taking (30%).

When asked what successful science education included, they answered:

- Hands-on science learning (50%)
- Fun science (36%)
- Student-centered learning (17%)
- Information relevant to students (14%)
- Incorporation of "other perspectives or issues" (12%)
- Inclusion of First Nations perspectives (1%).

Additionally, when asked what advice the participants would give to their former science teachers, the most frequent responses were:

- Use more hands-on, interactive approaches to teaching science (46%)
- Make science more fun and/or interesting (46%)
- Make science relevant to students (26%)
- Promote understanding rather than memorization (12%)
- Increase the use of labs or demonstrations (12%).

The participants' responses are reflective of the contemporary dominant discourse in science education, where the underlying goal is to provide more efficient ways to teach Western science content. The acquisition of Western academic content takes precedence over pedagogy, and laboratory experiments are understood as the quintessential science experience. In naming what they believe makes up successful science education, these participants also shed light on what is marginalized or excluded in the teaching and learning of science. It is what the participants leave out that is most telling of their subjectivity and the interpellation into contemporary science education. It should be noted that student responses do not entirely originate with them. Their responses highlight the discursive construction of what has been normalized and privileged in the academy. What is absent in the participants' understandings of science education is an examination or critique of the privileging of Western science and the impact this legacy has had and continues to have on everything occupying this planet. In the participant responses there was no critique of science or science education included in the advice given to teachers. Rather, their only advice was how to make the acquisition of Western science more effective, with an emphasis on using hands-on, relevant and fun methods. What was excluded was the need for a critical exploration of problematic colonized infrastructure, or outcomes, inherent in Western science and Western science education. While one participant suggested that critical thinking needs to occur in science resources to address stereotypes associated with gender disparities in the fields of science, he or she provided no further critique of how power is played out in science and science education in relation to economics, politics, race, class, heterosexism, ageism or speciesism.

In line with arguments by Angela Calabrese Barton (1998), Dawn Gill and Les Levidow (1987), Sandra Harding (1991, 1994), Kevin Kumashiro (2001) and Alison Sammel (2004), the findings of this section suggest that teaching science or science education uncritically promotes the status quo and invariably maintains infrastructural inequities. Since none of the participants spoke of conceiving a space for a critique of the privileging of Western science, this suggests that those who research and teach with the agenda of highlighting the relationship between culture, politics, nature and science still have a long way to go in reconstructing science education as a site for negotiating equity.

Thoughts on First Nations science education

When asked what the term "First Nations Science" would suggest, the participants responded:

- Including nature-based science content (such as sustainability, plants, animals and weather conditions) (35%)
- Learning First Nations culture or beliefs (13%)
- Learning how First Nations knowledge fits into Western science (13%)
- Teaching First Nations history (10%)
- Unsure of what First Nations science is (8%)
- Teaching the medicine wheel (5%).

First Nations science was strongly associated with the natural environment. First Nations peoples were described in this study as being the "first conservationists," "the biologists," rather than as cultural groups who also employed knowledge that Western science would call physics, chemistry, etc. As one participant commented, "if you were to teach First Nations science you would also need to teach physics and chemistry." Participants were concerned that if First Nations science were to be included in science education, "it could take away from the logical explanation of the biological and chemical parts of science," thereby implying a loss of logical explanations and/or Western science content. This was echoed by another student's fears that First Nations science was just a "dumbed-down version of science," and that those students pursuing university degrees would be penalized by this content inclusion/exclusion. Comments that Western science is "hard science" and "the truth" and that First Nations science has "not much content," "is not accurate" and "is not as advanced" were situated beside comments that stereotyped First Nations science as "nature based" and a "more primitive science." The invisible history of white privilege within science education is told by these participants' value judgements.

White privilege is "a set of locations that are historically, socially, politically and culturally produced and, moreover, are intrinsically linked to unfolding relations of dominance" (Frankenberg, 1993, p. 6). White privilege is symbolic rather than biological and therefore is better understood as a construct of racial dominance rather than as a personal or individual possession (Levine-Rasky, 2000). As a discursive practice, it sustains Eurocentric world views through policies and laws (Shome, 1999) and is held in place by inherited ideologies and infrastructures. The pre-service student responses of "physics envy" are a reflection of white privilege. Anne Fausto-Sterling (1991) suggests that physics is perceived as the pinnacle of a scientific pyramid. It is seen as the best model for doing science because it is believed to be more contextually stripped, that is, removed from socio-cultural influences. To these students—who seem unaware of any relationship between culture, science and nature—physics and chemistry are almost entirely removed from the biases of socio-cultural influences, existing as science should: objective, neutral and rational. In contrast, these students consider First Nations science to be inseparable from its context. Thus, without their knowing what it might consist of, but according to the standards of evaluation that Western culture has provided them to measure the legitimacy of science, they perceive First Nations science as less valid. This is very apparent in later discussions around spirituality.

How the students perceive what can be considered "science content" provides further insight into the impact of white privilege on the education of these students. The participants assume that First Nations knowledge is "isolated" content, devoid of time and location and universally agreed upon, a story that captures all and can be told anywhere and anytime and always make the same sense. According to the Western pedagogical model, the participants spoke of capturing and essentializing First Nations science in order to put it in digestible pieces of content for later student regurgitation. In contrast, Cajete (2000) explains that First Nations science cannot be reduced to agreed-upon concepts; nor can it be taught without connection to the local places where that knowledge was gained. The participants' responses reflect the metanarrative of Western science education, in which knowledge is depicted as universal, detached, cleanly captured, defined and unitary. This again speaks to the normalization of Western science, where Othered pedagogies are assumed to be "naturally" like Western concepts, processes and structures and can be easily assimilated if teacher-friendly resources are available. In this way, the dominant message the system provides is that a (white) teacher could simply add the allusive homogenous First Nations science content and consider that First Nations science has been "taught."

Anti-oppressive education and post-colonial pedagogies insist that students, teachers and teacher educators resist the alluring idea that simply adding First Nations content will address any inequity issues. Instead, these theories call for the deconstruction and questioning of deeply held beliefs, both individually and socially, that perpetuate the colonized agenda. They necessitate the problematization of how we have come to know science and science education, and how we negotiate the teaching and learning of science. In order to achieve this, teacher education institutions need to reflect on existing agendas, in which they act merely as First Nations "content" brokers, instead of helping students to deconstruct cycles of oppression and concepts of privilege, and to understand the importance of various protocols in forming relationships with local First Nations communities. As teacher educators we must reflect on the amount of support, resources and time we provide for pre-service students as they engage with the discomfort of unlearning normative values and as they begin the task of reconstructing a science education that addresses issues of oppression. We must ask ourselves to what degrees we are talking with, and listening to, our students to ensure we are using their resistance productively, while still remembering that they are continually growing, exploring and coming into being. Mostly, however, we need to consider the ways we model healthy allegiances with First Nations communities.

Participants' comments about the benefits of learning about First Nations science

When asked what benefits there were to including First Nations science in teacher education programs, the participants responded:

- It would add another perspective to the teaching and learning of science (41%)
- It would help First Nations students succeed in science (23%).

Answering the same questions in relation to their own classrooms, the participants responded with:

- It would add another perspective to the teaching and learning of science (37%)

- It would help First Nations students succeed in science (12%)
- It would make science more relevant to First Nations students (10%)
- This knowledge would benefit all students (4%).

Even though the majority responded that the benefit of adding First Nations science would provide another perspective, in an earlier question about what successful science education would include, only 12 percent commented that it would involve a broadening of students' perspectives. This indicates that, overall, they perceive broadening of perspectives to be a low priority in the teaching and learning of science. Further, in the earlier question, many of the students did not consider First Nations science to be as legitimate a science as Western science. The results from all participant groups illustrate that these students—whether from First Nations-affiliated teacher education institutions or not—are products of a colonial system in regard to a white-dominated ideology of science education.

The most telling comments in this study were those suggesting that First Nations science was merely a tool to help First Nations students succeed in Western science by finding alternative ways of explaining science. This poses the question: to what degree are teacher education institutions and formal educational systems communicating this message to pre-service students and the wider communities? Are these assimilationist practices indeed the desires we want future teachers to hold? Certainly the majority of the participants assumed First Nations science knowledge would fit within the boundaries of Western science and would help integrate or assimilate First Nations students into the learning of Western science in a faster and more efficient way. As one participant said, "if there is such a thing [as First Nations science], it would help relate science to First Nations people and they might become more interested in science and therefore learn more and learn it more quickly." What does the dominant Western science discourse perceive as the use for First Nations science? From this response, it would appear that First Nations science is simply a mechanism for more efficiently connecting Western science to First Nations students. Is the purpose of rapid assimilation what teacher education institutions are intentionally or unintentionally communicating, if they indeed even address this topic?

There are many problematic assumptions underlying this idea of using First Nations science as a bridge to learning Western science. The first is implicit in the fact that there was no mention of Western students being interested in or benefitting from First Nations science. Problematic, too, was the implication that First Nations science is acceptable or worthy of teaching or learning only if it corresponds to or endorses Western science paradigms. This is consistent with white privilege and reflects the normalization of Western concepts and pedagogies. Further, the successful acquisition of Western content by a First Nations student and the student's successful progression through the Western capitalist system is viewed as a solution to a repertoire of historical, infrastructural and socio-political problems. Unless this assumption is deconstructed and recon-structed with pre-service students within tertiary science pedagogy, science ed-ucation defaults to the dominant Western pedagogic and knowledge discourses that students have been indoctrinated to perceive as "normal." Instead, we ought to be helping our students to recognize that teaching is both a question of learn-ing and a question of politics, since learning both content and methods is deeply connected to the individual's understandings of diversity, race and equity.

Participants' perceived drawbacks in learning about First Nations science
The participants were asked what the drawbacks might be if First Nations science were included in teacher education programs or their own classrooms. The over-whelming response was the perceived discomfort of non-First Nations students, parents and the community. There was an assumption that First Nations students and parents would be supportive of the inclusion of First Nations science and that non-First Nations students and parents would not be. There was no mention of the comfort or discomfort of students with the indoctrination of Western sci-ence ideology in science education classrooms. This speaks to white privilege, where the "luxury of ignorance" (Howard, 1999) allows for the hegemonic group to function without any knowledge of the Other; however, in order to survive, the Other must inherently know the functioning of the dominating system.

The main discomfort the participants thought the non-First Nations com-munity would have is related to spirituality. Many participants said First Nations science involved spiritual dimensions that would make non-First Nations people uncomfortable. These participants communicated the assump-tion that Western science was objective and value-free, which was the ideal; however, First Nations science was biased, and therefore not as legitimate. They perceived an ideological conflict between First Nations spiritual beliefs and the school's beliefs. It was suggested that due to any discomfort around imposing a spiritual belief, a First Nations science that included the spiritual aspects should be avoided in science education. The participating students assumed that any First Nations science brought into the classroom would be in this "neu-tralized" form. These participants may not understand, or may not have been taught, that Western science is based upon a societal foundation of thought that is predominantly Judeo-Christian in origin. This origin has influenced how scientists have come to understand scientific data and to form hypotheses. Western religions, specifically Christian world views, ethics and morality, have influenced the very way in which we think and do Western science. An example of this is the hierarchical understanding of humans as compared to other "an-imals." Again, it is essential for science teachers to appreciate the cultural con-struction of science and how science in turn tells the powerful Western metanarrative through which we read the "natural" world.

Both telling of the students' educational journeys and reflective of white privilege, the answers these pre-service students give demonstrate that they lack an understanding of how science and science education normalizes and promotes Western ideologies, beliefs and agendas and thereby maintains certain political and economic priorities and cultural perspectives. Until their previously learned beliefs about the teaching and learning of science are disrupted, and until they start to understand how science and educational systems (including universities) and their own pedagogy are complicit with this oppression, they may find it difficult to consider First Nations science as anything but a marginalized topic. The responses of the participants illuminate normally unarticulated assumptions that can provide science teacher educators with insight into how to modify our pedagogies to acknowledge and confront prejudgments and to deconstruct these harmful images with our colleagues and students.

Interestingly, when asked what successful science education includes and what advice these participants/students would give to their previous teachers, one of the significant themes was to make science relevant to students. However, when we consider their responses regarding the use of First Nations science in the classroom, it seems that these participants believe that the need for science to be relevant is more appropriate for some students than for others. For if making science relevant for the First Nations students does indeed imply making the non-First Nations students uncomfortable, then this would not be as desirable a goal for science pedagogy. The responses that imply participants were more comfortable with the discomfort of First Nations students than with the discomfort of non-First Nations students suggest that infrastructural racism is normalized within the discourse of science education.

Summary and suggestions

The underlying assumption of these participating students was that First Nations science is worthy of "being infused into Western science" only if it promotes the meaning of Western science for First Nations students. It was commonly assumed that First Nations science should be "content" that is taught in higher educational institutions so that pre-service teachers would be better able to connect with the growing population of First Nations students who are thought to be marginalized by Western science. It was assumed that by acquiring this "content" (assumed to be acquirable—almost prepackaged—and universal) these pre-service students could highlight the relevance of Western science to these First Nations youths and, thus, accelerate understanding of Western science. Stating this goal succinctly, one participant said, "First Nations science is needed to promote more First Nations scientists." First Nations science was not widely understood as being beneficial to all students; instead, these soon-to-be teachers depicted First Nations students, as well as First Nations science, as deficient. It was assumed that First Nations communities would embrace First Nations science and that non-First Nations students, parents and the wider community would resist its inclusion. The students hold these perspectives due to their conscious or unconscious cultural articulation of hegemonic colonial Canadian values, and, as such, they give voice to the pejorative understanding of First Nations science. I would argue that the inclusion of First Nations science content designed primarily to benefit First Nations students is rooted in culturalist and culturalist revivalist discourses and therefore embodies a deficit approach. The understandings and images these participants have about First Nations science will, no doubt, influence how they choose to negotiate Western science and First Nations science in their future science pedagogies.

Within these responses, there were no critiques of power or oppression within Western science or of how colonization has impacted the teaching and learning of science. The responses the participants offered are reflective of larger infrastructural issues associated with what is being normalized, legitimatized, prioritized, taught and practiced in the name of science education in the institutions where the study was conducted and, arguably, elsewhere. The understandings that the pre-service students hold are representative of the power hierarchies and colonizing agenda embedded in Western societies. Tertiary institutions are a part of this agenda and will remain so, if they do not deliberately and consciously make the choice to resist this status quo.

These responses both identify and reflect the larger challenge for science education. Many post-colonial science scholars have identified the problematic nature of science and the reluctance of science to address these ideological critiques. Responding to these problems would mean teaching and learning science differently, since science education rarely discusses the implications of cycles of oppression, the complexity of colonization and how white privilege functions within this discipline. The subjective, changing and partial nature of knowledge construction in Western science must be exposed and examined with students, so that these students can begin to understand how Western science is embedded in the beliefs and ideologies that hold privileged positions of power within our societies and within the stories we tell about how the natural and social worlds are constituted and operate. Even though this anti-oppressive pedagogic sentiment has been expressed many times over the past decade, a thorough review would reveal that the literature echoes, for the most part, the sentiment of the participants in my study—that is, that this is not a priority for the field of science education. Clearly, for science education, it is not a priority to learn about our involvement in oppression and to unlearn our normative assumptions. This is not surprising, since research shows that learning something that challenges integrated world views, or beliefs we have previously held, is rarely easy (Britzman, 1998; Ellsworth, 1997; Kumashiro, 2001). However, pre-service science education must acknowledge that it is one of many sites where white privilege, or infrastructural racism, is normalized. If it does not, then it is unlikely that teachers or students will deconstruct inherent issues of power and assumptions about the legitimacy of knowledge. Further, it is unlikely that they will reconstruct a new pedagogy in science that works towards addressing these oppressive forces or that they will desire to introduce their students to a new ideological frame. Of course, even when teacher educators or pre-service teachers understand the complexities associated with oppression and whiteness, this does not necessarily translate into anti-racist classroom practices; however, perhaps injustice may be not quite as invisible as it once was.

In conclusion, this paper argues that the problem with contemporary science education is complex, revolving around its racist colonization agenda and, I argue, the reluctance of those involved with the teaching and learning of science to name this agenda. I suggest that as a field we should critique hegemonic Western science education, as well as what passes as First Nations science. I believe that it is not possible to teach First Nations science in an anti-racist, anti-oppressive way from within the dominant paradigms of Western science. Teaching First Nations science as an essentialist understanding of a people's identity and culture is unlikely to disrupt their marginalization. Instead, we need to reimagine another way of teaching science and to promote another science: to do this, a critique of the assumptions of Western science's objectivity and neutrality is crucial. Before we work with communities to discuss First Nations science, before we begin to teach First Nations science in our reimagined science classes, we need to recognize, deconstruct and resist the inherent racism in Western science, and Western science education, so that we can work individually, and collectively with our students to negotiate the effects of colonization and white privilege on all facets of the teaching and learning of science.

In this way, science education needs to move beyond the idea of giving time to First Nations content or perspectives in curriculum guidelines or classroom practices. Science education needs to become more reflective and critical of the ideological foundations and implementation of educational policy and to become more conscious of how curricula are actualized. As (science) educators we need to evaluate continuously and critique our socially constructed initiatives and assumptions for how issues of legitimacy, authenticity and quality perpetuate the status quo and exclude First Nations knowledge and peoples.

REFERENCES

Abd-Khalick, F., & Lederman, N. G. (2000). The influence of history of science courses on students' views of nature of science. *Journal of Research in Science Teaching, 37*, 1057–1095.

Abell, S. K., & Smith, D. C. (1994). What is science? Preservice elementary teachers' conceptions of the nature of science. *International Journal of Science Education, 16*, 475–487.

Aguirre, J. M., Haggerty, S. M., & Linder, C. J. (1990). Student-teachers' conceptions of science, teaching and learning. *International Journal of Science Education, 12*, 381–390.

Bianchini, J. A., & Solomon, E. M. (2003). Constructing views of science tied to issues of equity and diversity: A study of beginning science teachers. *Journal of Research in Science Teaching, 40*, 53–76.

Britzman, D. P. (1998). *Lost subjects, contested objects: Towards a psychoanalytic inquiry of learning.* Albany: State University of New York Press.

Bybee, R. (1997). *Achieving scientific literacy: From purposes to practices.* Portsmouth: Heinemann.

Cajete, G. (2000). *Native science: Natural laws of interdependence.* Santa Fe, New Mexico: Clear Light Publishers.

Calabrese Barton, A. (1998). *Feminist science education.* New York: Teachers College Press.

Ellsworth, E. (1997). *Teaching positions: Difference, pedagogy and the power of address.* New York: Teachers College Press.

Fausto-Sterling, A. (1991). Race, Gender and Science. *Transformations, 2*(2), 4–16.

Fensham, P. (2002). Science for all. In J. Wallace & W. Louden (Eds.), *Dilemmas of science teaching: Perspectives on problems of practice* (pp. 210–212). London: Routledge.

Frankenberg, R. (1993). *White women, race matters: The social construction of whiteness.* Minneapolis: University of Minnesota.

Gill, D., & Levidow, L. (1987). *Anti-racist science teaching.* London: Free Association Books.

Harding, S. (1991). *Whose science? Whose knowledge? Thinking from women's lives.* Ithaca, NY: Cornell University Press.

Harding, S. (1994). Is science multicultural? Challenges, resources, opportunities, uncertainties. In D. T. Goldberg (Ed.), *Multiculturalism: A critical reader* (pp. 344–370). Oxford: Blackwell.

Howard, G. (1999). *We can't teach what we don't know: White teachers, multiracial schools.* New York: Teachers College Press.

Kumashiro, K. (2001). "Posts" perspectives on anti-oppressive education in Social Studies, English, Mathematics, and Science classrooms. *Educational Researcher, 30*(3), 3–12.

Kyle, W. (2001). Towards a political philosophy for science education. In A. Calabrese Barton & M. Osborne (Eds.), *Teaching science in diverse settings* (pp. xi-xix). New York: Peter Lang.

Laplante, B. (1997). Teachers' beliefs and instructional strategies in science: Pushing analysis further. *Science Education, 81,* 277–294.

Lederman, N. G. (1992). Students' and teachers' conceptions of the nature of science: A review of the research. *Journal of Research in Science Teaching, 29,* 331–359.

Lee, O. (1999). Equity implication based on the conceptions of science achievement in major reform documents. *Review of Education Research, 69*(1), 83–115.

Letts, W. J. (1999). How to make "boys" and "girls" in the classroom: The heteronormative nature of elementary school science. In W. J. Letts & J. T. Sears (Eds.), *Queering elementary education: Advancing the dialogue about sexualities and schooling* (pp. 97–110). Lanham, MD: Rowman & Littlefield Publishers.

Levine-Rasky, C. (2000). The practice of Whiteness among teacher candidates. *International Studies in Sociology of Education, 10*(3), 263–284.

Mayberry, M., & Welling, L. (2000). Towards developing a feminist science curriculum: A transdisciplinary approach to feminist earth science. *Transformations, 11*(1), 1–22.

Murcia, K. (2005). *Science for the 21st Century: Teaching for Scientific Literacy in the Primary Classroom.* Draft paper presented at the 54th annual National conference of the Australian Science Teachers' Association: CONASTA54, University of Melbourne. Retrieved November 10, 2006, from www.conferences.unimelb.edu.au/conasta54/papers/B1S1KM/Paper%202%20 CONASTA%2005.doc

Peters, M. (1996). *Poststructuralism, politics and education.* Westport, CT: Bergin & Garvey.

Sammel, A., & Zandvliet, D. B. (2003). Science reform or science conform: Problematic epistemological assumptions with/in Canadian science reform effort. *Canadian Journal of Science, Mathematics and Technology Education, 3*(4), 513–520.

Sammel, A. (2004). *Teachers' understandings and enactments of social and environmental justice issues in the classroom: What's "critical" in the manufacturing of road smart squirrels?* Unpublished doctoral dissertation, University of Western Ontario, London, Ontario, Canada.

Sammel, A. (2006). Finding the crack in everything: Exploring the causal promise in science education. *Canadian Journal of Science, Mathematics and Technology Education, 6*(4), 325–337.

Schwartz, R. S., & Lederman, N. G. (2002). "It is the nature of the beast": The influence of knowledge and intentions on learning and teaching nature of science. *Journal of Research in Science Teaching, 39*(3), 205–236.

Shome, R. (1999). Whiteness and the politics of location. In T.K. Nakayama & J. N. Martin (Eds.), *Whiteness: The communication of social identity* (pp. 107–128). California: Sage Publications.

Southerland, S. A., Gess-Newsome, J., & Johnston, A. (2003). Portraying science in the classroom: The manifestation of scientists' beliefs in classroom practice. *Journal of Research in Science Teaching, 40,* 669–691.

Yerrick, R. K., Pedersen, J. E., & Arnason, J. (1998). "We're just spectators": A case study of science teaching, epistemology, and classroom management. *Science Education, 82,* 619–648.

Young, R. M. (1987). Racist society, racist science. In D. Gill & L. Levidow (Eds.), *Anti-racist science teaching* (pp. 16–42). London: Free Association Books.

CHAPTER 5

ENCOUNTERING STRANGERS: TEACHING DIFFERENCE IN THE SOCIAL WORK CLASSROOM

Donna Jeffery

> . . . encounters between others involve the production and over-representation of the stranger as a figure of the unknowable. That is, such encounters allow the stranger to appear, to take form, *by recuperating all that is unknowable into a figure that we imagine we might face here, now, in the street.* (Ahmed, 2000, original emphasis)

Sara Ahmed's rendering of the encounter "between others" captures an essence that resonates with social work education and practice. She captures the sense of that which cannot be fully known in the encounter with an other and the accompanying anxiety that is created by an unknowability that cannot be avoided. Typically, the meeting between professional caregiver and client/stranger—she who embodies difference and must be helped—is framed as an interaction between a competent, knowing professional and a fragmented, contingent client. In contrast, however, imagining social work practice through the lens of an encounter, as defined above in Ahmed, opens up the relationship in such a way as to destabilize the previously knowable subjectivity of the social worker. In my role as a professor of social work, I have been preoccupied with the question of how to dismantle the certainty of the caregiver subject who wants to "know" and "do," particularly within the context of professional education. Specifically, what pedagogical strategies might be best deployed in this education for recreating a subject who is less compelled towards certainty? With this question in mind, I take up the interconnections between experience, empathy and judgement in the social work classroom and the ways in which these interrelations play out as students anticipate, with some anxiety, the encounter between themselves and the mythical, (un)knowable "client" other.

An educational mission in social work schools is to prepare practitioners to work with vulnerable populations in multiple settings. Interpretation and implementation of this mandate shifts with the socio-political and economic context, but, no matter the particulars of the specific program or curriculum, teaching students about social difference and ways to intervene across differences is common ground in social work education. Some social work programs espouse an overtly anti-oppressive approach to education and practice, in which critical inquiry into dominance and subordination is foundational to the curriculum. Indeed, in a bid to emphasize the centrality of "making sense of" difference, anti-oppressive social work practice is sometimes referred to as "difference-centered" practice and is defined as "anti-oppressive approaches which interrogate normative assumptions and practices that exist in both marginalized and privileged spaces, resulting in the social exclusion of people on the basis of their difference from an assumed norm" (Moosa-Mitha, 2005, p. 63). Students enter such programs with the expectation that they will learn how to be effective, competent *and* anti-oppressive social work professionals. The challenge comes when we set out to center difference in the educational program without simultaneously disrupting the urge to *know* and *do* that lies at the core of professional practice. When we fail to disrupt assumptions about what it means to *know* and *do*, analyzing social difference is left vulnerable to being turned into just another skill to be mastered. The danger is, as Ahmed explains, that rather than seeing differentiation "as something that happens at the level of the encounter," we are inclined to identify difference as something that exists "in the body of an other with whom I am presented" (2000, p. 145). Thus, if we resist the urge to look at the examples of gender and race

> as something that this other has (which would thematise this other as always gendered and racialised *in a certain* way), we can consider how such differences are determined at the level of the encounter, insofar as the immediacy of the face to face is affected by broader social processes, that also operate elsewhere, and in other times, rather than simply in the present. (p. 145)

I have written elsewhere (Jeffery, 2002, 2005) about this dilemma in social work education. Those of us who approach social work education through anti-racist pedagogies struggle because, while anti-racism is something that we want to teach in a manner that holds relevance for practice, it has to fit within the accepted parameters of what *doing* is considered to be in social work education. So long as doing social work is synonymous with practices that amount to *managing* the lives of others, we end up with new variations of Western essentialized binary oppositions: public and private; bad and good; helper and victim. Students enter social work schools expecting to be taught a roster of skills that will enable them to feel ready to handle a range of situations and clientele when they go "out there" to practice. Educators who expect to teach critically and oppositionally face enormous challenges in the classroom, as we try to link complex theoretical perspectives with a requisite skillset demanded by students. The question for all of us in those social work classrooms is how we might integrate, creatively and critically, a conceptually more complex understanding of difference, dominance and subordination into something we might call "better practice."

I have found it useful to imagine the culture/race divide, as it is manifest in social work classrooms, through the image of the encounter as laid out by Ahmed. In professional practice, the drive to forge useful, applicable cultural knowledge often gives way to static and simplified depictions of cultures.[1] Culturalist paradigms focus, for example, on a service provider's lack of familiarity with clients' traditions, religious practices, food preferences or restrictions, family networks or cultural norms and the ways that this can make it more difficult for the social worker to provide for the "culturally different" client's needs. A cultural framework positions the culture of the Other as the problem, defined against white, Western standards. Racialized persons are seen to possess cultures, while the dominant culture is unnamed and unproblematized. Further, the move towards culture as the sole or central explanation for problems or barriers experienced by racialized persons may be erroneous. Medical sociologist Didier Fassin (2001) provides several excellent case examples of how cultural explanations served to overshadow and erase more likely socio-political explanations for poor access to health and social services. Similarly, Yasmin Gunaratnam (1997) describes the sense of professional unease workers face as they realize that they lack the skills to serve an increasingly wide range of clients. We can view a cultural competence approach as a variation on the problem of positing difference as something inherent to the person in need of care rather than to the encounter. The value of a cultural explanation to account for difference is in the way that it turns the problematic assignation of difference to the person-in-care, something that, ultimately, adds to the professional sophistication of the social worker. The more that difference is imputed to the client, the more professionally acute (and the more implicitly normative) the social worker appears. The result is that the cultural competence argument represents a more contemporary iteration of an older assertion of professional superiority on the part of the social work profession. Cultural competence takes the sting and uncertainty of difference out of the encounter; it puts difference aside and transforms it into something that, like the client's problems, can be managed. Framing the practice "problem" as one of cultural respect and sensitivity seems to be as close to anti-racism as we want to

---

1.   See Chapter 7, "The more things change . . . : The endurance of 'culturalism' in social work and health-
      care," in this volume.

venture, since culture gives the worker something to *do,* whereas an encounter with "race" does not. To talk about racialization is to destabilize the worker's sense of self as both a good person and a capable practitioner, thereby activating the distress of "getting it wrong" or being exposed as racist. The sense of anxiety and the requisite uncertainty that are built into the real and imaginary encounters that comprise social work practice lead the way to culture as the balm, as that which must be learned and applied.

An example will help to illustrate my point. In my classes, readings and discussions engage with issues of colonialism and post-coloniality: we talk about the need for an anti-racist curricula that troubles nationalist discourses of multiculturalism and the ways that it serves to reinscribe relations of domination (Schick & St. Denis, 2005); we take up Kevin Kumashiro's (2000, 2004) challenge that anti-oppressive practices begin with the goal of interrupting and disrupting notions of normalcy and common sense; we discuss culturalized racism and the ways in which racialized discourses underpin the moves in helping professions to seek cultural solutions for problems that are not cultural. And yet, when it comes time to prepare a class assignment in which these issues are taken up and applied to a specific context that is usually work/practice related, it is not uncommon for a student to present a paper or presentation that is embedded in a form of cultural consumption or exchange. The rationale provided is premised on the idea that oppression, and those who are oppressed, can be better understood through a cultural exchange. The student, by experiencing some element of the oppressed person's culture, will better understand and accept the imagined client and the suffering that she has endured and will be better able to empathize with her plight. The student will have brought the other closer and felt the client's oppression as if it were the student's own.

I struggle to respond to assignments that propose to educate non-indigenous participants about the negative impact of colonialism through an exercise wherein the group recreates artifacts that are specific to indigenous peoples or papers that draw on cultural and racial stereotypes in the name of creating an experience that will yield more "understanding" and, as a result, social change. This in itself is not unusual, as we know from a myriad of Orientalist examples of consumption of the other (for example, bell hooks' 1992 chapter, Eating the Other). What is compelling to me is the logic that underpins the translation from theoretically informed critique to practice, as well as the subsequent aftermath once the student is questioned about the assignment or exercise. From students' perspectives, the re-creation of an experience permits them to develop more effective skills—and the circle from experience to empathy to practice is complete. Thus it is not surprising that a typical response from students is an insistence that they be "told what to do" so that they can "get it right." These examples are not to suggest that students are incapable or inept; indeed, no matter how well-taught the point, the social work student is driven by the nature of social work itself to transform knowledge and complex ideas into competencies and techniques. Rather, the examples are significant for what they tell us about the difficulties of teaching this content and, for students, of incorporating it into their learning and practice. I highlight the examples in order to forward the claim that a phenomenon commonly found in the social work classroom is this: whatever we teach with regard to racialized hierarchy and domination, students very often "hear" and take away cultural solutions as the practical answer to inequality and oppression.

Culture is the conduit, in the above examples, that allows one to experience the other, to bring the other closer. No matter what we teach about a critical analysis of race, and perhaps in spite of it, people take away culture as the operationalization of the idea, as the way to make a racial analysis concrete in a way that brings the other closer. Experiencing culture can provide a way of finessing the encounter and bridging the "difference" gulf, while bringing an apparent sense of greater understanding. This is not to say that experience itself is the problem; rather, the ways in which people relate to and derive meaning, and presumed understanding, from their own experiences and those of others forestalls an analysis of experience itself. It is the sense of presumed "knowing" that accompanies a shared experience that allows for a sense of competence and skill. More than that, though, the cultural move serves to alleviate some of the anxiety that goes hand in hand with the uncertainty of encountering difference. Skills become the apparatus that contains the encounter and eases anxiety through the illusion of being able to manage such uncertainty.

The discussion in the rest of this chapter is based on the findings from a research project in which recent Bachelor of Social Work graduates were asked to reflect on their educational experiences, their current work experience and their insights into what an anti-oppressive perspective contributed to their social work practice and professional identity. Participants were asked, in individual interviews, to reflect on their learning, their challenges and their critiques of the social work educational experience. The interviews reveal some very interesting insights about the central role that the evidence of experience plays in the classroom and the ways in which, as Megan Boler (1999) notes, the "introductions of experiential truths into classroom debates dead-end the discussion" (p. 123).

Experience has always been a mainstay in professional programs like social work. It is in the discourse of experience that ontological and epistemological assumptions about professional practice merge: we draw on students' life experiences; we encourage them to relate course content to events past and present; we invite the linkages between experiential anecdote and theoretical analysis. In the next section, I look at the overlapping concepts of experience and empathy as they play out in the social work classroom amid ongoing demands for skills.

Experience

In their interviews, most research participants spoke about what they brought with them to the social work program—themselves as a particular kind of subject upon entering the classroom. The role of experience was central as they spoke of practicing anti-oppressively as "simply a way of life":

> I think anti-oppressive social work is a way of living and being in the world . . . and you can come in here and you can learn . . . I don't believe one comes in and learns skills through this process. You learn a way of thinking and you either learn from it and it shifts how you are or you go out and you just let go of it and it's almost like it never was. (INTERVIEW 5)

The role of prior experience is made even clearer by this person, who states that she works anti-oppressively because "I embraced it in my life [and] it's who I am, not just something I learned in school." Similarly, this participant said that

> I think people who are good anti-oppressive practitioners have lived it . . . until you've lived it, you can't get it. I feel I work anti-oppressively, but it's because I embraced it in my life. It's who I am, it's not just something I learned in school . . . I was a homeless mom. I was a poor student. I was on welfare. I was in a transition house—many years ago. I been there, done that. So anti-oppressive is very much a part of my life . . . I can never take off the AOP lens even if I want to. (INTERVIEW 3)

Those who spoke of embracing an anti-oppressive perspective spoke of embodying it—of living it: "AOP is something that you can't just put on, you have to really live it and kind of struggle with it in your personal life as well as your professional life" (INTERVIEW B). There was an overall sense of the importance of previous experience or perspective of a life already lived "anti-oppressively."

Each of these participants stresses the importance of shared experience—if I've suffered or been a victim of oppression or felt marginalized in my life, then I can understand what other people are feeling and that will make me an empathic worker, a *good* anti-oppressive social worker. If we are educators, what are we to do with statements like these? We cannot know what our students bring with them to the classroom. Nor can we admit only students with a very specific set of life experiences that are judged to be "the right kind." In a very real sense, the fact that students have had this prior experience of oppression does provide them, potentially, with insight and an aptitude for what it means to work with marginalized clients. The issue is not to eliminate experience from the equation entirely, but rather to flag the need to consider the language of experience in our classrooms and the ontological and epistemological assumptions embedded in these statements.

Experience is, of course, an important source of self-knowledge and certainly influences our relationships with others, both professionally and personally. We are both shaped by and draw on experiences and the influences around us in our self-construction. However, these comments also raise concerns about the essentialist qualities that are ascribed to experience and its significance. While shared experience can offer us insights into another's plight, we can't assume that similar experiences are conducive to understanding how another person feels or that similar events or circumstances are experienced in the same way by everyone. Empathy, built through shared experience, can help us to see common ground; yet, to deny the *lack* of common ground in how and for whom experience is lived is to forestall an analysis of "the difference that difference makes." The speaker who claims to be anti-oppressive because s/he has "been there" forecloses any possibility of critique or deeper exploration of what a statement about difference can mean. The speaker's victimization, and accompanying innocence, is laid bare, and critique comes to an abrupt end.

Historian Joan Scott (1992) argues, from a post-structural position, that experience is not a fact, something that people *have*, but rather that experience is a discursive practice. To use experience as naturalized evidence is to overgeneralize a group's history and to "take as self-evident the identities of those whose experience is being documented and thus naturalize their difference" (p. 777).

Scott suggests that experience should be the beginning, not the end point, of our analyses. That is, we should shift our focus from the event or the experience itself to the discursive systems that shape experience. Scott's suggestion is taken up by Allen and Cloyes (2005) in the context of nursing research. They note that nursing research literature (and I would suggest that the parallels in social work literature are obvious) is filled with articles whose titles indicate an interest in a group's "experience of" some event or phenomenon. In research where experience is the evidence, "experience is something about which a claim is being made," that is, experience is seen to have certain characteristics that are shared by all members of the group under study. Allen and Cloyes note that when we draw on experience to make a claim, an important shift occurs: rather than focusing on the event or the phenomenon, we emphasize the individual. This shift to the individual results in several things, the first of which is that these first-person statements "are taken to be uncontestable *facts*" (p. 99). When the experiencing subject is positioned as belonging to a marginal or oppressed group, to question the accuracy or partiality of these experiential facts "smacks of elitism" (p. 99) and further cements the conflation of experience with knowledge. To avoid these traps, the authors urge us to treat experiential accounts as "narrative testimony" that requires us to interrogate "the conditions under which it is produced, recalled and reported, and its relationship to others' accounts" (p. 103).

Returning to the research participants' claims about experience and its significance to anti-oppressive social work education and practice, the presumed direct link between experience and knowledge is made quite explicitly. It is commonly claimed that unless one has endured oppression in one's life, it is impossible truly to embrace an anti-oppressive perspective. I am arguing that those of us who try to teach in ways that work against multiple oppressions must turn our analytic lens towards this simplified and linear link—equating the experiencing of oppression with having an anti-oppressive perspective.

I want to pause here and repeat what it is that I am *not* saying. Students' life experiences are crucial to our pedagogical practices. They provide the concrete examples that students draw on to ground the theoretical concepts that we work with in class. These experiences shape, in large part, the ways in which students articulate their desire to work in the social services field, and these experiences provide educators with "raw material" to work from in the classroom. Thus, it is not the fact that students draw on their experiences to make sense of new learning that is problematic. Rather, what can be problematic is what we do with those experiences and the ways in which we use them to make claims about who we are—what we can and should (and cannot and should not) do, what we assume about other people and how we translate those life experiences, *unproblematically,* into direct knowledge about someone or something.

The conflation of experience and knowledge in this way requires us to ask about the students who do not have a repertoire of oppressive experiences upon which they can draw. When one of the assumptions operating in the anti-oppressive social work classroom is that experiencing oppression is a prerequisite for anti-oppressive practice, what occurs for those students who do not have comparable narratives to tell? Interview participants recognized this very situation from their classrooms, and while some felt that common experiences legitimized their understanding and allowed them greater authority to practice anti-oppressively, others, like this participant, also captured another side of this dilemma:

> . . . the work is about the relationship, right? It is a mutual thing. But what I see [others] do is say 'I'm not Aboriginal so how can I speak? How can I say anything?' And then there is silence. There is either silence or they are resigned to not even investigate what their part in that is and that becomes really confusing . . . if you never challenge yourself, then *you are always going to be in these binaries where I am the outsider of that experience and I can never know* so therefore I don't have to ask. (INTER-VIEW A, emphasis added)

This statement illustrates the point I am trying to make here: experience becomes necessary to relating to the Other and is seen to be the only (or primary) way to do so. This sets up an essentialist view of experience (and the people having it) by presuming that it is static, immune to context or discursive influence. Thus we see the situation play out in an educational context where some of the students have the experiential narratives of oppression and others do not. The former group, presumably, *gets* anti-oppressive practice because they have "been there," whereas the latter group can study the theory but remain on the periphery of "good anti-oppressive social work practice."

One of the participants noted that it seemed students without stories of oppression to tell were silenced, because their stories were about privilege and these experiences were less welcome. She felt that there was a trend towards thinking that "'privilege equals guilt' and 'privilege equals bad' . . . but that that was your experience and you need to be able to know that and you don't have to carry around shame and guilt because that is not going to be helpful" (INTERVIEW C). Another participant summed it up this way: " . . . there was this hierarchy happening . . . like, 'well, you're not "there" yet'" (INTERVIEW D).

I am not suggesting that the tendency to reify experience or construct hierarchies can be laid at the feet of a few particular students. On the contrary, students in any classroom learn very quickly which stories have currency and will be seen to legitimize their claims to being able to understand clients. My concern is to illuminate the productive conditions under which oversimplified dichotomies and experiential, self-reflective "truths"—in Megan Boler's words, "the uncontestable invocation of experience" (1999, p. 178)—become the dominant instructive tropes.

The binary traps of oppressed versus oppressor, and who "gets it" and who doesn't, serve to shut down critical explorations of social problems and remedies and the potential for interactions that challenge oppressive conditions. In addition, oppression and anti-oppressive work are seen to be models, prescriptive sets of directions, which can be followed and checked off as complete or not. This is antithetical to the work of anti-oppressive educator Kevin Kumashiro (2004), who notes that "[a]nti-oppressive education is premised on the notion that its work is never done" (p. xxvi).

Privileging experience in this way can lead to the situation described by one participant above, in which students won't think it is worth listening to the stories and histories of others with whom they perceive no common ground because there is no way in which they can *know* that experience or individual. Rather than leading to social justice or change, shared oppressive experiences as a direct route to empathy can simply create opportunities for misplaced identification; we are off the hook. The risks of pedagogical practices that encourage a passive empathy are addressed in detail by Boler (1999). She suggests that educators attend to the question of who and what (institutions, ideas, practices) benefits from empathy and its production: "what is gained by the social imagination and empathy, and is this model possibly doing our social vision more harm than good?" (p. 156).

Those who have "encountered" difference and oppression, as in the examples above, are positioned as "right"; they know and understand the other because they have "been there." At the same time, the other students, those who don't share the life stories of marginality, know that they, too, are "right." Therefore, it is through the discursive encounter that we all "make ourselves" as subjects: some through experiencing oppression and then assuming they know all about it and are "anti-oppressive" as a way of life, and others through constructing an encounter—in a cultural project or experiment—as in the classroom examples that I referred to earlier. To indulge in culture and experience it in the only way they can is the next best thing. In both cases, however, the encounter seems designed to help people feel "good" and innocent and to know themselves as capable of understanding and relating, skills essential to being a social worker.

What is interesting here is that the students who have experienced oppression see their "use" of the encounter as quite advanced, allowing them access to special knowledge. The so-called privileged, "inexperienced" students, on the other hand, appear to be lagging behind, unable to access that knowledge. Both they and the "experienced" students recognize this distinction between them as something most people know and feel, whether they describe it as a problematic hierarchy or simply a fact. Thinking about this differential access through the trope of the encounter, however, dissolves this binary, since in both cases the stranger encountered is reduced to a figure against which the subject can know herself better, feel good and learn "softly / gently," a learning priority identified in the next section. Thus the encounter and the stranger are both necessary in the making of self as a social work subject.

When we are caught up in binaries where some of us "get it" because we've "lived it," the stage is set for comparison and judgement. Indeed, one participant suggested that judgement is built into the very fabric of anti-oppressive practice. This sense of being judged is closely related to this discussion of empathy and experience.

Can the perils of judgement be "fixed" by a gentler classroom?

> We need to have a space to make mistakes. School is all about unlearning and unpacking a lot of baggage . . . and understanding your place and your privilege and really understanding what the impact [of that] has been. So I think a lot of people approach anti-oppressive practice as 'oh my god, I have to learn what not to say' as opposed to learning what to say and when to speak up. And I think folks actually need to know that it is totally okay to make mistakes and to just say the wrong thing as long as you are okay and super-forgiving to yourself, to say 'I can still learn that' . . . and to be comfortable with that place inside you that doesn't feel good. I think there needs to be room for people to learn [but] I think that people react from this place of 'oh no, I have been doing so many things wrong that I don't even want to open my mouth.' And there has to be a way of *teaching people gently.* (INTERVIEW C, emphasis added)

I begin this section with this lengthy quote from one of the participants because it so ably captures the challenges that learners and educators encounter in the anti-oppressive classroom. In naming the negative feelings and the desire for a gentler place to learn, this person identifies the inevitability of crisis, tension and complexity in the face of pedagogies that implicate us in social practices of marginalization. As one self-described "white, mainstream" person put it, "[t]o suddenly find out that you're way more oppressive, even racist, than you had ever imagined, there needs to be some space of acknowledging that . . . in a *softer way*." She was specifically not asking for "safe space" because "why do you expect to be safe in school anyway?" but she was insistent that this learning is "messy" for everyone and "there needs to be some place for [us] to learn instead of just stuffing and pretending [we] *get it*" (INTERVIEW A).

Kevin Kumashiro (2004) argues that one of the defining characteristics of anti-oppressive education is the use it makes of discomfort and crisis. More commonsense definitions of "good" teaching (or "good" social work for that matter) typically mean that "crisis is averted, that lessons are doable and comfortable, that problems are solved, that learning results in feeling better, [and] that knowledge is a good thing" (p. 47). However, as Kumashiro makes clear,

> if anti-oppressive teaching requires disrupting the repetition of comforting knowledges, then students will always need to confront what they desire not to confront. And since learning what we desire not to learn (as when learning that the very ways in which we think, identify, and act are not only partial but also problematic) can be an upsetting process, crisis should be expected in the process of learning, by both the student and the teacher. (2004, p. 47)

The discomfort of learning that which destabilizes us is further compounded for some respondents by the very public quality of the classroom, the sense of getting it wrong and being exposed in front of one's peers. One participant provided a very thoughtful analysis of the source of the fear that she and others experienced in the classroom:

> You need to be able to process, [have] a place where you can think—'what am I bringing here and what are my fears about this situation?' 'Are my fears that I am going to handle the situation wrong? Am I going to say something racist?' This is a new concept for [many] students [and] I think we need a space to work through that with our honest reactions and say 'this is what I feel in that situation' and have someone gently say, 'okay, how do you think we can look at this? What would an anti-oppressive approach to this situation be?' But having to be able to process that out loud without feeling . . . pretty judged (INTERVIEW A).

In this quote we see a restating of the longing for a place to practice, but the speaker raises two new concerns as well: the fear of "getting it wrong" and the accompanying dread of judgement when one does. Yasmin Gunaratnam (1997) cites a similar finding in that palliative care workers experienced tremendous anxiety over the possibility of doing something "wrong" when working with culturally different clients. She points out that the focus on task-based competencies has not served to allay such anxieties, but rather, that the emphasis on overly general information about people and their cultures may solidify the chances of getting it "wrong."

This sense of being judged harkens back to the earlier discussion of empathy and experience. When we are caught up in binaries where some of us "get it" because we've "lived it," the stage is set for comparison and judgement. Indeed, one respondent suggested that judgement is built into the very fabric of anti-oppressive practice. However, these comments point to something more fundamental—the question: *what is the sense of peril about?* It is this very fear of error, exposure and judgement that looms in the uncertainty that the encounter with the stranger presents. I think that, to understand this, we have to look to theorizations of the subject and the ways in which subjectivity is constituted. Drawing again on Ahmed's configuration of the encounter and its relevance for deconstructing the social work classroom, the stranger becomes the mechanism and the point of analysis for transforming the social worker's subjectivity.

Returning to the encounter

Thus far in the chapter I have shown how the problems of "passive empathy" and "experience as knowledge" are central issues for the encounter. Yet experience and empathy are, and will remain, indispensable features of professional education among social service providers. The question, then, becomes how experience and empathy might factor into social work education in ways that disallow the false certainty and crippling fear of censure that foreclose on further analysis of "modes of encounter (rather than particular others)" (Ahmed, 2000, p. 145). I have come to a crossroads of understanding the problem of negotiating difference in the social work classroom that stems from the entanglement of these issues: 1) the emphasis on experience for understanding oppression; 2) the substitution of the other's culture as the vehicle by which an experience, or encounter, can be created if one lacks direct prior experience; and 3) the encounter as a model through which people (differently) "meet" difference and negotiate it. The underlying problem remains: how are we, social work educators and students, to resolve the impasse that characterizes the irreconcilable requirements for both professional competency and the uncertain subject? It is the very fear of getting it wrong and the resulting judgement that makes social work students so likely to look to "cultural competence" as a way out of our impasse.

As suggested by one of the research participants quoted above, living in the uncertainty that the encounter brings—and not being afraid of that uncertainty, but learning from it—is a place to begin. Pedagogies must create classrooms that are both productive and transformative for professionals-in-training to refuse the notion of practice as something that exists outside of critique and is separate from the subject who practices. How are we to encourage students "to be comfortable with that place inside you that doesn't feel good" (INTERVIEW C), yet foster in them a productive relationship with their own experience and empathy without just converting it into professional competence that comes without risk, either to themselves or to the stability of their role vis-à-vis the other/client?

Recalling Joan Scott's argument that experience (and in this case, empathy that is born from experience) must be the beginning, not the end point, of our analysis seems a good place to begin. From here, students' experiences, and the passive forms of empathy that they yield, must form the basis of the work in the social work classroom. As we have seen above, the problem is not that some students have the right or wrong experiences; nor are we going to banish the exchange of experiences in the classroom. Indeed, the life stories that students bring to the classroom provide a rich starting point from which to explore notions of subjectivity and the making of self. Carol Schick and Verna St. Denis (2005) have described their use of critical autobiography as a teaching tool in their courses with teacher education students. Here they show us how they work with students to tell their own stories in a critical, conscious way that allows them to see what lies behind the autobiography—what we take for granted in the telling of ourselves. As a method for teaching about complex concepts such as whiteness, power, subjectivity and the ways that each of us is produced within these discourses, critical autobiography offers a way not only to work with the experience stories that fill the classroom but also to expose the social production of one's experience at the same time. In focusing on students' stories of who they know themselves to be, the encounter, together with all of the anxiety, judgement, confusion and ambiguity that are seen to abide within it, can be called upon as a site where we come to know ourselves in the social work classroom as the "right" kind of helper. Again, Sara Ahmed (2000) succinctly describes the relationship between identity and the shifting boundaries of familiarity and strangeness:

> We can ask: how does identity itself become instituted through encounters with others that surprise, that shift the boundaries of the familiar, of what we assume that we know? Identity itself is constituted in the 'more than one' of the encounter; the designation of an "I" or "we" requires an encounter with others. These others cannot be simply relegated to the outside: given that the subject comes into existence as an entity only through encounters with others, then the subject's existence cannot be separated from the others that are encountered. (pp. 6–7)

To theorize worker-client interactions in this manner creates gaping holes in the illusion that encounters with unknowable strangers, otherwise known as social work practice, can be managed through the proper application of the correct set of skills.

REFERENCES

Ahmed, S. (2000). *Strange encounters: Embodied others in post-coloniality.* London: Routledge.

Allen, D., & Cloyes, K. (2005). The language of "experience" in nursing research. *Nursing Inquiry, 12*(2), 98–105.

Boler, M. (1999). *Feeling power: Emotions and education.* New York: Routledge.

Fassin, D. (2001). Culturalism as ideology. In C. M. Obermeyer (Ed.), *Cultural perspectives on reproductive health* (pp. 300–317). Oxford: Oxford University Press.

Gunaratnam, Y. (1997). Culture is not enough: A critique of multi-culturalism in palliative care. In D. Field, J. Hockey, & N. Small (Eds.), *Death, gender and ethnicity* (pp. 166–186). London: Routledge.

hooks, b. (1992). *Black looks: Race and representation.* Toronto: Between the Lines.

Jeffery, D. (2002). *A terrain of struggle: Reading race in social work education.* Unpublished Ph.D. dissertation, University of Toronto.

Jeffery, D. (2005). "What good is anti-racist social work if you can't master it?": Exploring a paradox in social work education. *Race, Ethnicity and Education, 8*(4), 409–425.

Kumashiro, K. (2000). Toward a theory of anti-oppressive education. *Review of Educational Research, 70*(1), 25–53.

Kumashiro, K. (2004). *Against commonsense: Teaching and learning toward social justice.* New York: Routledge Falmer.

Moosa-Mitha, M. (2005). Situating anti-oppressive theories within critical and difference-centred perspectives. In L. Brown & S. Strega (Eds.), *Research as resistance: Critical, indigenous and anti-oppressive approaches* (pp. 37–72). Toronto: Canadian Scholars' Press.

Schick, C., & St. Denis, V. (2005). Critical autobiography in integrative anti-racist pedagogy. In C. Lesley Biggs & Pamela Downe (Eds.), *Gendered intersections: An introduction to women's and gender studies* (pp. 387–392). Halifax: Fernwood Publishing.

Scott, J. (1992). Experience. In J. Butler & J. Scott (Eds.), *Feminists theorize the political* (pp. 22–40). New York: Routledge.

CHAPTER 6
NATIVE STUDIES BEYOND THE ACADEMIC-INDUSTRIAL COMPLEX[1]

Andrea Smith

Before I went back to school for graduate work, I had been involved in Native sovereignty and other social justice struggles for a number of years. When I went back to school I was told that it was not possible for academics—even those rooted in Native studies and ethnic studies—to continue to do organizing and activist work while in academia. Despite this admonition, I have continued to be involved in a number of organizing projects, including Incite! Women of Color Against Violence and the Boarding School Healing Project.[2] Although there are real costs associated with taking such a stance, the assumption that organizing and academic work are incompatible speaks to the problematic way that Native American studies in particular and ethnic studies in general have been articulated within the academy.

Justine Smith (2005) criticizes the development of "indigenous" knowledges and epistemologies, an intellectual project that has become popular within

---

1. This essay in its entirety, as well as some short sections, has been previously published elsewhere. One short portion of this chapter was published in Andrea Smith, "Generative narratology and prolineal genealogy: Preface excerpts," in *Native Americans and the Christian Right*, pp. xxv-xxvii. © 2008, Duke University Press. All rights reserved. Used by permission of the publisher.

    Selections also appeared in Andrea Smith, "Social-justice activism in the academic industrial complex," *Journal of Feminist Studies in Religion*, 23.2 (2007), 140–145.

    An extended version of this essay previously appeared under the title "Native studies and critical pedagogy: Beyond the academic-industrial complex" in Julia Sudbury and Margo Okazawa-Rey, *Activist scholarship: Antiracism, feminism, and social change* (Boulder, CO: © Paradigm Publishers, 2009), 37–54. Used by permission of the publisher.

2. For more on these organizations, see Incite! Women of Color Against Violence, http://www.incite-national.org, and The Boarding School Healing Project, http://boardingschoolhealingproject.org.

Native studies. She argues that this project is unwittingly situated within a pro-capitalist and Western hegemonic framework because the concept of *epistemology* is based on the notion that knowledge can be separated from context and praxis and can thus be fixed, essentialized and commodified. She contests that a preferable framework for Native studies is the framework of performativity—that is, conceptualizing Native communities as bounded by practices that are always in excess but ultimately constitutive of the very being of Native peoples themselves. The framework of performativity is not static and resists any essentializing discourse about Native peoples, because performances by definition are always in flux.

Because Native studies focuses on epistemology, it becomes content driven rather than process driven. This content-driven approach in turn contributes to a fixation on essentialized debates about "what are Native knowledges" or "what is Native identity." Much of the energy in Native studies is directed towards "knowing" more about Native peoples and can be understood as reflecting a concern about what Mary Douglas (1995) terms *matter out of place* (p. 41). That is, in the context of centuries of genocide, Native peoples who continue to survive pollute the colonial body from the colonizer's perspective—they are matter out of place. To understand fully, to "know" Native peoples, is the manner in which the dominant society gains a sense of mastery and control over them. Furthermore, as Micaela Di Leonardo (1998) argues, there is a tendency among academics to study "Native people" as a means for those in the dominant culture to learn more about themselves. Either Native communities have "ancient wisdom" to bestow upon others or they represent the "savage" that proves the superiority of the dominant society. "Primitives are ourselves, or our worse or best selves, or our former selves, undressed: human nature in the buff" (p. 147).

A Native studies approach that replaces a content-driven epistemological framework with a performative narrative is evident in Audra Simpson's (2003) groundbreaking study of Mohawk nationalism. What is significant in this work is the conscious refusal to reveal excessive ethnographic detail about the Mohawk communities in which Simpson situates her work. This absence coincides with Justine Smith's (2005) analysis of indigenous texts as aporetic texts. That is, what is significant about indigenous texts (*texts* understood in the broader sense of the term) is as much what is *not* in the texts as in their positive textual content. The aporetic nature of Simpson's text serves several functions. First, it serves to decenter whiteness and the white gaze from her project. This decentering is reinforced by the absence of any explanation of her methodological shift. In this sense, she echoes the work of Janelle White (2004) on Black women in the anti-violence movement. Reflecting on the dilemmas facing Black women writers, one of White's interviewees states:

> It is okay to dislodge [white people from the center] . . . as long as you [explain it]. It's kind of like the way bell hooks appeals to white women

because she talks explicitly about how we need to shift white women from the center and put Black women in the center. But if she had just done it? For example, if you think about Pat Parker compared to Audre Lorde. Pat Parker just talked about Black people. She was just into addressing Black people's lives . . . Audre Lorde really addressed white women more. I mean, I still very much value what Audre Lorde wrote, but I think that's part of why Audre Lorde was heard of so much. (J. White, 2004)

Janelle White concludes: "Does acknowledging that white people are not at the center of academic discourses actually serve to affirm and sustain their perceived and/or material centrality?"

Similarly, Simpson (2003) does not discuss the imperative to decenter whiteness and re-center Native peoples in her work; her aporetic text simply does it. Thus, her work becomes a project of generative narratology, rather than the site for a voyeuristic examination of the Mohawk community. That is, her text generates a praxis of nation building involving multiple narratives, including her interlocuters, herself and her readers. This text does not simply describe Mohawk nationalism; rather, the narration itself becomes a moment of nation building. It is a text that invokes a collective participation of what could be, rather than a description of what is. Hence, Simpson's work can be described as a *prolineal genealogy* of the Mohawk nation. That it is; her focus is not just on writing "a history of the present" (Foucault, 1977)—an analysis of what nationhood has meant for Mohawk peoples today. Rather her prolineal genealogy tells a *history of the future* of the Mohawk nation—what nationhood *could mean* for Mohawk peoples specifically and Native peoples in general.

In addition to pointing to the need to develop performance-based indigenous intellectual projects, Justine Smith's analysis has even more dramatic implications for Native studies. If we understand epistemology as rooted in the commodification of knowledge, then it is apparent that the academy becomes the site where knowledge is bought and sold in the academic marketplace. In this sense, we can identify the existence of an "academic-industrial complex," a synergistic relationship between capitalist accumulation and academic knowledge production and dissemination. The academic-industrial complex is the site where intellectual labour is alienated from peoples and communities, and is thus constitutive of capitalism. Additionally, if we articulate Native studies within a framework of performativity and praxis, then we must articulate these practices within our current context, which is a context of multinational capitalism, u.s. empire and white supremacy. Consequently, we must center performances of liberation and sovereignty within Native studies, with the understanding that liberation and sovereignty are not fixed concepts either but are always performed and never finished. Consequently, we must ask ourselves whether the future of Native American studies is in the academy at all.

Can the Academy Be Decolonized?

Some of the intellectual projects that have emerged recently call on Native peoples to "indigenize" or "decolonize" the academy (Mihesuah & Cavender Wilson, 2004; Mihesuah, 1998; Wilson, 2005). These projects are important and have created a critical space for Native scholars to interrogate their position in the academy. Given the interest in this topic, the extent to which Native scholars fail to address the colonial structure of the academy itself is surprising. That is, Native scholars will complain about racism in academic institutions without acknowledging that racism and colonialism are inseparable from the very structure of these institutions.

Louis Althusser (1971) argued that educational systems are an "ideological state apparatus" by which the capitalist system reproduces itself ideologically. "Education" is not innocent or neutral; it is designed to teach peoples to accept their subjection to colonial and capitalist structures. Similarly, as Pierre Bourdieu (1998) elaborates, dominating classes ensure their position through domination not only over economic capital but also over cultural capital, a form of domination that enables them to secure the terms of discourse and knowledge to their benefit. The educational system is particularly important in the reproduction of symbolic capital under capitalism. The standardization of academic qualifications—a given amount of labour and time in academic apprenticeship is exchanged for a given amount of cultural capital, the degree—enables a differentiation in power ascribed to permanent positions in society and hence to the biological agents who inhabit these positions. Such standardization encourages a system of power and domination between institutions through "socially guaranteed qualifications and sociologically defined positions," rather than directly through individuals (Bourdieu, 1998). Thus, according to Bourdieu, what is significant about the educational system is not just the set of ideologies that it promotes but the set of tacitly unequal institutional power relations it ensures through the fiction of equal access to education. Good intentions on the part of academics do not render those academics innocent of reinscribing prevailing power relations in society. Thus, racism and sexism in universities are not products of racist or sexist individuals in the academic system; they are endemic to the system itself.

Consequently, it is necessary to question whether the presence of people of colour in the academy is an unquestioned good. Does tenuring more Native or ethnic studies scholars necessarily contribute to a decolonized academy, or does it serve to retrench further a colonial academic system by multiculturalizing it? Does our position in the academy help our communities, or does it enable us to engage in what Cathy Cohen (1999) describes as a process of secondary marginalization, creating an elite class that can oppress and police the rest of the members of our communities? Have we fallen into the trap that Elizabeth Povinelli (2002) describes of simply adding social difference to the multicultural academy without social consequence? Does our presence help challenge the political and economic status quo, or does our presence serve as an alibi for the status quo? In asking these questions, I do not suggest that there is politically pure space from which to work *outside* the academic-industrial complex. As Dorinne Kondo (1997) notes, "Opposition can be both contestatory and complicit, and yet still constitute a subversion that matters." However, it is an imperative to ensure that our opposition within the academy is more contestatory and less complicit.

Decolonization Through Collective Power

To foster oppositional work, it is important to examine to whom we are structurally accountable. "Decolonization" is a political practice that is rooted in building mass-based movements for social change. The implications of this conceptualization are that those in the academy who are committed to decolonization would actually need to be part of or to develop relationships of accountability to movement-building work. By movement-building work, I mean work that is focused on organizing people politically who are not already activists for the purpose of building a sufficiently large base of resistance to challenge the status quo.

If we see the need for such grassroots movements for social justice, what should be the relationship of Native American scholars to these movements? Are good intentions on the part of scholars good enough, or do we need formal relationships of accountability to these movements? Can we further social change when currently our only formal relationships of accountability are to tenure committees and other groups that represent those in power, with no corresponding relationship of accountability to those we claim to represent? To create "people power," we need to develop formal relationships of accountability to movement-building groups. How that accountability can be structured will take different forms—whether it involves formally joining a group or developing a formal relationships where an academic provides expertise that supports movement work. The point is that, if we are going to challenge the individualistic system, we need to engage in collective action through relationships built on mutual responsibility and accountability. The system can handle thousands of "oppositional" academics who do work on their own; it is not until these thousands begin to act collectively that the system can be challenged.

The excuses given by academics who argue that they cannot engage in collective action are indicative of the extent to which academics become unconsciously (or consciously) loyal to the current capitalist system. Academics will often say, for instance, that they are "too busy" to do activist work. The reality, however, is that everyone is "too busy" for organizing. So, the assumption behind this excuse is that academics should have some kind of special dispensation from activist work. But why should academics be any less responsible for taking part in activist work than florists, garbage collectors or beekeepers? The assumption that academics should have some special dispensation suggests an investment in social elitism that would hold academics in a special category from other workers of the world.

That said, it is also true that a significant problem for *anyone* doing organizing work is that much of the social justice work in North America uses a non-profit model. Activists and organizers often have difficulty conceiving of developing organizing structures outside this model. At the same time, however, social justice organizations across the United States are critically rethinking their investment in the "NGOization" of social movements. Funding cuts from foundations as a result of the current economic crisis, as well as increased surveillance on social justice groups in the United States through "homeland security," have led social justice organizations to assess whether there are possibilities for funding social change that do not so heavily rely upon state structures. In 2004, Incite! Women of Color Against Violence co-organized a conference, in conjunction with Grace Chang of the University of California-Santa Barbara, entitled "The Revolution Will Not Be Funded: Beyond the Non-Profit Industrial Complex." This conference became the basis of a book published by Incite! under the same name. In this work, Dylan Rodriguez defined the non-profit industrial complex (NPIC) as the set of symbiotic relationships that link together political and financial technologies of state and owning-class control and surveillance over public political ideology, including especially emergent progressive and leftist social movements. He argued that the NPIC is the natural corollary to the prison-industrial complex (PIC) in that, whereas the PIC overtly represses dissent, the NPIC manages and controls dissent through incorporating it into the state apparatus.

The NPIC encourages us to think of social justice organizing as a career—that is, you do the work if you can get paid for it. But the mass movements needed to topple the existing capitalist hierarchy requires the involvement of millions of people, most of whom cannot get paid to do the work. Or, as Arundhati Roy (2004) says, "Real resistance has real consequences. And no salary." By trying to do grassroots organizing through this careerist model, we are essentially asking a few people to work more than full time to make up for the work that needs to be done by millions of people. The NPIC therefore contributes to a mode of organizing that is ultimately unsustainable.

As Paula Rojas (2007) and Adjoa Jones de Almeida (2007) point out, it is important to look outside the United States for alternatives models for social change. In other countries such as India or those in Latin America, social movements are not necessarily dominated by non-profits. Rather, the constituents fund movement building. These movements might strike alliances with non-profits or they might develop their own non-profits as intermediaries to fund specific aspects of their work. But these non-profits are accountable to social movements, and they are not seen as being part of the movements themselves. Furthermore, if a non-profit is defunded, it does not significantly impact the movement, because the movement's constituents primarily provide its resources.

Consequently, these organizing models are based on people being able to integrate organizing into their everyday lives, rather than making organizing a career vocation. Thus, although everyone might not be able to spend twenty hours a week over and above their paid jobs to do organizing work, they can probably each spend one hour a week—and if millions of people all contributed one hour a week to political organizing we could challenge the system significantly.

Beyond Anti-Racism to Movement Building

Many Native scholars and ethnic studies scholars today seem to be overly pre-occupied with legitimizing Native studies in the academy. However, achieving legitimation by the ideological state apparatus may have unintended conse-quences. First of all, it does not challenge the capitalist notion that knowledge should be a commodity sold through the academic system. Rather, it adds Native knowledges to the range of academic expertise available for exchange. This is where we can perhaps be informed by the struggle of indigenous peoples in Latin America, who charge that they cannot build a movement on a foun-dation of illiteracy—everyone must be educated. For that to happen, however, education must become part of the praxis of everyday life, because not everyone can go someplace to be educated. So, for instance, the landless movement uses the concept of "education on the run," in which, no matter what is going on in the community, the educational process never ceases. If we are really about de-colonizing Native nations and ending all forms of oppression globally, we need to think about providing education outside the academic walls.

The second problem is that we spend an excessive amount of our time com-plaining about racism in academia. While anti-racism work is important, it is important to consider that academia, as the ideological apparatus of a colonial state, is itself racist and will never legitimate a truly liberatory Native studies. To challenge racism anywhere, including in academia, we have to build our own power. We cannot keep using what I call the Native caucus or the people of colour caucus approach for making interventions, because it constantly places us in the position of marginalization. This "caucus" approach involves com-plaints about how the larger group, of which the caucus is a part, is oppressive. If caucus members are sufficiently skilled in complaining, white people might eventually pay them to berate them, in the form of anti-racist training. A more productive approach entails building "people power" inside and outside the academy to build mass movements for sovereignty and social justice. Instead of worrying about why white people don't like us, we can start to create our own autonomous power, our own frameworks and our own visions for Native studies that are not rooted primarily in the academy. Only when we have people power behind us can we force changes in institutions like the academy; after all, it is people power that forced Native studies and ethnic studies into academia in the first place (Davis, 1988). Here again we can be informed by the organizing concepts of what the Brooklyn-based community organization Sista II Sista describes as "taking power" and "making power." That is, while it is necessary to engage in a politics that opposes corporate and state power (taking power), if we engage only in the politics of taking power, we will tend to replicate the hierarchical structures we are opposing in our movements.

Consequently, it is also important to "make power" by creating structures within our organizations, movements and communities that model the world we are trying to create. Many groups in the United States try to create separatist communities based on egalitarian ideals. However, if we "make power" without also trying to "take power," then we ultimately support the political status quo by failing to dismantle those structures of oppression that will undermine all our attempts to make power. Muscogee scholar Roberto Mendoza (1984) makes an important critique of some indigenous approaches towards "making power." He notes that Native thinkers valorize "Native solutions" to our problems without spelling out what they are. Native activists are fond of saying, "We won't follow socialism or capitalism; we'll do things the Indian way." Often the political strategy espoused is one that advocates that Native nations simply separate from the larger colonial system rather than contesting the colonization system of North America itself. Native activist Lee Maracle (1998) argues: "AIM did not challenge the basic character or the legitimacy of the institutions or even the political and economic organization of America; rather, it addressed the long-standing injustice of expropriation" (p. 100). And, she notes, it was the power of this u.s. political/economic system that devastated AIM.[3]

This approach is not sufficient to dismantle multinational capitalism, argues Roberto Mendoza (1984), because it does "not really address the question of power. How can small communities tied in a thousand ways to the capitalist market system break out without a thorough social, economic and political revolution within the whole country?" (p. 8). A separatist approach can contribute to a reluctance to engage with other social justice movements. But Mendoza concludes: "I feel that dialogue and struggle with Left forces are necessary rather than rejection and isolation" (p. 39).[4]

We might need to clash with institutions, but the clash is effective only insofar as we make power. If we start to build our own educational system and start creating the society we would actually like to live in, we can more effectively challenge the mainstream institutional frameworks with an alternative one. We can set the terms of the debate rather than react to a debate set by those in power. Many writers have argued that the critical issue is that Native studies needs to be in autonomous departments, complaining that the inclusion of Native studies within ethnic studies has contributed to its marginalization

---

3. It should be noted that AIM (American Indian Movement) is not a monolithic entity and many sectors of it did and continue to organize against the u.s. empire here and abroad.

4. At the same time, because of the relatively small numbers of Native peoples in the u.s., they have often had to create some of the most creative and effective alliances with other communities in their struggles for sovereignty. See Smith, A. (2002). *Bible, gender and nationalism in American Indian and Christian Right Activism.* Santa Cruz: University of California-Santa Cruz.

within the academy. I would suggest, by contrast, that Native studies *and* ethnic studies are marginalized within the academy because they are not tied to mass movements for social change. If Native studies were tied to a power base, it would then be in a position to dialogue with ethnic studies or other academic projects without fear of co-optation or marginalization.

Surviving the academic-industrial complex

Does this mean that issues about tenure, student recruitment and retention, and representation are unimportant? On the contrary, until such time as we do truly decolonize our educational systems, we will have to have day jobs so we can pay our bills, and some of us will have jobs in academia. Consequently, sharing short-term strategies for survival is important. What becomes problematic is when our activism and organizing are solely focused on these short-term strategies. Without a longer-term vision, we have no basis on which to judge the efficacy of our short-term strategies to ascertain if they are bringing us closer to our vision. Furthermore, if we become focused solely on academic survival on an individualized, short-term basis, we will never build the power to set the agenda in the long term.

Of course, many Native peoples and people of colour support capitalism and empire and desire only to further their careers. They use the cultural capital their racial or cultural difference is supposed to represent to further individual aspirations at the expense of working for the survival of all Native peoples. But what they do not realize is that this strategy ultimately undermines their individual aspirations, because capitalism is an unsustainable system that deprives 95 percent of the world's population of real control over their lives even as it destroys the environment that we all need to survive. Such scholars are "included" in the academy because they support the interests of the academy, not because the academy actually values their work. Hence, they are also easily dispensed with if the academy does not find their presence to be cost-efficient. And then there are other scholars who, while not *opposed* to social justice, simply do not see how another world can be created. In either case, it is easy to dispense with more radical visions as "impractical." I would argue, however, that the current system is impractical. It is killing millions of people through poverty, war and environmental degradation. If we care about the survival of these people, it is our responsibility to imagine alternative possibilities. Activist scholar Beth Richie's (2000) analysis of the anti-violence movement can be rephrased to sum up the imperatives facing Native studies: First, we have to understand that the goal of Native studies is not for diversity and not for inclusion. It is for liberation. For if we're truly committed to the well-being of Native communities, we must start in the hardest places—the places where our work has not had an impact yet. We must not deny the part of ourselves and the part of our work that is least acceptable to mainstream academia. We must not let those who really object to all of us and our work co-opt some of us and the work we're trying to do.

As if Native studies could ever really be legitimate in a capitalist, colonial and white supremacist society. We must take leadership in this movement from those who, up until now, have been excluded from this movement. Not just by white people, but by some Native people, too. And ultimately Native studies needs to be accountable not to those in power, but to the powerless. The relevancy of Native studies and the integrity of our work is only as solid as what we do to end all forms of oppression. For if we understand the work of Native studies, we understand that it is not about affirmative action, it is about liberation. It is not about multicultural programming—it is about freedom and sovereignty. It is not about tenure—it is about justice.

REFERENCES

Althusser, L. (1971). *Lenin and philosophy and other essays.* New York: Monthly Review Press.

Bourdieu, P. (1998). *Outline of a theory of practice.* Cambridge: Cambridge University Press.

Cohen, C. (1999). *The boundaries of blackness.* Chicago: University of Chicago Press.

Davis, A. (1988). *Angela Davis: An autobiography.* New York: International Publishers.

Di Leonardo, M. (1998). *Exotics at home.* Chicago: University of Chicago Press.

Douglas, M. (1995). *Purity and danger.* London: Routledge.

Foucault, M. (1977). *Discipline and punish.* New York: Vintage Books.

Jones de Almeida, A. (2007). Radical social change: Searching for a new foundation. In Incite! (Ed.), *The revolution will not be funded: Beyond the nonprofit industrial complex* (pp. 185–195). Cambridge, MA: South End Press

Kondo, D. (1997). *About face.* New York: Routledge.

Maracle, L. (1988). *I am woman.* North Vancouver, b.c.: Write-On Press.

Mendoza, R. (1984). *Look! A nation is coming.* Philadelphia: National Organization for an American Revolution.

Mihesuah, D., & Cavender Wilson, A. (Eds.). (2004). *Indigenizing the academy.* Lincoln: University of Nebraska Press.

Mihesuah, D. (Ed.). (1998). *Natives and academics: Researching and writing about American Indians.* Lincoln: University of Nebraska Press.

Povinelli, E. (2002). *The cunning of recognition.* Durham: Duke University Press.

Richie, B. (2000). Plenary presentation. In Incite! (Ed.), *The color of violence conference: Violence against women of color* (p. 124). University of California–Santa Cruz: Incite! Women of Color Against Violence.

Rojas, P. (2007). Is the cop in our head and our hearts? In Incite! (Ed.), *The revolution will not be funded: Beyond the nonprofit industrial complex* (pp. 197–214). Cambridge, MA: South End Press.

Roy, A. (2004). Tide or Ivory Snow? Public power in the age of empire. Keynote address for the American Sociological Association, San Francisco, August 16, 2004. http://www.democracynow.org/2004/8/23/public~power~in~the~age~of

Simpson, A. (2003). *To the reserve and back again: Kahnawake Mohawk narratives of self, home and nation.* Montreal: McGill University.

Smith, J. (2005). Indigenous performance and aporetic texts. *Union Seminary Quarterly Review, 59*(1,2), 114–124.

Turner, D. (2006). *This is not a peace pipe.* Toronto: University of Toronto Press.

White, J. (2004). Our silence will not protect us: Black women confronting sexual and domestic violence. Unpublished doctoral dissertation, University of Michigan.

Wilson, W. A. (2005). *Remember This!* Lincoln: University of Nebraska Press.

CHAPTER 7

THE MORE THINGS CHANGE . . . : THE ENDURANCE OF "CULTURALISM" IN SOCIAL WORK AND HEALTHCARE

Donna Jeffery and Jennifer J. Nelson

. . . despite theoretical understandings of 'race' and ethnicity as relational and socially constructed, there is still a voracious appetite for approaches that freeze, objectify and tame 'race'/ethnicity into unitary categories that can be easily understood and managed. (Gunaratnam, 2003, p. 33)

. . . whatever we teach about racialized hierarchy and domination, students very often 'hear' and take away cultural solutions as the practical answer to inequality and oppression. Culture is the conduit . . . that allows one to experience the other, to bring the other closer. (Jeffery, this volume)

Introduction

In the arenas of social work and healthcare, dialogues over the best approaches to service provision for culturally, racially or ethnically marginalized groups have thrived over the last several decades. Knowledge about the nature of difference and the meanings of race and culture has underpinned these debates, and various strategies have been developed and practiced. Many scholars have critiqued approaches like "cultural competence" or sensitivity training, noting the tendencies of these approaches to overgeneralize and essentialize knowledge about cultures or groups, as well as other limitations. Culture itself, as a social category, has been highly contested due, in part, to a fundamental lack of clarity over its various meanings and deployments.

In this chapter, we take up these issues to explore a central question: After so much criticism of cultural formulations around problems of difference, why do these models prevail despite growing awareness of their dangers and pitfalls? What is the ongoing appeal of culture-based approaches to understanding problems and providing services? For although approaches like cultural sensitivity and competency in professional education are generally considered outdated, we see them alive and well in social work and related "helping" professions, and we see their ongoing appeal for practitioners as they struggle to develop practice to meet a growing diversity of needs. Our intention is to reinforce and augment the important critiques that have been made, while also proceeding beyond them towards less rigid and more socially and politically contextualized ways of thinking about difference.

This chapter explores discourses of culturalism, through which the problems of racial and cultural difference have been centrally addressed in social work and healthcare settings. This exploration illustrates that culturalist thinking shapes approaches to "difference" in service delivery in ongoing and profound ways. We follow with an exploration of the drawbacks of these approaches and account for some alternatives that have been employed more recently. We pose suggestions for a way forward that incorporates critical theory that is not commonly considered in health and social service fields. The theorists on whom we draw urge us to be vigilant about culturalism and essentialist notions of diversity, while negotiating the still-deeply-entrenched categories of difference that pervade knowledge and practice.

Essential differences and cultural meanings

Essentialism refers to the practice of seeing certain characteristics or intransient qualities as inherent, definitive and unchanging. When a group sees itself as uninfluenced by historical, social and other contextual circumstances, the insiders will say their cultural group is "like this," as opposed to, and much different from, "that other group." Difference is seen as fixed and, consequently, unbridgeable.

Essentialism is not merely interchangeable with the concept of culturalism, a term which we use to represent the attribution of minority groups' characteristics—including behaviours, traditions, problems, barriers—to their cultural backgrounds. Indeed, culturalism is a particular form of essentialism whereby the so-called essential characteristics of a group are attributed to the group's cultural characteristics, performances and forms of knowledge. This is in contrast to a type of essentialism that has been based on assumptions about innate racial or biological facts.

Culturalist thinking tends to overgeneralize about and homogenize "all" members of said cultures and to construct non-dominant cultures as inferior to the dominant group. For instance, much of African-American culture in North America has been characterized in dominant discourses as a self-perpetuating, degenerate existence marked by broken families, single mothers, poverty, crime, gangs and violent black men (see, for example, Lewis, 1966; Moynihan, 1967). What is often erased in these essentializing discourses is the historical and ongoing violence in black communities imposed through slavery and newer forms of institutionalized racism at every level of society (Bennett & Reed, 1999). While it is no longer socially acceptable in many circles to express racism publicly, expressions such as "It's nothing against them as people, it's their culture" are now made acceptable by attributing signs of inequality to a group's innate cultural practice.

Situating ourselves

As sociologists with appointments in public health and social work departments, the authors' research interests converge around anti-racist education and practice in the helping professions. In our joint research, we have been interested in how the demand for multicultural service provision, in the context of growing racial/ethnic diversity in Canada, is operationalized by professionals in practice. This conceptual discussion about approaches to difference has emerged as we prepared a grant application and carried out a pilot study to examine social work practice in oncology settings. While our research is set in Canada, we have found that similar issues pervade social work and healthcare literature from various parts of the world (Gunaratnam, 2003; Lewis, 2000; Park, 2005; Polaschek, 1998; Smye & Browne, 2002) and in a variety of sites and disciplines.

In Canadian settings, the urgency to develop multicultural competence in social service delivery is typically linked to two federal policies: one being the change in immigration policy to facilitate entry for non-European (and specifically non-white) immigrants; the other being the 1971 multiculturalism policy, which was later incorporated into the *Constitution Act* of 1982 within the *Canadian Charter of Rights and Freedoms*. Josephine Naidoo and R. Gary Edwards (1991) explain the "ideal of multiculturalism [as] that of a 'mosaic' wherein ethnocultural groups may retain their distinctive characteristics— customs, languages, traditions—with official financial and moral support" (p. 217). This national narrative is often expressed in contrast to the American cultural paradigm of the "melting pot," whereby groups are expected to renounce their distinct identities and assimilate "American" values and ways of life. Following an increase of immigration from non-European countries in the 1960s and 1970s, Canadian health and social service agencies have been serving a growing number of non-European/non-white cultures and "races." The client populations with whom they work are increasingly diverse. As a sector study on social work in Canada notes, the skill and service needs of the future will require a curricular focus on Aboriginal and immigration issues. This study found that in a context of globalization, fiscal cutbacks, a national ethos of multicultural tolerance for diversity and demands for racial equity in health and social services, the long-term needs of these populations, and "especially cultural aspects that might impact on health and family," will be central areas for skill development (Stephenson et al., 2001, p. 200).

In social service contexts, culture has become the most prevalent framework through which ethnic and racial differences are understood (Altman, 1996; Galambos, 2003; Kai et al., 2001; Leigh, 1998), and "cultural competence" the most common strategy for addressing these issues. Understandably, a lack of familiarity with clients' traditions, religious practices, foods, family or cultural norms can make it difficult to address clients' needs. This can create a sense of professional unease as workers realize they lack the skills to serve an increasingly wide range of clients. The most common response to this unease has been the application of research to address gaps in knowledge, and the cultivation of skills, knowledge and attitudes that are seen as suitable to cross-cultural practice (for example, Daley & Wong, 1994; Faulkner et al., 1994; Jackson et al., 2000; Lum, 1999; McKennis, 1999; Olandi, 1992; Purnell, 2002).

Jennifer Nelson has often observed the centrality of this approach in her work with racialized communities in cancer care.[1] Frequently, health and social service professionals refer to the "cultural barriers" faced when working with non-dominant groups, including cancer "myths" held in different communities and cultural "taboos" against discussing illness or bodily functions. These differences are seen as problems to be overcome through cultural competence training for professionals, as well as better education of the marginalized populations to correct misinformation. In supportive care circles in health settings, "diversity" and "culture" are the common terms for discussing difference, while there is very little discussion of inequality or power relations.

Attempts to address what is widely termed "the challenge of diversity" have meant equipping practitioners with information that allows them to identify the characteristics of those who belong to non-dominant cultural groups and to draw on their traditions in addressing their needs. Such cultural competence is defined by characteristics like awareness of one's own cultural limitations, openness to differences, expertise in the use of cultural resources and respect for cultural integrity (Betancourt et al., 2003; Dhooper & Moore, 2001; Green, 1999; Paasche-Orlow, 2004; Purnell, 2002). It is underpinned by values such as: respect for the uniqueness of the client's culture; a commitment to "preserving" the dignity of the client by "preserving" their culture; being sensitive to the value conflicts experienced by cultural groups in relation to dominant societal values; and advocating for culturally sensitive services for minority groups (Sowers-Hoag & Sandau-Beckler, 1996, p. 39).

Competency, then, comprises the multiple components of "cultural awareness, knowledge acquisition, skill development, and continuous inductive learning," resulting in a social worker who "reaches a point of comprehension and relative mastery" (Lum, 1999, p. 3). In order to teach and learn such skills, social work as a profession must rely on specific modes of knowledge-making about difference. The prevalent forms of *knowing* about cultural Others mirror

---

1.   See Chapter 2, "Lost in translation: Anti-racism and the perils of knowledge," in this volume.

those in much healthcare research literature (Betancourt et al., 2003; McKennis, 1999; Mir & Tovey, 2002; Shen, 2004; Waxler, 1990;). And in the context of our current research, a review of psychosocial oncology literature reveals that culture remains the dominant entry point into discussions about difference and service provision. Such work tends to focus on different help-seeking, screening and other health behaviours, or on the level of knowledge of various groups, including the health "myths" they believe (Bourjolly et al., 2003; Guidry et al., 2003; Kinney et al., 2002; Phillips et al., 2001). Oncology support services and information both address and normalize a dominant, white, middle-class patient; efforts to serve other groups typically draw on culturalist models of knowledge and service. In the following sections, we explore several criticisms of this approach.

Culture as a marker of Otherness

It is important to note, first of all, that "culture" as a concept is usually applied only to specific groups who are designated "Other," those who fall outside the norms and privileges of the dominant society. As such, these groups are seen to embody "difference," which professionals must learn to overcome when serving them. Significantly, similar behaviours, reactions or practices, when echoed in the dominant, white population, tend not to be culturalized. For instance, Nelson has noted through her work that mainstream cancer "survivor" stories from middle-class white women often contain experiences, fears and concerns similar to those of women of colour. Such things as body image concerns (Delinsky, 2001; Kaye, 1991; Nash, 2002), the use of alternative therapies (Davis, 2002; Thompson, 2002) and reference to spiritual beliefs (Asti, 2002; Pooley, 2002) are not considered "cultural" in mainstream accounts, but become points of difference or barriers when expressed by women of colour.

Already, the concept of culture, employed in this manner, has become a way to understand deviations from an unmarked norm. It is clear which groups comprise cultures, and which groups *have* culture, but this specificity is never named. (How many of us, when we hear about a researcher who does work on "culture," picture that person researching affluent white non-immigrants?) As Yoosun Park remarks:

> That "culture" is conflated with race and ethnicity is conceptually and methodologically dubious; that it is invariably equated with minority races and ethnicities is cause for consternation. Deployed as a synonym for race, the traditional demarcator for difference in us society, and ethnicity, the sophisticated multifarious variant of "race," "culture" functions in this discourse as a referential demarcator measuring the distance these Others stand in relation to the Caucasian mainstream, inscribed in its turn as the "culture-free" norm. (2005, p. 21)

This act of demarcation has important consequences in terms of which groups are studied by researchers—and how they are studied—as well as which groups and practices escape scrutiny. It influences what questions are asked and how "the problem" is framed.

Culture as a barrier

Social work, as a multidisciplinary profession, draws on the knowledge created in fields such as psychology, sociology and anthropology—all disciplines that have, in various ways, attempted to describe and explain "other" cultures. It also draws increasingly on business and management models. The drive to forge practical and applicable knowledge often gives way to static and simplified depictions of cultures. For example, Yasmin Gunaratnam (1997) has analyzed "factfiles," or checklists, for palliative care professionals, which provide a descriptive summary of information about various cultures. While granting that this cultural information can be useful, she finds that general descriptions focusing on foods, holidays and funeral traditions often serve to reify beliefs that cultures are fixed and frozen in time. Such conceptualization also suggests that we can "know" other cultures and therefore do service provision the "right" way, by getting cultural facts and their application correct.

This approach may be, understandably, appealing to professionals, as it engenders concrete tools and methods for practice. However, culture often becomes framed as a marker of implicitly backward beliefs and traditions that interfere with the correct understanding of healthcare needs, making the work of social workers and healthcare providers more difficult. Importantly, this interpretation allows a problematic sense that a "correct" understanding—and thus something of a "recipe" for practice with particular groups—is possible. Mir and Tovey (2002), in their study of cultural competence healthcare approaches in a South Asian community, note how cultural models fail to account for cases that do not fit a generalized stereotype; they found that workers were taught that South Asian families value and rely on extended family networks, preferring to "look after their own." In practice, this was not always the case, and some families were not offered the support they required. This speaks to how preconceptions on the part of the worker, informed by cultural knowledge, can have a direct detrimental effect on service.

Such failures of generalized information are not lost on the worker, who is placed in an untenable position when it comes to applying cultural knowledge in practice. Ellison Williams and Ellison (1996) examined interactions between American Indian clients and non-Indian professionals, finding that, although workers felt they needed cultural information, they "were unsure how much weight to place on the cultural characteristics and were uncomfortable gathering the information" (p. 147). Gunaratnam (1997) also found that palliative care workers experienced tremendous anxiety over the possibility of doing something "wrong" when working with culturally different clients. She points out that the focus on task-based competencies has not served to allay such anxieties, but rather, that the emphasis on overly general information may solidify the chances of getting it "wrong," heightening a sense that culture and cultural others are "knowable" entities that can be studied and correctly treated. Such static concepts of culture run counter to the fluid and changing nature of cultures and of the individual negotiations of culture in which all humans engage. As Chandra Talpade Mohanty (1993) insists, culture is better understood as "a terrain of struggle," rather than as a collection of "discrete consumable entities" (p. 52).

Importantly, the move to instantiate culture as the central explanation for barriers experienced by racialized persons has particular consequences. Medical sociologist Didier Fassin (2001), for example, has observed the ways in which cultural explanations can serve to overshadow the more likely socio-political reasons for poor access to health services. His research with Indian Equadorean women reveals how health professionals and researchers attributed the women's distrust of healthcare systems and subsequent failure to seek obstetric care to their cultural beliefs, while ignoring their extreme poverty and the racism they often faced in hospitals. When the "other" culture is implicitly centered, professionals are not required to examine critically either their own practices or the systemic inequities embedded in the institutions in which they work. The life circumstances of impoverished and marginalized groups are also erased, and the dominant culture, along with the barriers *it* might invoke for newcomers, remains unexamined.

Conceptual confusion

Donna Jeffery (2002) notes a profound lack of clarity in understandings of culture and difference among social work educators, practitioners and scholarship on cultural and racial diversity in prominent American, Canadian, British and Australian journals between 1985 and 2000. From our more recent research and observations, we suggest that this conceptual confusion is far from over.

Yoosun Park (2005), writing about social work, identifies a central problem for a profession that consistently designates culture as the "key signifier of difference in our discourse" (p. 13) but employs the term unselfconsciously, as if its meaning were uncontested or self-evident. This presumption is in sharp contrast to writers such as Raymond Williams who have cited culture as "one of the two or three most complicated words in the English language" (Williams, 1976, cited in Park, 2005, p. 87). Park speculates that perhaps it is the "sheer slipperiness of the term that deters social work from examining the construct" (p. 14), or alternatively, the fact that the profession has a propensity to focus on "measurement rather than premise." Whatever the reason, the end result is that "the problem is conceived as the need for epistemological refinement rather than ontological scrutiny" (p. 15).

Gail Lewis (2000) has usefully employed the term "ethnic absolutism" to convey a similar problem in the context of social welfare service delivery in the

United Kingdom. Lewis notes that implicit notions of difference underwrite the literature and professional debates on social work service provision (p. 119–20). When difference is demarcated around notions of essential cultural or ethnic otherness, then the seemingly appropriate professional response to a racially diverse population is to ensure that representatives of those populations are available to deliver "ethnically sensitive" welfare services (p. 37). Culture is the privileged site of differentiation, and service provision is the sole focus.

> Because the assumption has been that the "black/white" divide equals the "client/social worker" one, the key issue was initially seen to be how to ensure that in areas of high "ethnic minority" populations social work staff would become equipped to deal with clients who had "racially" or ethnically defined needs and were therefore "different" by definition from the "normal" social services client. Already in this situation we enter the terrain in which certain sections of the population have become racialized or ethnicized. "Racial" or ethnic belongingness is not seen as something applicable to all people—including those implicitly defined as the (de-ethnicized) *majority*. It is not a field of ethnic differences that is conceptualized, but a difference from the otherwise universal structuring of need. (Lewis, 2000, p. 120)

Lewis found that the strategy employed to accommodate the differences that certain populations were seen to embody and to remedy "white bias in social work" (p. 120) was twofold: train white social workers to be more ethnically and culturally aware and recruit and hire new workers from those populations who could both provide services and decode difference, providing translations to white workers. The key point here is that difference, interpreted this way, creates a sense of naturalized barriers that are inevitable and eternal.

Multicultural encounters

Moves towards cultural competence in the helping professions have often failed to consider how contemporary racism is expressed through a language of culture. Today, scientific racism has largely been supplanted by newer forms of racism and exclusion that may be more difficult to identify and name. Scientific racism, and its commitment to biological reductionism, refers to how "[h]uman behaviour, intelligence, and the capacity for civilization and culture were seen as a product of some underlying biological essence, made visible principally through features such as skin colour" (Mulholland & Dyson, 2001, p. 17). Philomena Essed (1991) has argued that old colonial models of race oppression, rationalized as they were with "pseudoscientific 'race' theories," have lost ground since World War II and that, in their place, culturalized racism has come to the fore. Older, more blatant ideas of race inferiority have been "replaced by a much more subtle ideology, built on the bedrock of cultural inferiority" (p. 13).

Harkening back to the ongoing conceptual muddle in which "culture" is mired, Yoosun Park (2005) notes: "While stereotypes of racial characteristics are vehemently repudiated in social work discourse, stereotypes fashioned from 'culture,' a term used interchangeably with, and as a descriptor for race, escapes [*sic*] equal censure" (p. 24). Because cultural competence is frequently explained as an expression of respect for difference, socio-political hierarchies are often masked. Critics of "culture talk" point to how such emphasis on cultural diversity too often leads to a superficial reading of differences that makes power relations invisible (Razack, 1998).

Lena Dominelli (1997) reminds us that "racial inequality has not disappeared because white people understand better the customs, traditions, and religious activities of ethnic minority groups" (p. 2). Similarly, addressing the perils of a "colour blind" approach, June Yee and Gary Dumbrill (2003) write, "much multicultural social work practice responds to various cultures as though we live in a land in which all ethno-racial groups are equal and those who deliver services and produce discourses about social work practice are colourless" (p. 101). By establishing that groups are simply "different but equal," culture discourse seems to express liberal good intent, but obscures systemic inequities. Dominant society continues to function through hierarchies, even as it purports to appreciate and include the diverse qualities of different cultures.

Sara Ahmed's analysis (2000) of the post-colonial "encounter" across difference allows us to build on the previous concern. Those whom we identify as Other, from other cultures, she notes, become strangers "only through coming *too close to home*" (p. 12, original emphasis). The figure of the stranger is invested "*with a life of its own insofar as it cuts 'the stranger' off from the histories of its determination*" (p. 5, original emphasis). The proximity of the Other to the dominant self becomes a necessary component of the other's perceived natural and factual difference. It is not that the stranger is rebuked or excluded; rather, in contemporary societies that see themselves as progressive and welcoming to immigrants, the stranger is imbued with all the attributes of the Other in the dominant imagination. Applying this notion to multiculturalism and the construction of nationhood, Ahmed poses the question: "what happens to the nation when 'strange cultures' are not only let in, but are redefined as integral to the nation itself?" (p. 97). Acts of multicultural inclusion, she finds, produce further Othering: "the act of welcoming 'the stranger' as the origin of difference produces the very figure of 'the stranger' as the one who can be taken in" (p. 97).

Multiculturalism, then, seems consistent with current social work practice guidelines that stress the need to respect and "work with" a client's difference. The practice goal shifts, but what remains constant is the notion that difference resides in the body of the Other—whether it is defined as a deficit or an asset. The multicultural paradigm, while embracing inclusion and respect for difference, reifies this difference in a way that leaves relations of domination intact.

Moving beyond culture: one step forward, two steps back

In the last two decades, Canadian social work programs have begun to problematize de-historicized and stereotyped approaches to conceptualizing social difference in general and cross-cultural practices specifically. Several schools have adopted an anti-oppressive practice (AOP) stance, sometimes referred to as a "difference-centered approach" (Moosa-Mitha, 2005), as the foundation upon which professional education is based.

Attempts to move beyond culture, however, also run into complex dilemmas, such as in Donna Jeffery's work (2002, 2007)[2] , which both criticizes culturalist approaches to service provision and looks critically at the application of anti-oppressive approaches in the social work classroom. Jeffery finds that newer frameworks also invoke a particular set of problems for instructors and new practitioners. For instance, although cultural competence paradigms are no longer taught in her social work program, she notes that problems still arise when she teaches a more politicized anti-racist analysis to the extent that students translate even anti-racist theory into cases of cultural difference. Jeffery observes that students' foremost expectations and demands are for skills and practice recipes to enable them to handle fieldwork with diverse clients. She struggles with the difficulty of linking this demand for skills to a more critical understanding of dominance, subordination and how these operate systemically.

Jennifer J. Nelson has encountered similar complexities in her research setting, as practitioners demand solutions and techniques for "working with different Others" while remaining indifferent to a critique or analysis of how those differences are constituted and operate to mark some groups as inferior. Although we certainly do not dispute this need for skills and for active change, we often note what feels like an urgency simply to skip the critical reflection—the processes of learning how to think critically and engaging with anti-racist analysis—and move automatically to a prescribed "action" that will correct the problem. The feeling is that researchers and educators must simply "tell us what to do differently," not that we first need to understand the deeply entrenched, problematic knowledge and practices that have long gone unexamined. This sense remains despite educational attempts to engage students in self-reflective practice.

As Barbara Rittner et al. (1999) note, social work education about diversity "is based on the premise that the content will enhance students' abilities to transcend the misunderstandings and biases that exist between and among groups" (p. 422). In confronting their own prejudices, students are presumed to be able to practice "without prejudgments and presuppositions" (p. 422). In reality, however, most enter and leave graduate programs "with a limited understanding of how cultures, particularly their own, influence their belief and value systems,"

---

2.   See also Chapter 5, "Encountering strangers: Teaching difference in the social work classroom," in this volume.

yet presuming that diversity content will allow them to "work effectively with various groups" (p. 422). Similarly, Donna Jeffery's research (2005) and classroom experiences have led her to identify several trends in education around anti-oppression principles, namely: 1) many students resist systemically informed theories of racism, finding them too academic and theoretical; 2) even though students sometimes engage meaningfully with anti-racist and postcolonial theories, they often express frustration that they are not being taught "skills" or "told what to do"; 3) students from dominant groups find that, in classroom contexts where experience has considerable currency, they have no experiences of oppression on which to draw to relate to their marginalized clients and thus feel a degree of frustration and alienation in relation to their ambitions to be competent helpers[3]; and 4) students feel guilty and ill-equipped either to comprehend or resist racism in their workplaces and interactions with clients. Because the notion of understanding the culture of the client is the default approach, the assumption is reinforced that there are tools and methods that can be learned and applied in order to "bridge" differences.

This more recent emphasis on self-reflection can serve to entrench further essentialist thinking, insofar as marginalized identity, experience and group belonging are uncontested as sites of knowing, while lack of experience of oppression is seen to preclude any valuable forms of knowledge, understanding or action. Importantly, this reifies various binaries: race vs. culture, theory vs. practice, thinking vs. doing—not to mention oppressor vs. oppressed.

Some thoughts on how culture does matter

Despite its limitations as an explanatory framework, culture does play an integral part in some group identifications, and practices cannot be simply dismissed. In the case of Aboriginal communities, their situation demands an understanding of colonial histories and how both racism and culture are lived in the wake of present-day versions and consequences of colonialism (Chevannes, 2002; Fiske & Browne, 2006; Hagey, 2000). While "narrow understandings of culture and culturalist discourses" create an array of problems in the relationships between healthcare providers and Aboriginal people (Browne, 2005, p. 81), cultural revitalization has in some ways provided a powerful response to the institutional and structural devastation of colonialism. Smye and Browne (2002) also illustrate how "cultural safety," a concept developed by Maori nurses in New Zealand (see also Polaschek, 1998), can guide health professionals to focus on initiatives that will improve "life chances" through access to education and housing, rather than the more unspecified conditions variously described as "lifestyle" choices. They write that cultural safety "involves the recognition of the social, economic and political position of certain groups within society" (p. 46).

---

3. See Chapter 5, "Encountering strangers: Teaching difference in the social work classroom," in this volume.

Cultural safety, as it developed in the New Zealand context, then, means something quite different from cultural competence or sensitivity in the work settings with which we are familiar.

In spite of some critical reconsideration of social work education around culture and diversity, however, a recent scan of social work and healthcare literature suggests that cultural competence and its variations remain deeply entrenched, perhaps most particularly in the American context. This echoes our concern above that the terms and definitions used to discuss difference must not be taken to have an assumed or preset meaning. The key is how, for whom and by whom "culture" is defined and applied.

In criticizing culturalist models, then, we are not suggesting that culture is unimportant or irrelevant in shaping experience, nor that it is in any way a separate issue from systemic oppression. Cultural differences can exist, and they do matter. There must be ways to acknowledge this without making assumptions about how, why and to whom cultures matter, and without assuming that cultures have innate meanings and characters that stay fixed, that they are outdated, backward, inferior, *or superior*, or that they matter similarly—or indeed, *at all*—to all their potentially associated members. As Lena Dominelli (1997) notes, social workers need to be able to "understand the significance of cultural factors without laying the responsibility for everything that goes wrong at culture's door" (p. 123).

Avtar Brah (1992, 1996), too, is concerned with questioning the ways in which we understand a complex category like culture. She notes that, while there is "no single 'right' definition of the term . . . [t]here is a tendency to regard the social processes which produce cultural differences as being unproblematic" (1996, p. 18). As Brah suggests, cultural differences are patently *not* unproblematic:

> Our lives encompass such an immense range of variability—geographical, environmental, physical, emotional, psychological, psychic and social, all imploding into one another, that meaning constantly eludes compartmentalisation and totalisation. In this sense, *cultural diversity* is the refusal of "fixity" of meaning . . . (1996, p. 91)

Invocations of cultural "separateness" and unity, then, can be engaged to mobilize and motivate marginalized groups. At the same time, however, such groups remain vulnerable to appropriation by others who seek to erect rigidly bounded borders between "us" and "them." The crux of the matter, writes Brah (1996), is this: "the meaning of 'cultural difference' is contingent not only on social and political circumstances but also upon the extent to which the concept of culture is posited in essentialist or non-essentialist terms" (p. 91). She argues that we should be able to recognize and act on cultural difference as something that integrates the "historical specificity of a particular cultural formation" in a way that allows for commonalities and similar experiences, without resorting to notions "of ultimate essence that transcend historical and cultural boundaries" (p. 92).

In other words, cultures need to be viewed as dynamic processes, not "reified artifacts" (p. 92). This, she argues, would permit us to be attentive to the ways in which needs—for our purposes, service provision needs—are constructed and talked about. For Brah's purposes, this yields the potential for feminists, for example, to confront particular cultural practices without condemning an entire cultural group as "inherently 'such and such'" (p. 92). In the case of social and health service delivery, we see a parallel argument in the idea that, while cultural practices are an important part of our interactions, clients need not be reduced to cultural or ethnic essences that determine their every need.

Similarly, Gail Lewis (2000) notes that, "more complex and fluid understanding[s] of culture have far more potential as a basis for developing policy and practice that will be flexible enough to meet the differential needs which a highly diverse society will produce" (p. 123). Indeed, if the goal for social work and other health professionals is to move beyond knowing enough about someone's cultural characteristics to avoid offending or discriminating against them, then, as Lewis suggests, we are going to have to "develop an analytical framework which will allow [us] to recognize ethnic difference in all its complexity but without being reductive or simplistic, . . . as a social category which carries a multiplicity of meanings" (p. 131).

The ongoing appeal

We are conscious of a predominant sentiment, in many social work and health professional circles, that cultural competence is passé: everyone is aware of the pitfalls, and culturalism is no longer the dominant discourse. It is beyond the scope of this chapter to conduct an exhaustive search of the ways in which culture is used throughout health and social work fields; however, a recent scan of health, social work and related social science literature since 2005 found close to 300 articles[4] about cultural competence, many of which still treat it as a novel and innovative concept. While there are a range of applications and understandings represented, rarely do the authors problematize culture as a concept, and the focus is overwhelmingly on skill development and organizational policy for service provision. Overall, the literature suggests that the language of culture and cultural competence, understood as meaningful terms with little explanation, is still pervasive. In healthcare contexts, moreover, it seems especially apparent that criticism has had little to no impact; on the contrary, many health practitioners and researchers are unaware that "culture" is vehemently contested by various social scientists. As some of our examples suggest, health dialogues and conferences on service provision tend to remain embedded in the culturalist paradigm. And although social work as a field claims to have moved on, stu-

---

4.   See, for example, Bussema & Nemec, 2006; Cronin, 2005; Davis & Rankin, 2006; Doutrich & Storey, 2006; Finnstrom & Soderhamn, 2006; Fowers & Davidov, 2006; Raso, 2006; Reeves & Fogg, 2006; Teasley et al., 2005; Todd & Baldwin, 2006; Vega, 2005; Xu et al., 2006; Yip, 2005.

dents continue to fall back on romanticized notions of how to experience other cultures as a path to greater understanding and better practice.[5] Even when the language of culture is not used, culturalism is at work in shaping the sense of "what to do" based on what is understood to be prescriptive practice. Throughout this critique, we have been able to point to what we see as several possible reasons for the pervasiveness of culturalist frameworks. What follows is a summary with a brief examination of these points.

Cultural models for learning and practice fit very well with the demand for skills and translatable actions that can be easily observed and evaluated. In their study of contemporary Canadian social service needs, Marylee Stephenson et al. indicate that there is a "substantial gap between what the demand side sees as the skills and knowledge that are called for in employees . . . and the basic preparation provided in the formal educational system at the post-secondary level" (2001, p. 200). The authors convey that "[e]mployers want people with the standard 'employability skills.' They want employees to be skilled at applying their intervention and communication skills to specific target groups, such as Indigenous peoples and immigrant populations." Strategies like cultural competence are seen to offer concrete tools and skills; they afford a worker the ability to act, and a sense of mastery over difference that is not simply an asset but is demanded by the profession and its client base. We are constantly bombarded by the demand to "do something." In Nelson's work, this is especially evident in health research, where the pressure lies in making sure that the research changes or fixes a service demand as quickly as possible. It is also present in Jeffery's classroom experiences where students insist that they be "told what to do," rather than taught how to think critically about their practices.

Yoosun Park makes a related point, noting that

> . . . the reification of culture is maintained, since if social work cannot claim a body of objective, transmissible, and acquirable knowledge from which measurable outcomes and interventions can be built, it also cannot claim the legitimate disciplinary status in the academy it has for so long pursued. (2005, p. 28)

We find this institutional situation especially relevant in light of a recent trend towards "knowledge translation" in health and social science research. Nelson has written critically about this imperative and its impact on the kind of knowledge that can be produced and legitimized through research.[6]

She links the prevalence of culturalist approaches to the need for researchers and practitioners to demonstrate clear and immediate applications of the

---

5.   See Chapter 5, "Encountering strangers: Teaching difference in the social work classroom," in this volume.

6.   See Chapter 2, "Lost in translation: Anti-racism and the perils of knowledge," in this volume.

knowledge they generate, even before they know what their findings will be. This should be a warning signal that more exploratory, theoretically complex and critical approaches to knowledge production are at risk. In particular, work that critiques existing processes and practices and does not provide simple and immediate alternative solutions is increasingly devalued. This means that problems such as systemic and institutionalized racism—and other problems that are not amenable to simple solutions—are met with only superficial attempts at accommodation. What is offered instead is cultural competence, a solution that comes from a decontextualized and vastly undertheorized analysis of what the problem actually is.

Culturalist thinking also allows professionals a sense of having addressed a problem or learned to work across differences without the disruption of steadfast social hierarchies. It is a more comfortable way to explore difference and to feel professionally competent and tolerant, while having reinforced the idea that the problems reside in that very difference one is learning to manage. Examining our own investments and collusions in systems of domination is difficult on many levels, and requires much more work than the provision of services in the familiar ways. We have few models for this kind of critical reflection. Moreover, we have few models for how to teach it and how to cope with either students' emotional resistance or their anxiety over the sense that it does not foster useful skills. As post-colonial theorists remind us, there is a dearth of alternative terms and models for thinking and talking constructively "beyond culture." We are only beginning to develop language and conceptual frameworks that disrupt and overwrite the unhelpful binaries we have attempted to outline.

So, what *do* we do?

Our overarching point may sound simple, but it is, nevertheless, a crucial cautionary note—namely, that it is too early to assume we have adequately critiqued and disbanded culturalist models of knowledge production and practice. In light of the concerns expressed here, one recommendation would be that we should not rush to develop a new and alternative recipe, for instance, to "replace" cultural competence models; rather, we must continue to talk about how and why recipe approaches have not effectively addressed the challenges that diversity and difference are seen to pose. And we should be cautious and reflexive about the potential ongoing essentialist underpinnings in newer strategies.

We also believe it is important to resist, where possible, the demand that everything we teach or research should translate in a simplistic and obvious manner into a skill or "outcome." We can, at least, ask for more than these cramped and reductionist pedagogical and research directions afford.

Centrally, we think it is important to resist the notion that mere critical thinking is somehow antithetical to change. There is an assumption that to think analytically and theoretically about systemic oppression precludes "doing something" or enabling anything to change in practice, as if we cannot be both analyzing and changing at the same time. This so-called common sense position would deny that to think differently and invoke new dialogues *is* to initiate change. On the contrary, it is possible to develop skills and carry on with practice while also contesting old, essentialist categories and engaging with critical and post-colonial theories that have new things to teach us about culture and race. One does not preclude the other.

In this sense, we borrow and extrapolate Patti Lather's concept (2001) of "doubled practice" in research and representation. She suggests that we must unveil and contest the implicit essentialist categories in the knowledge we produce, while also working to connect theory to lived experience and to account for people's identities in specific historical contexts. We suggest that both critical thinking and practice can and must exist simultaneously and that they will shape and transform one another.

REFERENCES

Ahmed, S. (2000). *Strange encounters: Embodied others in post-coloniality.* London: Routledge.

Altman, R. (1996). *Waking up/fighting back: The politics of breast cancer.* Boston: Little, Brown & Co.

Asti, J. (2002). *A spiritual journey through breast cancer: Strength for today, hope for tomorrow.* Chicago: Northfield.

Bennett, L., & Reed, Jr., A. (1999). The new face of urban renewal: The Near North Redevelopment Initiative and the Cabrini-Green neighborhood. In A. Reed, Jr. (Ed.), *Without justice for all: The new liberalism and our retreat from racial equality* (pp. 175–211). Boulder: Westview Press.

Betancourt, J. R., Green, A. R., Carrillo, J. E., & Ananeh-Firempong, O. (2003). Defining cultural competence: A practical framework for addressing racial/ethnic disparities in health and health care. *Public Health Reports, 118*(4), 293–302.

Bourjolly, J. N., Barg, F. K., & Hirschman, K. B. (2003). African-American and white women's appraisal of their breast cancer. *Journal of Psychosocial Oncology, 21*(3), 43–61.

Brah, A. (1996). *Cartographies of diaspora.* London: Routledge.

Brah, A. (1992). Difference, diversity, and differentiation. In J. Donald and A. Rattansi (Eds.), *'Race,' culture and difference* (pp. 126–145). London: Sage.

Browne, A. (2005). Discourses influencing nurses' perceptions of First Nations patients. *Canadian Journal of Nursing Research, 37*(4), 62–87.

Bussema, E., & Nemec, P. (2006). Training to increase cultural competence. *Psychiatric Rehabilitation Journal, 30*(1), 71–73.

Chevannes, M. (2002). Issues in educating health professionals to meet the needs of patients and other service users from ethnic minority groups. *Journal of Advanced Nursing, 39*(3), 290–298.

Cronin, M. S. (2005). Enhancing the cultural competence of social workers. *Dissertation Abstracts International, A: The Humanities and Social Sciences, 66*(2), 758-A.

Daley, J., & Wong, P. (1994). Community development with emerging ethnic communities. In A. Faulkner, M. Roberts-DeGennaro, & M. Weil (Eds.), *Diversity and development in community practice* (pp. 9–24). New York: Haworth Press.

Davis, S. (2002). Never give up. In E. Bodai and J. F. Panneton (Eds.), *The breast cancer book of strength and courage: Inspiring stories to see you through your journey* (Hardcover ed.) (pp. 166–169). Roseville, CA: Prima.

Davis, P. C., & Rankin, L. L. (2006). Guidelines for making existing health education programs more culturally appropriate. *American Journal of Health Education, 37*(4), 250–252.

Delinsky, B. (2001). *Uplift: Secrets from the sisterhood of breast cancer survivors.* New York: Washington Square Press.

Dhooper, S., & Moore, S. (2001). *Social work practice with culturally diverse people.* Thousand Oaks, CA: Sage.

Dominelli, L. (1997). *Anti-racist social work: A challenge for white practitioners and educators* (2nd ed.). Basingstoke: Macmillan Education.

Doutrich, D., & Storey, M. (2006). Cultural competence and organizational change: Lasting results of an institutional linkage. *Home Health Care Management and Practice, 18*(5), 356–360.

Ellison Williams, E., & Ellison, F. (1996). Culturally informed social work practice with American Indian clients: Guidelines for non-Indian social workers. *Social Work, 41*(2), 147–151.

Essed, P. (1991). *Understanding everyday racism: An interdisciplinary theory.* Newbury Park, NJ: Sage.

Fassin, D. (2001). Culturalism as ideology. In C. M. Obermeyer (Ed.), *Cultural perspectives on reproductive health* (pp. 300–317). Oxford: Oxford University Press.

Faulkner, A., Roberts-DeGennaro, M., & Weil, M. (Eds.). (1994). *Diversity and development in community practice.* New York: The Haworth Press.

Finnstrom, B., & Soderhamn, O. (2006). Conceptions of pain among Somali women. *Journal of Advanced Nursing, 54*(4), 418–425.

Fiske, J., & Browne, A. (2006). Aboriginal citizen, discredited medical subject: Paradoxical constructions of Aboriginal women's subjectivity in Canadian health care policies. *Policy Sciences, 39,* 91–111.

Fowers, B. J., & Davidov, B. J. (2006). The virtue of multiculturalism: Personal transformation, character, and openness to the other. *American Psychologist, 61*(6), 581–594.

Galambos, C. M. (2003). Moving cultural diversity toward cultural competence in health care. *Health and Social Work, 28*(1), 3–22.

Green, J. W. (1999). *Cultural awareness in the human services: A multi-ethnic approach* (3rd ed.). Boston: Allyn and Bacon.

Guidry, J. J., Matthews-Juarez, P., & Copeland, V. A. (2003). Barriers to breast cancer control for African-American women: The interdependence of culture and psychosocial issues. *Cancer, 97*(S1), 318–323.

Gunaratnam, Y. (1997). Culture is not enough: A critique of multi-culturalism in palliative care. In D. Field, J. Hockey, and N. Small (Eds.), *Death, gender and ethnicity* (pp. 166–186). London: Routledge.

Gunaratnam, Y. (2003). *Researching "race" and ethnicity: Methods, knowledge and power.* London: Sage.

Hagey, R. (2000). Cultural safety: Honoring traditional ways. *Alternative and Complementary Therapies, 6*(4), 233–236.

Jackson, J. C., Taylor, V. M., Chitnarong, K., Mahloch, J., Fischer, M., Sam, R., & Seng, P. (2000). Development of a cervical cancer control intervention program for Cambodian American women. *Journal of Community Health, 25*(5), 359–375.

Jeffery, D. (2002). *A terrain of struggle: Reading race in social work education.* Unpublished doctoral dissertation. University of Toronto.

Jeffery, D. (2005). What good is anti-racist social work if you can't master it? Exploring a paradox in anti-racist social work education. *Race, Ethnicity and Education, 8*(4), 409–425.

Jeffery, D. (2007). Radical problems and liberal selves: Professional subjectivity in the anti-oppressive social work classroom. *Canadian Social Work Review, 24*(2), 125–139.

Kai, J., Bridgewater, R., & Spencer, J. (2001). "Just think of TB and Asians," that's all I ever hear: Medical learners' views about training to work in an ethnically diverse society. *Medical Education, 35,* 250–256.

Kaye, R. (1991). *Spinning straw into gold: Your emotional recovery from breast cancer.* Lamppost Press.

Kinney, A. Y., Emery, G., Dudley, W., & Croyle, R. (2002). Screening behaviors among African American women at high risk of breast cancer: Do beliefs about God matter? *Oncology Nursing Forum, 29*(5), 835–843.

Lather, P. (2001). Postbook: Working the ruins of feminist ethnography. *Signs, 27*(1), 199–227.

Leigh, J. W. (1998). *Communicating for cultural competence.* Toronto: Allyn and Beacon.

Lewis, G. (2000). *Race, gender, social welfare: Encounters in a postcolonial society.* Cambridge: Polity Press.

Lewis, O. (1966). *La Vida: A Puerto Rican family in the culture of poverty–San Juan and New York.* New York: Random House.

Lum, D. (1999). *Culturally competent practice: A framework for growth and action.* Pacific Grove: Brooks/Cole Publishing.

McKennis, A. T. (1999). Caring for the Islamic patient. *Association of Operating Room Nurses Journal, 69*(9), 1185–1206.

Mir, G., & Tovey, P. (2002). Cultural competency: Professional action and South Asian carers. *Journal of Management in Medicine, 16,* 7–19.

Mohanty, C. T. (1993). On race and voice: Challenges for liberal education in the 1990s. In B. Thompson & S. Tyagi (Eds.), *Beyond a dream deferred: Multicultural education and the politics of excellence* (pp. 41–65). Minneapolis: University of Minnesota Press.

Moosa-Mitha, M. (2005). Situating anti-oppressive theories within critical and difference-centred perspectives. In L. Brown & S. Strega (Eds.), *Research as resistance: Critical, indigenous and anti-oppressive approaches* (pp. 37–72). Toronto: Canadian Scholars' Press.

Moynihan, D. P. (1967). The Negro family: The case for national action. In L. Rainwater & W. L. Yancey (Eds.), *The Moynihan report and the politics of controversy* (pp. 41–124). Cambridge: MIT Press.

Mulholland, J., & Dyson, S. (2001). Sociological theories of "race" and ethnicity. In L. Culley & S. Dyson (Eds.), *Ethnicity and nursing practice* (pp. 17–37). Houndmills, UK: Palgrave.

Naidoo, J., & Edwards, R. G. (1991). Combating racism involving visible minorities: A review of relevant research and policy development. *Canadian Social Work Review, 8*(2), 211–236.

Nash, J. (2002). *The* Victoria's Secret *catalog never stops coming—and other lessons I learned from breast cancer.* Plume.

Olandi, M. (1992). Defining cultural competence: An organizing framework. In M. Olandi (Ed.), *Cultural competence for evaluators: A guide for alcohol and other drug abuse prevention practitioners working with ethnic/racial communities* (pp. i-x). Rockville, MA: Department of Health and Human Services.

Paasche-Orlow, M. (2004). The ethics of cultural competence. *Academic Medicine, 79*(4), 347–350.

Park, Y. (2005). Culture as deficit: A critical discourse analysis of the concept of culture in contemporary social work discourse. *Journal of Sociology and Social Welfare, 32*(3), 11–33.

Phillips, J. M., Cohen, M. Z., & Tarzian, A. J. (2001). African American women's experiences with breast cancer screening. *Journal of Nursing Scholarship, 33*(2), 135–140.

Polaschek, N. R. (1998). Cultural safety: a new concept in nursing people of different ethnicities. *Journal of Advanced Nursing, 27*(3), 452–457.

Pooley, S. M. (2002). God, the unseen physician. In E. Bodai & J. F. Panneton (Eds.), *The breast cancer book of strength & courage: Inspiring stories to see you through your journey* (pp. 17–22). Roseville, CA: Prima.

Purnell, L. (2002). The Purnell model for cultural competence. *Journal of Transcultural Nursing, 13*(3), 193–196.

Raso, R. (2006). Cultural competence: Integral in diverse populations. *Nursing Management, 37*(7), 56.

Razack, S. (1998). *Looking white people in the eye: Gender, race, and culture in courtrooms and classrooms.* Toronto: University of Toronto.

Reeves, J. S., & Fogg, C. (2006). Perceptions of graduating nursing students regarding life experiences that promote culturally competent care. *Journal of Transcultural Nursing, 17*(2), 171–178.

Rittner, B., Nakanishi, M., Nackerud, L., & Hammons, K. (1999). How MSW graduates apply what they learned about diversity to their work with small groups. *Journal of Social Work Education, 35*(3), 421–431.

Shen, M. Z. (2004). Cultural competence models in nursing: A selected annotated bibliography. *Journal of Transcultural Nursing, 15*(4), 317–322.

Smye, V., & Browne, A. (2002). 'Cultural safety' and the analysis of health policy affecting Aboriginal people. *Nurse Researcher, 9*(3), 42–56.

Sowers-Hoag, K., & Sandau-Beckler, P. (1996). Educating for cultural competence in the generalist curriculum. *Journal of Multicultural Social Work, 4*(3), 37–56.

Stephenson, M., Rondeau, G., Michaud, J. C., & Fiddler, S. (2001). *In critical demand: Social work in Canada.* Ottawa: Canadian Association of Schools of Social Work.

Teasley, M. L., Baffour, T. D., & Tyson, E. H. (2005). Perceptions of cultural competence among urban school social workers: Does experience make a difference? *Children and Schools, 27*(4), 227–237.

Thompson, M. (2002). Miracles can happen. In E. Bodai & J. F. Panneton (Eds.), *The breast cancer book of strength & courage: Inspiring stories to see you through your journey* (Hardcover ed.) (pp. 126–134). Roseville, CA: Prima.

Todd, J., & Baldwin, C. M. (2006). Palliative care and culture: An optimistic view. *Journal of Multicultural Nursing and Health, 12*(2), 28–32.

Vega, W. A. (2005). Higher stakes ahead for cultural competence. *General Hospital Psychiatry, 27*(6), 446–450.

Waxler-Morrison, N. (1990). Introduction. In N. Waxler-Morrison, J. M. Anderson, & E. Richardson (Eds.), *Cross-cultural caring: A handbook for health professionals in Western Canada* (pp. 3–10). Vancouver: UBC Press.

Xu, Y., Shelton, D., Polifroni, E. C., & Anderson, E. (2006). Advances in conceptualization of cultural care and cultural competence in nursing: An initial assessment. *Home Health Care Management and Practice, 18*(5), 386–393.

Yee, J., & Dumbrill, G. (2003). Whiteout: Looking for race in Canadian social work practice. In A. Al-Krenawi and J. Graham (Eds.), *Multicultural social work in Canada: Working with diverse ethno-racial communities* (pp. 98–121). Don Mills: Oxford University Press.

Yip, K-S. (2005). A dynamic Asian response to globalization in cross-cultural social work. *International Social Work, 48*(5), 593–607.

CHAPTER 8
WELL-INTENTIONED PEDAGOGIES THAT FORESTALL CHANGE

Carol Schick

The problem

"Who do you think you are?" is a question I pose in almost every course I teach, where the question becomes the underlying, and sometimes not-so-hidden, focus of all subsequent discussions. I present the question in written form rather than speaking it aloud because the provocative nature of the question changes with each inflected word. I continue to ask the question, however, because for most meanings that it can have, the answers are always under negotiation. This lack of a definitive answer is not to suggest that students are unstable people, but rather that identifications are always partial and in flux and that they are not necessarily chosen, even by oneself. For example, the category "teacher" (which is of particular interest to my students in the Faculty of Education) refers to an identity that is always emerging against a backdrop of fictionalized im/possibilities. My purpose, then, in asking and re-asking the question "Who do you think you are?" is to invite the students I teach in this settler colonial landscape of the Canadian prairies to explore the fluid nature of who the gendered, classed, raced citizen-teacher can be and to consider the impossible fictions of their own identifications and subjectivities.

Discourses in a particular geographic location or site have effects on how students and their teachers are able to recognize themselves within histories of colonization, race, gender, class and sexuality; discourses also affect the disruption and the reproduction of power relations that are commonplace within schooling. Curricular choices reflect social, historical and political discourses in which practices of schooling are embedded. The contrasting curricula of anti-racist pedagogy versus an emphasis on various aspects of a people's culture have been discussed throughout this book. It would be a mistake, however, to pit these discourses of anti-racist/anti-oppressive pedagogies against discourses of cultural familiarity and relevance as if they were binaries and opposites. There are areas of overlap and distinction as well as times when one will be more useful than the other. Each has a particular purpose, as well as strengths and weaknesses. The point of comparison that I wish to investigate involves the discourses of teacher identity that are accomplished through these orientations. Specifically, how do these discourses that are productive of teacher identity promote or detract from the goal of socially just teaching? What this chapter offers is a consideration of the identities that these pedagogical and curricular choices afford and the extent to which these choices may very well have unintended consequences that are counterproductive to the process of decolonizing schooling practices.

It would be disingenuous to suggest that the purpose of this chapter is simply to compare the relative merits of the two curricular forms mentioned above. If forced to choose one orientation over the other, I am more clearly in support of a critical, anti-racist, justice orientation to teacher education and public schooling. Yet, in spite of the limits of culturalism as a means of promoting socially just teaching, cultural display remains a popular discourse that is well rehearsed locally and historically. Kevin Kumashiro (2000), in his excellent review of anti-oppressive pedagogies, lists four main approaches, each with its own strengths and weaknesses. Each approach is necessary for particular purposes. Insofar as curricular discourses produce subjectivities and identifications in schools, I am interested in what is accomplished by popular pedagogies and discourses in spite of their limitations and outcomes. Furthermore, what are the desires that are being reinforced among white students/teachers in my courses and the changes that are otherwise forestalled?[1]

The question of what is forestalled is posited against what is instantiated by discourses that construct the ongoing identifications of white teachers and white settler citizens. In the next section, I offer a description of the geographic and historical context in which these questions have particular meaning, followed by a discussion of the effects of well-intended pedagogies that reproduce relations of domination, regrettably with a renewed access to white entitlement and agency through discourses of cultural proficiency.

The context
Statistics
The geographic area of Saskatchewan is the ancestral home of indigenous peoples whose descendents comprise approximately 14 percent of the province's

---

1.   A worthwhile study that is not taken up in this paper is the way in which anti-oppressive and cultural pedagogies reinforce and produce identifications of racial minority, First Nations and Métis students who comprise approximately 10 percent of undergraduate courses.

total population. The 2001 census indicates that, on average, the Aboriginal population is younger than the non-Aboriginal population at 18.4 and 38.8 years respectively. Following the 2006 census, the projection is for continued faster growth among Aboriginal populations.[2] One-third of all new school entrants in Saskatchewan are Aboriginal children.[3] In the area of teacher education, First Nations and Métis peoples have established successful teacher education programs that continue to graduate teachers, administrators and other education professionals. However, the long history of the colonial process has also resulted in several social indicators of below-average standing for indigenous people, including lower rates of school success[4] and employment,[5] and higher rates of incarceration.[6] Most Aboriginal people are at or below the poverty line.[7] The effects of residential school experiences, cultural genocide and economic exploitation are part of the ongoing legacy of colonialism that marks Aboriginal/settler relations in the Canadian prairies.

In the teacher education program that I describe, 90 percent of students identify as white; roughly 75 percent are female. The settler/colonial era is still within memory of some white families, who can tell the immigration stories of ancestors and the upward mobility of the second, third and fourth generations of the descendents of those immigrants. These most recent success stories of hard work and industry reinforce the common notion that success or the lack thereof is based on merit. Since the in-migration of racial minority people at 2 percent of total population is very low in Saskatchewan compared to other places in Canada, the history of unearned white privilege and entitlement is rarely named, nor is its complex progress challenged—most certainly not by pre-service teacher education students.

The discourse of culture and multiculturalism in Canada

The emphasis on cultural relevance and cultural celebration lies at the heart of some of the nation's best-known narratives. Official multiculturalism is a well-

---

2.   Projections of the Aboriginal populations, Canada, provinces and territories. Retrieved from *http://www.statcan.gc.ca/pub/91-547-x/2005001/4072106-eng.htm* Aboriginal Children's Survey, 2006: Family, Community and Child Care. Retrieved from *http://www.statcan.gc.ca/pub/89-634-x/89-634-x2008001-eng.htm*

3.   2000. *Aboriginal Awareness Training Manual: Two Worlds Meet,* p. 2. University of Regina and Saskatchewan Association of Health Organizations.

4.   Back to School—September 2008. Retrieved from *www.statcan.gc.ca/pub/81-004-x/2008003 /article/520323*

5.   Labour Force Survey: western Canada's off-reserve Aboriginal population. Retrieved from *www.statcan.gc.ca/daily-quotidien/050613/dq050613a-eng.htm*

6.   Collecting Data on Aboriginal People in the Criminal Justice System: Methods and Challenges. Retrieved from *www.statcan.gc.ca/daily-quotidien/050510/dq050510b-eng.htm*

7.   *Aboriginal Awareness Training Manual: Two Worlds Meet,* p. 3.

known trope of Canadian identity and a popular discourse for ostensibly promoting harmony and understanding, if not equality, between cultural groups in Canada. There is a broad and commonsense appeal for culturally relevant modes of schooling as a way to remedy the failure of public education for Aboriginal children. A move towards cultural revitalization is an important part of this goal. The pedagogy of culturalism is not restricted to education processes in Saskatchewan but is well-rehearsed in the national narrative in which the "celebration of culture" is synonymous with being a good Canadian.

The cultural approach in Saskatchewan schools

A cultural approach is the predominant discourse in Saskatchewan schools regarding First Nations and Métis education. This dominant discourse is found in curriculum policy at the highest levels of educational administration and is duly repeated throughout school divisions and individual schools in the province. Curriculum policy for Aboriginal education mandated by Saskatchewan Learning can be found in *Action Plan 2000–2005*, a ministry document prepared by the Aboriginal Education Program Advisory Committee. Briefly stated, one of the goals of the *Action Plan* is to address the problem of schooling failure and Aboriginal students' lack of preparation for and success in the adult workforce. A second goal is to see that Aboriginal and non-Aboriginal people are knowledgeable "about Aboriginal peoples and their history."[8]

The four recommendations that support these goals call for input into decision-making, a commitment to lifelong learning and two other points that are especially germane to this topic. Simply put, but large in scope, is the recommendation to implement and actualize Aboriginal content and perspectives within the curriculum with a "concern for quality and authenticity." Promoting "quality and authentic" information by and about Aboriginal people and their cultures occupies a considerable part of curriculum development, planning, implementation and in-servicing of all teachers and administrators. Equally important is the recommendation to develop a positive school climate, especially in light of research that reports: "many Aboriginal students in the province do not find schools to be culturally affirming places."[9] These last two recommendations, which focus on culture, are central to the Ministry's approach for addressing unequal educational outcomes.[10]

---

8.   "Our goal is to see the following: 1) Aboriginal young people with grade 12 and post secondary educations, flourishing in all professions; 2) Aboriginal and non-Aboriginal students and young people knowledgeable about Aboriginal peoples and their history." Retrieved from *http://www.sasklearning.gov.sk.ca/docs/policy/aboriginal/action/index.html*

9.   "Our recommendations in this area are aimed at ensuring that schools promote the well being of each individual and community by affirming the cultures, traditions, languages, spirituality, and world views of all the students." From *Action Plan 2000–2005.*

10.   Back to School—September 2008. Retrieved from *www.statcan.gc.ca/pub/81-004-x/2008003/article/520323*

Teaching options

In this province the expectation and mandate for curriculum and instruction is that it will be reflective of, and relevant to, the culture of First Nations and Métis peoples. The fact that the relevance of schooling for First Nations and Métis students has to be mandated is an indication that this very legitimate and real expectation has not been fully realized. At first glance, relevant schooling seems responsible and entirely necessary given the failure of the education system to educate Aboriginal students adequately; therefore, raising questions about these goals and recommendations might seem nonsensical at the very least. However, the question is not whether classrooms should be culturally relevant, non-relevant or irrelevant, but whether this culturally relevant approach is *sufficient* to overcome and unsettle the social positioning and "commonsense" assumptions of racialized white people who would be effective teachers. Promoting cultural relevance as a solution to inequality is problematic when this approach presupposes and reproduces an innocent white teacher whose task is to supply those qualities that marginalized students are said to lack. What further renders the provincial goals and recommendations problematic is the absence of a serious consideration of the effects of racialization and racism on Aboriginal schoolchildren and on the prior education of their white teachers.

With the best of intentions, pre-service students make plans to adopt culturally relevant curricular topics, teaching methods and school resources that are said to reflect the knowledge and world view of First Nations and Métis peoples. However, cultural references also appear in teachers' conversations in less picturesque, benign and folkloric ways. Aboriginal culture is cited as the reason for family transience, for ineffective parenting styles, for poverty or for inferior facility with language,[11] and all of these are linked to lack of school success. When cultural attributions and culturally specific ways are used as explanations for school failure, these discourses amount to nothing less than the il/logic of biological essentialism in which cultural attributes are made to seem like inborn traits with inevitable outcomes. The contradictions are well-rehearsed and stand for "commonsense" policy: the *absence* of indigenous culture in schools is the de facto explanation for lack of success for Aboriginal students, whereas the "innate" *presence* of indigenous culture is a predictor of failure and explanation for inequality. In both discourses, cultural ways serve as a stand-in for discredited assumptions of racial categorization and the insupportable notion that racial difference is biologically determined.

Teacher education students at the graduate and undergraduate levels are well-schooled in the taken-for-grantedness of a culturalist approach, even before they begin their teacher education certification programs. The popularity of this orientation is in contrast to courses that offer a critical, post-structural, anti-oppressive orientation to justice and equality. Ann Berlak (2004) offers a

---

11.   See Chapter 1, "Language as an agent of division in Saskatchewan schools," in this volume.

succinct description of a justice-oriented course that mirrors the pedagogy that I am working towards in my own practice:

> My primary goal for the diversity course is to encourage students to *re-think their assumptions* about race, class, gender, culture, language, and sexual orientation *that predispose them to reproduce rather than challenge injustice.* I want them to recognize forms of injustice, including those that are least visible, and to become aware that as teachers they will have many opportunities to choose between collaborating with or challenging individuals and institutions that encourage indifference to oppression. (Berlak, 2004, p. 124, emphasis added)

In my own teaching, I am encouraged that many students are excited to find a critical analysis that emphasizes how they might "challenge injustice" by first recognizing how they are implicated in relations of inequality. A great deal of learning goes on during and after the courses, and former students report on their growing interest in activist causes. These are bright, hard-working students who see connections to their own work that go beyond what I have taught them. They are developing an anti-racist literacy and an ongoing critique of what constitutes "good teaching." These responses are some of what I have hoped would take place in courses that are dedicated to anti-oppressive education.

What, then, is the problem?

There are many contrasting responses described elsewhere in this book[12] that trouble the way a critical approach, which I favour, is either not taken up or is sidelined in one way or another. My interest, therefore, is not simply about "best practices," but about the potential for a socially just orientation to produce unintended outcomes given the hegemonic discourses of schooling and citizenship that are already in place. These unintended outcomes are what motivate my investigation of this issue.

In spite of a critical approach that follows the norms of critical teaching mentioned above—including a social/political analysis, examination of one's own subject positioning, the necessity of social action against inequitable structures and policies—the fallback position used repeatedly by in-service and graduate students is a technical rational application of cultural expression. I am willing to offer that the failure on the part of some students to comprehend the meaning and significance of a critical approach may be found in my abilities as a teacher and my social positioning as a white, middle-class woman. There is, however, significant literature, including Berlak's chapter cited above, to indicate that doing anti-racist teaching and learning can be emotional, confrontational,

---

12.   See Chapter 5, "Encountering strangers: Teaching difference in the social work classroom," and Chapter 9, "From *Stonechild* to social cohesion: Anti-racist challenges for Saskatchewan," in this volume.

frequently traumatic (Chubbuck & Zembylas, 2008). It must be noted that some students understand very well what I am teaching and choose to resist on ideological grounds. There are, however, many students who mistakenly imagine that they are following precisely where I have led and who turn again to a familiar—and what I regard as a cultural and racially-oriented—narrative as an explanation for student failure. What continues to puzzle me about their reliance on and comfort with a cultural emphasis is the appeal this approach has for so many students, teachers and administrators such that leaving it behind seems unfathomable and incommensurate with good teaching and good educator identity.

Clearly, I am not alone in my puzzlement over the popularity of culturalist discourses and the default to cultural solutions, as other articles in this volume suggest.[13] In this geographic location, however, a measure of teacher competence has been a generous application of "culturally relevant" events as a provincial and national response to the failure of schools to educate Aboriginal students. It is not surprising that pre-service and in-service teacher solutions echo the mandates of school authorities for curricular relevance and positive climate-setting by means of information by and about Aboriginal peoples.

Whether a student takes up an anti-racist analysis or focuses on aspects of cultural revitalization, the questions at hand involve the identities and subjectivities that are produced through each discourse. For white teachers engaged in pre-service and in-service instruction, then, what do the discourses of anti-racism and cultural revitalization accomplish?

THEORETICAL DISCUSSION

Identities and subjectivities

Identities/identifications can be understood, in part, as performative actions, shaped through various discourses circulating with and in the social relations to which one has access. Tracing the effects of teacher identifications is integral to my teaching because of the performative nature of interpersonal relations between students and teachers. Identifications are always significant to how and what one teaches, as in the case of my own teaching and that of my students. For many white students the invisibility and neutrality of whiteness is an assumption that can only be dislodged by looking directly at power relations that construct identifications and subjectivities. A teacher's identification is always read by others in the classroom through the performativity of values and desires, worst and best qualities as an aspect of the lived curriculum. At the same time, however, the identification of the category "teacher" is illusory, unstable and an

---

13.   See Chapter 5, "Encountering strangers: Teaching difference in the social work classroom," Chapter 2, "Lost in translation: Anti-racism and the perils of knowledge," and Chapter 9, "From *Stonechild* to social cohesion: Anti-racist challenges for Saskatchewan," in this volume.

impossible perfection. In its embodied form, the identity of "teacher" is a learned performance whose dramatic effect is assessed through normative expectations of race, class, gender, sexual orientation, language, ability, religion and so forth.

The reason I want to talk about identifications and subjectivity is twofold. First, one's identification—at least how and with whom one identifies—is a dynamic and evolutionary process. Because it is subject to change, one's identification is, to some extent, something that one may alter, adjust and take responsibility for. Educators are often surprised to learn that most teachers pay the greatest attention to students whose backgrounds and socio-economic status are similar to their own, even when the teachers are aware of this biased tendency. Awareness of how one's identity significantly influences the curriculum is unknown to many dominant culture students. For many white teachers, the challenge of seeing outside of their social positioning is disrupted for the first time by Peggy McIntosh's entry-level discussion of white privilege (1998). This articulation of white privilege on the part of racially dominant teachers, however, is no guarantee that their racial minority colleagues and students will be treated more justly or that the overt and hidden curriculum of white supremacy will fall away. Students will continue to learn the normative assumptions that Aboriginal children are not expected to graduate from high school, that merit is attributed to social class and that being a sexual minority is something to be ashamed of; furthermore, the disembodied male voice coming from the loudspeaker still retains more authority in most places than the female version. Because identifications and subjectivities are not simply one's destiny, learning some of the effects of one's subjectivity and calling into question the repetition of harmful practices may have some potential to inform and promote change.

Second, schooling practices and discourses in this place and others have already been shaped through colonialism, immigration and other relations of empire. There is no neutral space in what or how we teach. Failing to understand this has every potential to avoid change, or worse, as Cameron McCarthy (1998) states, "to deliver . . . (neo)colonial effects" (p. 5), which is to retrench inequality as normative. Teacher identities have also been shaped through colonial relations, especially if teachers are educated in Canada. Uncovering and making conscious the effects of this colonial shaping is a lifelong challenge requiring a healthy skepticism of one's own assumptions (Fendler, 2003; Pillow, 2003). Examining the effects of identity production illustrates that curriculum is not benign or neutral. Furthermore, these examinations can have the effect of further retrenching relations of domination even while purportedly "doing the right thing."

"Identification has a history—a colonial history" (Fuss, p. 141). Knowing how identification takes place is not merely interesting nor an abstract indulgence; it also affords a way of tracing the imperial process, of coming to understand how domination and imperialism have come to be justified as positive social acts. A colonialist project is not merely a thing of the past, but continues today through schooling practices, including teacher education programs. As socially authorized discourses, particular schooling practices have every possibility of reproducing "the ontological privilege of the colonizer and the subjugated condition of the colonized" (Fuss, p. 141) even if only one or the other is present. Knowledge of how identifications are implicated in imperialism can radically inform practical applications that intend to interrupt the colonial project and even perhaps destabilize taken-for-granted privilege and unacknowledged dominance.

Invisibility of whiteness

Even though the concept of "race" does not hold, the material effects of racialization do. I speak of whiteness as a construct that is produced through the effects of racial hierarchies and constructed dominance. Whiteness is an unstable identity that depends on various performances of language, gender, religion, sexual orientation, social class, geographic location and several other means of identification, including skin colour. The instability of whiteness and its prize of respectability and legitimate citizen status render it a necessary and uneasy performance and one in need of constant vigilance. "To study race, identity, culture and to intervene in their field of effects, one must be prepared to live with extraordinary complexity and variability of meaning" (McCarthy, 1998, p. 6).

"Race" doesn't consciously figure in the self-identity of most white students and the invisibility of their whiteness equates to a kind of racelessness. This lack of awareness and the invisibility of their whiteness, however, throws the "difference" and otherness of racialized minorities into sharp relief. Discourses that omit talk about race depend on and reinforce the social meanings of who is "normal" and who is "the other." Furthermore, there is no way to make sense of privilege, inequality and racialized schooling practices—in other than biologically determined and racist ways—without the language of racial identity, race privilege and white supremacy.

In my focus on teacher education, I cannot assume that white students already have an understanding of the effects of white privilege and the overwhelmingly white space of their classrooms, let alone are aware that their racialization has an effect on what they can know and say. Therefore, as significant as culturally relevant teaching will be for certain students, I employ critical race theory and anti-racist teaching from an anti-oppressive perspective to address the needs of white teacher education students in their roles as teachers. I try to address what they need to know about themselves and the pedagogies that are available to them. This critical approach is distinguished in several ways from a culturalist approach, one of which is to reconsider who it is that has the problem and who or what it is that has been failing First Nations and Métis students.

Socially just teaching

There is a distinct lack of clarity over what is considered "socially just teaching." Sharon Chubbuck and Michalinos Zembylas (2008) offer an excellent discussion about what the concept of socially just teaching might be, given a consideration of its goals, methods, curricula and respective audiences. They conclude with this summary definition: Teaching for social justice involves

> . . . a teacher's efforts to transform policies and enact pedagogies that improve the learning and life opportunities of typically underserved students while equipping them and empowering them to work for a more socially just society themselves. This composite definition includes *intrapersonal development* in the teacher, pedagogy[,] curriculum . . . and [the work of] activist teachers engaged in challenging and transforming equitable structures and policies in schools and society. (Chubbuck and Zembylas, 2008, p. 284, emphasis added)

Since students of the dominant society are the ones who populate the classrooms where I teach, I try to ensure that part of their learning entails "intrapersonal development" and consciousness-raising about the implications of their own positioning. This process of self-development that complicates students' own identity construction also makes it possible for them to recognize the heterogeneity of minority student experience, a realization that is otherwise obscured when all experiences and explanations of difference are presented as originating in culture. They also learn that ignoring the systemic nature of inequality denies the salience of their own racialization and confirms the commonplace impression that marginalization of minority students is naturally occurring and that, simultaneously, privilege, entitlement and success for white students are natural phenomena. The heterogeneity of all students produced through their gender, class, sexual orientation, language, religion and other identifications is overlooked when "difference" (a.k.a. culture) is simply designated as "theirs" and "ours."

Telling one's story is a frequent vehicle for the process of intrapersonal development. Kevin Kumashiro (2001) warns that "'telling one's story' not only presumes a rational development of a singular subject from ignorance to enlightenment, but also privileges the developmental model as 'the story,' making other stories unthinkable and untellable" (p. 9). The personal story told as a method of learning about oneself has every possibility of repeating what one already knows and, hence, the telling fails to disrupt "commonsense" notions of power, place and identity that play out in one's practice. Socially just teaching is not necessarily comfortable or easy and includes, as stated above, "teachers engaged in challenging and transforming equitable structures and policies in schools and society" (Chubbuck & Zembylas, 2008, p. 284). Telling one's story in a way that is unfamiliar and uncomfortable "involves desiring a working through crisis rather than avoiding and masking it" (p. 9). It also involves imagining new possibilities for who we think we are and can be, rather than transmitting notions that confirm only more of the same.

WHAT IS ACCOMPLISHED BY DISCOURSES OF RACE, CULTURE, AND EQUITY?

Positive Outcomes

I have mentioned Kumashiro's typology (2001) with four approaches to anti-oppressive education, with each approach having particular strengths and weaknesses. The first approach, "education *for* the other," is mainly about the benefits marginalized people can take from learning about their own customs and traditions. The second, "education *about* the other," considers the anticipated benefits of learning about First Nations and Métis students on the part of white students.

"Education for the other" produces solidarity and group recognition

Among First Nations and Métis students, the value of learning about and being immersed in their own cultural practices cannot be underestimated. Verna St. Denis (2004) describes her significant experience of formally learning alongside other Métis students about her Aboriginal heritage and language while at university. It was transformative for St. Denis to be able to identify openly with traditions that were often denigrated, minimized and far removed from formal education. "These moments of having one's life and cultural heritage acknowledged and legitimated are profoundly moving and powerful . . ." (p. 35). She notes that cultural teachings and the instilling of cultural pride have had life-changing effects on peoples who have been discouraged from identifying with their communities and traditions.[14] Teaching about one's cultural history and traditions "challenges the goals of colonization that eradicate the cultural practices and identities of Aboriginal people" (p. 45). Learning the politics, history and economic lives of one's ancestors supports people in establishing their rights and furthering political claims; it helps peoples gain strength against the threat of assimilation. The teachings not only make possible political action and cohesion in the present; they also ensure that the history, culture, protocols, language and respect for traditional ways are maintained and lived out for future generations.

The work of Paulo Freire is an example of the positive effects of learning that one's history, culture and social positioning are worthy of dignity and respect, including most notably, one's self-respect. Posing problems about the nature of inequality and injustice as described by Freire (1970) are among the first steps to "reading the world"; this is a reading that lays claim to "intrapersonal development" and an emancipatory stand against oppressive systems.

---

14.   It would be a misrepresentation of St. Denis's work, however, to suggest that she favours a culturalist approach to teacher education. She advocates a vigorous anti-racist analysis for addressing racism and other forms of marginalization that occur routinely for Aboriginal students and others. See St. Denis, V. (2006). Aboriginal education and anti-racist education: Building alliances across cultural and racial identity. *Canadian Journal of Education* 30(4), 1068–1092.

"Education about the other" leads to sameness

There are positive aspects to the practice of teaching white education students about the historical, economic, social and political practices of other people who are not necessarily like them. Perhaps the most significant benefit of what is most often referred to as cross-cultural learning is its potential to enrich a person's understandings of different ways of being. At the very least, such learning can bring to light unexamined assumptions about sameness and difference between people. It is possible that, in learning about others, one may develop a sense of empathy, recognition and mutuality towards people who were once considered different. Applied as formal curriculum on the part of Saskatchewan Learning, this approach ostensibly informs the knowledge gaps of all students. Students may also learn that their former knowledge about others was based on stereotypes, myths and incomplete knowledge, as well as exclusion, invisibility and silence. Students may learn that their own social location and experience has been a barrier to learning about others or even about themselves and that, in the politics of knowledge, what they learned about "difference" patronized, distorted, disparaged and marginalized "the other." Ideally, in "learning *about* the other," there is an appreciation that the heritage, language, customs and self-identification of the other are as significant, diverse and fluid as one's own. These are some of the positive outcomes of learning about the culture, language, history and spirituality of First Nations and Métis peoples on the part of white teacher-education students in this location.

These two models of how inequality is to be overcome through education processes—education *for* the other and education *about* the other—are the most common methods employed throughout systems of education in this province. Mandated by the Saskatchewan Ministry of Education, they have become the default for doing social justice teaching in classrooms. While they have some benefits, these methods and their variations have been critiqued extensively for their limitations. According to Carla O'Connor, Amanda Lewis and Jennifer Mueller (2007), the problem is twofold: first, the heterogeneity of minority experience is frequently overlooked, especially when all experiences and explanations of difference are presented and explained as originating in cultural experience; and second, most studies ignore the institutionalized production of race and its significance in creating inequality and then uniformly and ideologically defending inequality as if it were naturally occurring.

In the last part of this chapter, I describe what such orientations and curricular practices produce in the identity construction of white pre-service education students, as well as what these methodologies forestall in the larger picture of colonizer/colonized relations.

Negative Outcomes: Teaching that fixes relations with no signs of changing them

The question of teaching about race and/or culture provides insight into the construction of teacher subjectivities. I argue that a cultural display, as described in the previous paragraphs about education *for* and *about* the other, provides partial access to notions of "the other" that serve to "fix" both dominant and subordinate selves into discourses of unequal relations that have been prepared historically, socially and economically. Learning about the other in these culturally specific ways goes further: it prepares and fixes subjectivities available to dominant students so that they can be readily inserted into and allow themselves to find their places within newly created and already-old stories of progress, professionalism, pastoral authority and identifiers of people in charge.

In a liberal democracy, where "difference" is assigned to others, the taken-for-grantedness of dominant identifications actually serves to confirm and produce normative relations of domination/subordination. In this binary, the colonizer requires a particular fiction of the subordinated subjectivity and the performance of difference. According to Fuss's reading (1995) of Frantz Fanon: " . . . the Imperial Subject imposes on all others, as a condition of their subjection, an injunction *to mime* alterity. The colonized are constrained to impersonate the image the colonizer offers them of themselves; they are commanded to imitate the colonizer's version of their essential difference" (p. 146). The stereotypes and binary positionings of both the enlightened helper and the subjugated other only "work" if colonized peoples are themselves offered as cultural artifacts devoid of politics and agency.

This repetition of sameness found throughout processes of colonization forestalls change by incorporating the language of liberal democracies and reinforcing an "improved" type of white subject. In this section, I discuss processes of enlightenment available to white subjectivities that maintain the discursive construction of the subjectivity of "others" through an education system organized for the consolidation of white students. Diana Fuss (1995) says that, "For the white man, the considerable cultural capital amassed by the *colonization of subjectivity* amounts to nothing less than the abrogation of universality" (Fuss, p. 143). This "abrogation of universality" has already been precluded by the imminent lack of the universal in conditions of liberalism—based as it is on European self-interest—as David Goldberg (1993) so eloquently describes.

One of the attractions for white students in taking up cultural and anti-racist approaches is that this is part of what constitutes the rhetoric of being a "good citizen." There are various ways that learning the discourses of anti-oppressive and cultural education positions white students as "good teachers," superior to their peers who do not have their awareness or facility with anti-oppressive language. In their care to "do the right thing," they also become better at being white. Alice McIntyre (1997) describes these students as "white knights," because of the goodwill they demonstrate to passive recipients in their classrooms. The emphasis on right actions and "best practices" that is part of teacher education "training" predisposes white students to imagine that anti-racist teaching is another set of prescriptive actions—rather than a set of power relations constitutive of self and others, continually under negotiation. Right action in cultural education means learning *about* aspects of other and self (you are other; I am not) that can be accomplished with some degree of certainty. With their enhanced knowledge, white anti-racist students may further perform their new roles with redoubled impunity as role models, saviours, helpers and charitable guides. Not surprisingly, these roles are like the static positionings of development workers who venture into unknown territory with unfamiliar people in need of assistance. On return, the workers invariably declare that they got more out of the experience than they gave (Heron, 2005), an outcome that is, after all, the quintessential purpose of colonization.

"Doing the right thing" ensures that certain white types are as good or better than other uninformed whites, when knowing about "others" and having access to "them" is understood to be a moral good. Insisting on the difference of the other is what preserves one's own uniqueness, as both "not other" and "better white." It also provides access to opportunities for consuming or becoming the other through having knowledge about and access to others' lives and experiences (Jones, 1999). Promise of access has no small attraction for mainstream white students, in that "the other" renders a common scene "diverse" simply because "they" are among "us." We are not only changed, but we come away with something extra. As Sara Ahmed (2006) explains: "[Diversity] also transforms difference into a property: if difference is something they are, then it is something we can have" (p. 120). The significant reward of "having" the other explains, in part, the attraction to cross-cultural work and the resistance to more critical inquiry that fails to confirm entitlement and actively works to disrupt it. The paradox is that white subjectivities desire to *be* or to consume the other in a way that still leaves white entitlement and subjectivities intact. Learning about otherness becomes a performative act in which white subjectivities may consume the other in an education ritual that becomes an end in itself.

Fuss, citing Gail Ching-Liang Low, suggests that "the primary attraction of the cross-cultural dress is the promise of 'transgressive' pleasure without the penalties of actual change" (Fuss, 1995, p. 148). The transgressive pleasure of identifying with the other available to white students "is the detour through the other that defines a self" (Fuss, 1995, p. 2). The pleasures in this seductive detour through the other are many (McWilliam, 1999). The detour is an act of agency that performs the identification that is, "from the beginning, a question of *relation*, of self to other, subject to object, inside to outside" (p. 3). Throughout the process of learning about the other, it is the white student who maintains agency as the one who may change or not, cross over or not, transgress or not.

In the midst of questions about the efficacy of formal cross-cultural education for white pre-service education students, there also resides the overwhelming influence of the informal, tacit curriculum. This "hidden" knowledge often carries—indirectly, pervasively, and often unintentionally—more educational significance than the official curriculum. The production of subjectivities in the classroom also takes place as part of these so-called hidden processes. Here, too, the colonizer makes claims on colonized space by requiring the other to be static, while the colonizer can be both traditional and up-to-date, value-free and universal. The other must remain a stereotype and must imitate the version that is selected, understood and desired by the colonizer.

CONCLUSION

This chapter contends that cultural displays are available to dominant teacher education students as real and symbolic evidence of both the difference of others and of the dominant students' own superiority. One of the worst outcomes of culturalist display among white students is that its seeming naturalness fulfills a desire for and consumption of difference and otherness, even as it reaffirms a sense of innocence among dominant students. Their subjectivities are reinforced in the way that missionaries, tourists and travellers—by accessing the spatialized discourses of others—emerge from their journey with an enlarged sense of self. Unfortunately, the subjectivity of a white student—as a liberal, self-determining and well-intentioned individual—is accomplished by cathartic notions of pleasure and entitlement (Ahmed, 2004; Boler, 1999; Goldberg, 1993) that continue to confound the project of social justice through schooling.

White teachers in this historic and geographic location, including this author, are socially positioned as settler colonizers because, and in spite of, our social histories and chosen means of identifications. Regardless of intentions, our attempts to promote justice issues and disrupt inequality are compromised by the effects of social in/justice education that reproduces social subjectivities in which identifications of self and other are, for the most part, confirmed, if not enhanced.

Possibilities for change and transformation that often go missing in educational practice are exacerbated by notions of fixed subjectivities of colonizer/colonized. Addressing these lost performances directly and organizing a curriculum around issues of injustice is one recommendation by Chubbuck and Zembylas (2008): "problem-pose the ordinary, taken-for-granted events of life that are in fact hegemonic expressions of injustice" (p. 282). Donna Jeffery (2007), in describing the limits of anti-oppressive education for social workers, suggests that what is wanted is "a critical ontology that allows the social worker to reinvent, explore, and otherwise make transparent the professional self in the classroom or in real-world practice" (p. 129). This critical ontology could begin again by asking the original question—"Who do you think you are?"—and forever problematize the answer. For disrupting notions of both culture and identity (McCarthy et al., 2005) might make possible the porosity of human endeavour that shapes educational exchange.

REFERENCES

Ahmed, S. (2006). The nonperformativity of anti-racism. *Meridians: Feminism, race, transnationalism, 7*(1), 104–126.

Ahmed, S. (2004). *The cultural politics of emotion.* New York: Routledge.

Berlak, A. (2004). Confrontation and pedagogy: Cultural secrets, trauma, and emotion in anti-opressive pedagogies. In M. Boler (Ed.), *Democratic dialogue in education* (pp. 123–144). New York: Peter Lang.

Boler, M. (1999). *Feeling power: Emotions and education.* New York: Routledge.

Chubbuck, S., & Zembylas, M. (2008). The emotional ambivalence of socially just teaching: A case study of a novice urban schoolteacher. *American Educational Research Journal, 45*(2), 274–318.

Fendler, L. (2003). Teacher reflection in a hall of mirrors: Historical influences and political reverberations. *Educational Researcher, 323*(3), 16–25.

Freire, P. (1970). *Pedagogy of the oppressed.* (M.B. Ramos, Trans.). New York: Continuum.

Fuss, D. (1995). *Identification papers.* New York: Routledge.

Goldberg, D. (1993). *Racist culture: Philosophy and the politics of meaning.* UK: Blackwell Publishers.

Heron, B. (2005). Self-reflection in critical social work practice: Subjectivity and possibilities of resistance. *Journal of Reflective Practice, 6*(3), 341–351.

Jeffery, D. (2007). Radical problems and liberal selves: Professional subjectivity in the anti-oppressive social work classroom. *Canadian Social Work Review, 24*(2), 125–139.

Jones, A. (1999). The limits of cross-cultural dialogue: Pedagogy, desire, and absolution in the classroom. *Educational Theory, 49*(3), 299–316.

Kumashiro, K. (2001). "Posts" perspective on anti-oppressive education in social studies, English, mathematics, and science classrooms. *Educational Researcher, 30*(3), 3–12.

Kumashiro, K. (2000). Toward a theory of anti-oppressive education. *Review of Educational Research, 70*(1), 25–53.

McCarthy, C. (1998). *The uses of culture: Education and the limits of ethnic affiliation.* New York: Routledge.

McCarthy, C., Giardina, M., Harewood, S., & Park, J.-K. (2005). Contesting culture: Identity and curriculum dilemmas in the age of globalization, postcolonialism and multiplicity. In C. McCarthy, W. Crichlow, G. Dimitriadis & N. Dolby (Eds.), *Race, identity, and representation in education* (2nd ed.) (pp. 153–165). New York: Routledge.

McIntosh, P. (1998). White privilege: Unpacking the invisible knapsack. In P. S. Rothenberg (Ed.), *Race, class and gender in the United States: An integrated study* (pp. 165–169). New York: St. Martin's Press.

McIntyre, A. (1997). Constructing an image of a white teacher. *College Record, 98*(4), 653–681.

McWilliam, E. (1999). *Pedagogical pleasures.* New York: Peter Lang.

O'Connor, C., Lewis, A., & Mueller, J. (2007). Research "Black" education experiences and outcomes: Theoretical and methodological considerations. *Educational Researcher, 36*(9), 541–552.

Pillow, W. S. (2003). Confession, catharsis, or cure? Rethinking the uses of reflexivity as methodological power in qualitative research. *International Journal of Qualitative Studies in Education, 16*(2), 175–196.

St. Denis, V. (2004). Real Indians: Cultural revitalization and fundamentalism in Aboriginal education. In C. Schick, J. Jaffe & A. Watkinson (Eds.), *Contesting fundamentalisms* (pp. 35–47). Halifax: Fernwood.

CHAPTER 9

FROM *STONECHILD* TO SOCIAL COHESION: ANTI-RACIST CHALLENGES FOR SASKATCHEWAN[1]

Joyce Green

The frozen body of Neil Stonechild, a seventeen-year-old Cree university student, was found on the outskirts of Saskatoon, on November 29, 1990. While his body bore cuts and marks that suggested he had been assaulted, the cause of death was determined to be freezing. He was last seen in the back of a police car by a friend, Jason Roy, to whom Stonechild was appealing for help. Denying Roy's account and attacking his credibility, the police officers in question also denied having Stonechild in police custody that night.

Neil Stonechild was not the first, nor the last, Aboriginal man to freeze to death in apparently similar circumstances. Indeed, the police practice of taking Aboriginals out of town and leaving them even had its own moniker, "Starlight Tours," used by both the police service and the Aboriginal community.

Ten years after Stonechild's body was found, Darrel Night was taken out of town and left to his fate. Night survived, and later filed a complaint. Two police officers were subsequently charged and convicted of unlawful confinement for their actions in his case. That same winter, in February 2000, the frozen bodies of Lloyd Dustyhorn, Lawrence Wegner and Darcy Dean Ironchild were also found, on separate occasions, in the same area. Within a few weeks, the RCMP was called in to investigate the matter, and in 2001 it produced a report. No charges were laid. The

---

1. First published in *Canadian Journal of Political Science / Revue canadienne de science politique* 39:3 (September/septembre 2006) 507–527. (c) 2006 Canadian Political Science Association (l'Association canadienne de science politique) and/et la Société québécoise de science politique. Reprinted with the permission of Cambridge University Press.

public inquiry looking into the circumstances surrounding Neil Stonechild's death, headed by Mr. Justice David Wright, was not struck until September 2003. According to one researcher in this matter, it was struck primarily because of sustained pressure for a public inquiry by Saskatoon lawyer Donald Worme, who was acting on behalf of Stonechild's mother, Stella Stonechild Bignell.[2]

In October 2004, Mr. Justice David Wright submitted the report of the Commission of Inquiry Into Matters Relating to the Death of Neil Stonechild (hereafter referred to as the *Stonechild* report), a provincial investigation. The report criticized the police investigation into Stonechild's death: "The deficiencies in the investigation go beyond incompetence or neglect. They were inexcusable" (Harding, 2004; Wright, 2004, p. 199). Moreover, Wright condemned not just the individual behaviour of those involved, but the command structure of the Saskatoon Police force, writing that these deficiencies "would have been identified and remedied before the file was closed if the file had been properly supervised" (2004, p. 200). Wright concluded that the Saskatoon Police Service had conducted the investigation in a fashion that obfuscated the matter and, in particular, the role of officers on the force in the event. Wright found that Stonechild had been in the custody of the police on the night he was last seen alive and that his frozen body bore injuries and marks likely caused by handcuffs. He found that the principal investigator on the case, Keith Jarvis, carried out a "superficial and totally inadequate investigation" of the death and "dismissed important information" provided to him by members of the police. Wright wrote: "The only reasonable inference that can be drawn is that Jarvis was not prepared to pursue the investigation because he was either aware of police involvement or suspected police involvement" (2004, p. 200).

Despite the Stonechild family's highly publicized concerns that racism was a factor in the quick closure of the file, the police chose not to investigate the officers implicated in the Stonechild death or to address racism in the Saskatchewan Police Service (Wright, 2004, p. 201–202). Wright found that in subsequent years "the chiefs and deputy chiefs of police who successively headed the Saskatoon Police Service, rejected or ignored reports . . . that cast serious doubts on the conduct of the Stonechild investigation." Finally, he found that "[t]he self-protective and defensive attitudes exhibited by the senior levels of the police service continued . . . (and) were manifested by certain members of the Saskatoon Police Service during the Inquiry" (Wright, 2004, p. 212). Stonechild's family is now suing the Saskatoon Police Service for $30 million: for costs, exemplary and punitive damages; for special damages, for behaviour characterized as trespass, assault and battery, deceit and conspiracy by police officers (CBC 2005d; Adam, 2005).

---

2.   Susanne Reber, personal interview, Regina, September 16, 2005. Reber, a CBC reporter who had covered the Stonechild incident, and Robert Renaud are co-authors of *Starlight Tour: The Last, Lonely Night of Neil Stonechild.* Random House Canada, 2005.

On November 12, 2004, Saskatoon Police Chief Russell Sabo fired Constables Larry Hartwig and Bradley Senger, announcing that they were "unsuitable for police service by reason of their conduct" (Harding, 2004, p. A6). Despite Wright's finding that Stonechild had been in police custody on the night he died, no charges were laid in connection with this. And what was the impugned conduct that cost the men their jobs with the Saskatoon Police Service? Not racism, not criminal negligence, and not manslaughter; instead, their failure was characterized as administrative. Chief Sabo said they had failed to properly report information and evidence about Stonechild being in their custody on November 24, 1990. The fired officers appealed the Sabo decision.[3]

More recently, Saskatoon Deputy Police Chief Dan Wiks was disciplined with a one-day unpaid suspension for giving inaccurate information to a Saskatoon *Star Phoenix* journalist. Wiks, in 2003, had told the reporter that "the police had no indication of officer involvement" in the Stonechild death, although he testified in 2004 to the Wright Inquiry that the Saskatoon police had, since 2000, known that the RCMP suspected constables Hartwig and Senger (Haight, 2005). The Saskatoon Police force, under Chief Sabo's direction, appealed, seeking a more severe ruling. However, sources in the police force reported to the media that some officers disagreed with the decision to appeal, demonstrating that Chief Sabo faced some internal challenges to his approach and, possibly, to his policy direction on Aboriginal policing (CBC, 2005d). Perhaps not coincidentally, upon review in March 2006, Sabo's contract was not renewed, and the chief, who had been recruited particularly to repair the police-Aboriginal relationship post-Stonechild, did not enjoy much support from the Saskatoon Police force. However, obviously taking a different view, the Federation of Saskatchewan Indian Nations honoured Sabo at its winter legislative assembly for "healing the rifts between police and the First Nations community" (CBC, 2006; Warick, 2006, p. A7).

Aboriginal activists and organizations have called the police force racist. Spokespersons for the police have denied the accusation and defended the force's reputation and the claims of the individuals involved in the Stonechild matter. And yet, a number of factors suggest something is amiss: the pattern of denial and obfuscation around the Stonechild case, which ultimately led to the Wright inquiry; the high degree of public awareness regarding the "Starlight Tours"; and the anger towards and fear of cops in the sizeable Aboriginal community. In the white community[4] in Saskatoon, opinion was polarized between

---

3. The hearing into the matter concluded on October 31, 2005, though a decision was not then made (CBC 2005c).

4. I use the term "white" for two reasons. First, empirically, Saskatchewan's population is predominantly white, with the balance being almost entirely Aboriginal. Only a tiny percentage of Saskatchewan residents are "visible minorities," something less than 4 percent. Second, "white" is intended to invoke the privileged component of a race-stratified society. Therefore, I also refer to "white racism," and have not taken up the ways in which non-white members of settler society may also be racist, or affected by racism.

those supporting the police position, and especially that of the officers involved, and those criticizing what appeared to be racism, apparent criminal behaviour on the part of some officers and institutional practices violating human rights.

In this chapter, I look at the Stonechild and related incidents as exemplars of the racism in Saskatchewan's (and Canada's) political culture, and consider what possibilities exist to erode this damaging and sometimes deadly phenomenon. I argue that the processes of colonialism provide the impulse for the racist ideology that is now encoded in social, political, economic, academic and cultural institutions and practices, and which functions to maintain the status quo of white dominance. I suggest that decolonization, rather than "revolt," "assimilation" (Memmi, 1965) or "cultural understanding," is the necessary political project to eradicate the kinds of systemic practices that arguably killed Neil Stonechild et al. I argue that decolonization is a political project capacious enough to include colonizer and colonized without erasing or subordinating either.

Census projections suggest that the very young Aboriginal population will continue to increase rapidly, and that by 2010 Aboriginal people, predominantly youth, will be the majority ethnic group in Saskatchewan. Given Saskatchewan's demographic trajectory, a failure to deal with white racism guarantees that there will continue to be social stresses between Aboriginal and non-Aboriginal populations, damaging the province's economic and social viability into the future. A proactive, self-reflective, anti-racist policy and a strategy for building public support should be a priority for any Saskatchewan government. Social cohesion, a necessary condition for a healthy citizenship regime and a notion of considerable interest to provincial and federal politicians and to academics in Saskatchewan,[5] cannot be constructed without tackling racism.

Individual acts of racism are often identified as such and condemned by members of the dominant community. However, the same community displays much less consensus over the existence and nature of a systemic racism that implicates all community members. And, as Stephanie Irlbacher-Fox (2005) shows, legacies of historic acts of racism are often discounted as though they were simply historic artefacts replaced by newer understandings and "renewed relationships." This formulation avoids the questions of agency, in/justice and responsibility.

Allegations of systemic racism are generally rejected by those who suggest that the way things are done, the status quo, is simply the product of social and intellectual consensus and is not laden with relations of dominance and

---

5. A Google search of "government of Saskatchewan social cohesion" raised about 11,400 invocations of the phrase. Notably, this includes a speech by Regina-Wascana MP (and then federal finance minister) Ralph Goodale: "[W]e're building homes as a way to invest in Saskatchewan's centennial year and thereby leave a lasting social and human legacy . . . It's all about building better futures in a community that truly cares about all its members—meaning greater inclusion and social cohesion" (2003).

subordination, nor the result of malicious intent. In order to challenge this, it is useful to employ the conceptual lens of Albert Memmi to Canadian colonial history. In Memmi's (1965) account, colonialism is tied to oppression and is conditioned by "the oppressor's hatred for the oppressed" (p. xxvii). This hatred is manufactured and perpetuated by sets of racist assumptions that form the ideological foundation for the systematic, bureaucratic and individual implementation of racist practices, while also constructing "self-absolution" of the racists (1965, p. xxvi). The consequence, racist ideology, facilitates the maintenance of both the economic potential and the processes of colonialism, while simultaneously explaining its ineluctability and positive significance (1965, pp. 82–83). The combination of oppression and publicly disseminated racist ideology functions to affect the self-image and political capacity of the colonized, creating wounded people who are vulnerable to internalizing the racist stereotypes (1965, pp. 87–89; see also the works of Frantz Fanon). A consequence is the impossible situation where assimilation of the colonized is the putative goal, but it cannot actually be achieved by reason of racism, while political and cultural autonomy is denied to the colonized for the same racist reasons.[6]

Racism never happens in the absence of relations of privilege: "privilege is at the heart of the colonial relationship—and . . . is undoubtedly economic" (Memmi, 1965, p. xii; see also Cesaire, 1972, pp. 10–11; van Dijk, 1993, pp. 21–22). And what is the nature of this economic privilege? It derives from the obliteration of the political, cultural and economic processes of the colonized, and their replacement by colonial models. This is done not to aid the "development" of the colonized, but rather to appropriate their land and resources for economic and political gain by the colonizers (Memmi, 1965, pp. 3–18). And that, after all, is the primary motivation of most Canadians' ancestors in immigrating: there were opportunities, especially economic opportunities, and access to cheap or free land here, that were not available at home. "Colonization is, above all, economic and political exploitation" (Memmi, 1965, p. 149). Colonial ventures are attractive because of the potential for profits, advancements and opportunities that exceed those the colonizers could reasonably expect to receive "at home" (Memmi, 1965, p. 4). In choosing the colonies, the immigrant chooses these benefits while also knowing that the indigenous peoples will be constrained in relation to the newcomers, thus creating privilege (Memmi, 1965, p. 8). "To different degrees every colonizer is privileged, at least comparatively so, ultimately

---

6. A pejorative term in the Canadian context, assimilation is, for Memmi, "the opposite of colonization. It tends to eliminate the distinctions between the colonizers and the colonized, and thereby eliminates the colonial relationship" (1965, pp. 149–50). Irlbacher-Fox considers assimilation a rhetorical device to "reinforce the colonizer as a norm to which Indigenous peoples must conform" (2005, p. 16). I prefer to conceptualize the potential of decolonization, rather than assimilation (Green, 2005; see also Irlbacher- Fox, 2005, p. 22). The difference is a new, mutually designed and beneficial politico-social order, as opposed to the erasure and imposition implied by assimilation.

to the detriment of the colonized" (Memmi, 1965, p. 11). The governing institutions and the assumptions of those who populate them are designed for the advantage of the newcomers and to the detriment of the indigenous (Memmi, 1965, pp. 11–13); this makes all newcomers complicit in the oppression of colonialism, "a collective responsibility by the fact of membership in a national oppressor group" (Memmi, 1965, p. 39).

Now, what might be termed "second-generation colonialism" includes the expectations of the benefits that accrue to those with privilege, precisely because of the colonial conditions that created the privilege and that deny it to the colonized, and because of those normalized assumptions that form the dominant political culture. Most of those with privilege are happily unaware of the particulars of Canada's colonial past and also of the contemporary consequences of colonialism, which include both Aboriginal trauma and white privilege. Yet, white privilege is a consequence of racism (as male privilege is a consequence of sexism) and so, too, is Aboriginal suffering. As Joel Olson writes, "Contemporary white privilege is like an 'invisible weightless knapsack' of unearned advantages that whites draw on in their daily lives to improve or maintain their social position, even as they hold to the ideals of political equality and equal opportunity" (2002, p. 338).

These liberal ideals include beliefs in a neutral, equitable meritocracy in which the most competent will succeed. Hence, the socio-economic indicators that measure appalling levels of Aboriginal suffering are assumed to be consequences both of Aboriginal inadequacy, best remedied by the bracing application of measures of progress and development, and of ineffable cultural differences.

Confronting and eradicating racism requires unmasking the white-preferential, male-preferential processes that facilitate access to power, privilege, education, influence, employment, political positions and so on. Because the effects of racism are unintended by individuals, and because most people in the dominant community are well-intentioned and truly believe that their privilege is solely the result of their merit and diligence, the existence of intentional systemic patterns of discrimination and privilege is denied by most members of the settler population. This results in what Sherene Razack calls "the dominant group's refusal to examine its own complicity in oppressing others" (1998, p. 40). Thus, systemic racism is embedded in Canadian political culture, in the service, first, of colonialism and, subsequently, in the maintenance of settler and white privilege.

"Race" is colloquially used to refer to categories of people who share broadly similar physical characteristics. However, critical race theorists and post-colonial scholars have shown that race is a socially constructed category that has shifted over time and across cultures, but is typified by the legitimation of relations of dominance and oppression, linked to categories of people. Reviewing that important corpus of literature is beyond the purview of this paper, and unnecessary for its argument. Still, it is useful to note that there are still some contemporary scholars who write and teach about race using discredited definitions and analyses.[7]

Such scholarship contributes to knowledge reproduction and perpetuates the mindless racism that sustains relations of dominance and subordination in which we are all implicated (Green, 2002; Razack, 1998; Smith, 1999, pp. 58–77; van Dijk, 1993, pp. 158–196). This racism was most notably transmitted via public education, "a central element in the colonial discursive apparatus which produced, and formed the 'truth' of racial hierarchies employed to justify the denial of human and civil rights to some groups of people deemed inferior" (Comeau, 2004, p. 2). While "race" is a constructed and hence contestable and arguably fallacious category, racism is not. Racism occurs when people behave as though race were a real category and when they act on the privileges or liabilities conferred by racist processes.

The systemic racism embedded in our political culture is inherited from the colonial relationships that have now been transmuted into the Canadian social context, where descendants of settler populations carry with them a preferential entry into social, political and economic institutions and see themselves reflected in those institutions, and in the dominant culture, in ways that Aboriginal populations do not. Further, the very fact of normativeness is a social asset to those who enjoy it. Finally, this asset is especially strongly correlated with white skin privilege, rather than with those racialized Canadians that our society labels "visible minorities." Ultimately, this phenomenon perpetuates both racist assumptions and racist processes, even as it is so normalized as to be invisible and non-controversial (Green, 2005).Yet, it is inescapably visible to those whose "race" constructs them as subordinate, and this realization is accompanied by anger at and resentment of those who benefit from race privilege while denying the existence and consequences of racism (for a good personal account of this, see Fourhorns, 2005).

Systemic racism has material consequences, both for those who enjoy privilege and for those who are subordinate. Statistics Canada data show that the likelihood of Aboriginal people completing school or acquiring post-secondary education is improving, but it is still significantly less than the national average (48 percent of Aboriginal youth did not complete secondary school as of 2001; 37 percent of non-reserve Aboriginal people had completed post-secondary studies, compared with 58 percent for the total Canadian population). Health problems are distinctive and prevalent for Aboriginal populations: "For every

---

7.   Without suggesting that the following is either the most important or the worst of this phenomenon, I offer the example of Mark Dickerson and Tom Flanagan (1999, p. 51): "A race is a biologically defined group whose members share a gene pool, giving them common physical characteristics, such as skin, eye, and hair colour. A race is the same as a subspecies; members of a race are physically identifiable and distinctive, but they can interbreed with members of other races and produce fertile offspring (as well as new races). A race differs from a nation in that it is only a biological group."

10-year age group between the ages of 25 and 64, the proportion of Aboriginal people who reported their health as fair or poor was about double that of the total Canadian population." Economic marginalization also shows up in the lack of adequate housing and childcare facilities (Statistics Canada, 2003; Saskatchewan Labour, 2003).

Mylène Jaccoud and Renée Brassard (2003) make the point that Aboriginal marginalization "begins in early childhood and is rooted in a much broader social context associated with the consequences of (the) colonization" (p. 143). This context becomes what they call a "defining path" that makes marginalization probable: "poverty, non-integration into the conventional job market, involvement in gainful activities that are socially frowned upon, unacceptable or even criminal, violence, alcohol, drugs, homelessness, reliance on food banks and shelters" (p. 143). These kinds of circumstances are incompatible with social cohesion.

Colonialism and its accompanying racism are practiced through "extreme discursive warfare" (Lawrence, 2004, p. 39). The trenches of this warfare lie in the media, in government bureaucracy and legislation, and in universities. The media write, speak and produce for the "average reader," the normative working-class or middle-class white model, with its set of social assumptions about the world. The advertisers that underwrite the media pitch to this category. For the most part, Aboriginal peoples do not exist for the media, except as practitioners of violence or political opposition, as marketing stereotypes or as bearers of social pathologies. Virtually no real Aboriginal people write for or are portrayed in the media, especially the private media, for Aboriginal or settler consumption. (Doug Cuthand's occasional columns in the Regina and Saskatoon newspapers are so exceptional as to prove the rule.[8]) The creators and enforcers of the laws and policies of the state are overwhelmingly non-Aboriginal, implementing regimes that are seldom directed at Aboriginal peoples and almost never with Aboriginal stakeholder or citizen participation. The knowledge producers, universities, construct and replicate forms of knowledge that they also have the power to determine; in so doing, they mostly legitimize forms of knowledge that are alien to and hostile to Aboriginal forms and to critical contestation (Green, 2002; Kuokkanen, 2005; Smith, 1999). Universities are overwhelmingly populated by those who know little or nothing about Aboriginal peoples and issues, and teach to student bodies that have only a few Aboriginal members. Thus, in both the knowledge presented and recruited, the ivory towers remain white, and the graduating elites carry with them this white-preferential way of seeing and organizing the world.

The Wright report leads logically to the conclusion that the incident concerning the death of Stonechild is a manifestation of structural and individual racism in institutional culture, and the report documents the obdurate denial

---

8.   Cuthand, a freelancer, was terminated by the Regina *Leader-Post* in February 2009, thus eliminating the only indigenous writer, or writer on indigenous issues, in the paper.

of this finding, especially by the Saskatoon Police force. That such incidents could possibly be a consequence of institutional or structural racism is denied by many non-Aboriginal members of Saskatchewan society, who prefer to see such events as isolated acts by individuals.

Institutional racism is diffused throughout the professional cultures and practices of state and private institutions. Structural racism is similarly encoded in the apparatus and practices of the agents of state and corporate and cultural power, such as politics, economics and universities. Racism, like other forms of political culture, is transmitted intergenerationally and is thus rendered non-controversial. Destabilizing it is enormously difficult: first, a critique must make the practices visible, frame the issues, to denormalize them; second, one must provide theories and strategies for change.

Stonechild provides us with a moment of opportunity and is a call to arms for all who were appalled by this incident and who are committed to transformation of this damaging and sometimes deadly phenomenon. It is a moment when even those who have no race analysis, and no understanding of colonialism,[9] are united with Aboriginal people in condemning the particular police actions that arguably led to the death of Neil Stonechild, and undeniably led to a set of institutionally sanctioned practices of police behaviour that frustrated the justice system. If we can trace the parameters of racism in political culture, it may be that the repugnance of those who reject police calumny and violence may also move them to reflect on our racist political culture, and how we are variously constructed within it. Then, we can move to strategies for building social solidarity and for undermining race privilege as well as race discrimination.

Stonechild shows us that racism kills. The same lesson emerged from the Pamela George case, in which the young Saulteaux woman was assaulted and killed by two middle-class white men in Regina (Razack, 2002), and from the murders of Eva Taysup, Calinda Waterhen, Shelley Napope and Mary Jane Serloin by a white man, John Crawford (Goulding, 2001). Racism maims, as demonstrated by the 2001 case of the 12-year-old Cree rape victim from the Melfort-Tisdale area, assaulted by three white adult males (Buydens, 2005; Coolican, 2001; Prober, 2003).[10] Its pervasiveness limits opportunities and experience, depriving us all of human capital even as individuals' lives are marred.

When individual cases, like that of the 12-year-old rape complainant, reach the justice system, powerful actors participate in the adversarial justice system to show that the victim is in fact responsible personally, while no party explores

---

9. Colonialism is an always exploitative relationship, in which the political, cultural and economic autonomy of one society or nation is appropriated by another via coercion. It is legitimated by myths of superiority, inevitability and racism, and it is enforced by the socio-political institutions of the colonizer. These myths and the practices of colonialism are transmitted intergenerationally through political culture.

10. See also James McNinch's examination of the trial transcripts for this case in Chapter 10, "I thought Pocahantas was a movie," in this volume.

the broader collective context for individual actions. Thus, the medical doctor providing evidence to the court in that case could state that the girl had reached "full physical maturity" and was "very attractive," and the court, which referred to the rapists as "the boys" (Prober, 2003, p. 2), could comfortably move to the question of the victim's participation—and instigation—of her rape by three older white defendants, who were, according to their lawyers, "aroused" by her (Buydens, 2005).

In the case of convicted murderer John Martin Crawford, Mr. Justice Wright (the same judge who would later be the commissioner in the Stonechild inquiry) noted: "Mr. Crawford was attracted to his victims for four reasons: one, they were young; second, they were women; third, they were Native; and fourth, they were prostitutes. . . . He seemed determined to destroy every vestige of their humanity" (Goulding, 2001, p. 188). In other words, the Aboriginal identity of the murdered women was part of what marked them as targets for murder, in addition to their other shared attributes.

Sherene Razack argues that racism in Canada has a spatialized component. She suggests that the colonial society disciplines the colonized into particular and least valuable portions of communities. It is not only the bodies of people that are raced, but geographical space in communities, where whiteness constitutes a pass to all areas, but an exclusive pass to exclusively white areas, and where areas of predominantly Aboriginal occupation are coded as dangerous, degenerate spaces still available for white (and especially white male) tourism. It is in this white adventure into degenerate Native space, Razack claims, that raced and gendered identities are enacted and confirmed—by the white agents, against the Native ones. Thus, "the Stroll" in Regina, Saskatchewan, is worked predominantly by Aboriginal women, and white men can venture there for risky adventure, confirming the power relations between all as they act out their raced sexuality on Aboriginal bodies. However, the likelihood that the women would similarly enter the primarily white residential space of the murderers is slim. This spatialized relationship maintains the focus on the indigenous as needing to be controlled, for racism suggests they are ultimately not fit for civilized society (Razack, 2002). The "Starlight Tours" also fit with Razack's analysis, as they served to eject Aboriginal men from the primarily white urban society of Saskatoon.

Razack uses this analysis to illuminate the processes that played out in the murder of Pamela George. Her analytical framework can be applied to other situations to show similar or identical processes: the murdered women in Vancouver's notorious pig farm; the murdered sex workers in Edmonton and Saskatoon; the scores of missing Aboriginal women across the country. These cases show us the racial definition of space, into white space and Other space, and the racial conflation of Aboriginal with available and ultimately disposable women. In this way, the white public "knows" there is no need to be concerned about these issues, for it believes (it is taught) that these women brought themselves into danger by "choosing their lifestyles." Consider the numbers of missing Aboriginal women whose cases are being documented and publicized by the Native Women's Association of Canada in its *Stolen Sisters* campaign and by Dr. Brenda Anderson at Luther College, University of Regina, through her groundbreaking Women's Studies course on missing indigenous women. These women have been disregarded as objects for state concern and action because of the many factors in their lives that are a direct consequence of being Aboriginal; ultimately, they are ignored precisely because they are Aboriginal.

All of these factors—white racism, sexism, indifference and ignorance, lack of public policy and lack of political and judicial attention—come together in the media treatment of matters Aboriginal. And yet the media, the fifth estate, is the primary source of political information for most Canadians and is thus deeply implicated in the maintenance of a political culture and dominant ideology of white racism: it is both institutional and structural in its construction and in its effects; it is white-preferential and thus racist in its content, context and agenda setting; and it dominates public consciousness and opinion formation and shapes "public cognitions" (van Dijk, 1993, pp. 241–282). "White group interests, including the privileges and power that are implied by white group dominance, thus find their cognitive counterpart in fundamental norms, values, and ideologies" (van Dijk, 1993, p. 246).

In his book *Just Another Indian*, Warren Goulding explores the context for the murders of four Aboriginal women by John Martin Crawford: the lack of media and state attention paid to the murders; Crawford's eventual trial and conviction in Saskatoon, Saskatchewan; and the "lurid details of a triple sex murder." Goulding points out that, in contradistinction to the Paul Bernardo trial, the media didn't seem interested: the story had the ingredients of sex and violence, but it was about Aboriginal victims, not middle-class white girls. Racism played, and plays, a role; it was the in/significance of the Aboriginality of the victims to authorities, media and the white public that resulted in the lack of urgency around the case. Contrasting the response to the Crawford murders with those committed by Paul Bernardo and Karla Homolka, Goulding implies that the middle-class whiteness of the latter's victims rendered them subjects of empathy and interest. "The mainstream media, conservative and decidedly non-Aboriginal in terms of working journalists, were unable to empathize with the perpetrator or the [Aboriginal] victims and their families" (2001, pp. 210–11). Crown prosecutor Terry Hinz told Goulding: "The media responds to victims they can empathize with." The indifference of white media and the white public to the violence and misery that attend to many Aboriginal lives is a deeply racist position.

Goulding also faults the organization of the media; many media outlets, particularly in the wake of private media mergers, have eliminated or scaled back or in other ways reduced focused positions such as the "Indian beat" (2001, p. 216; see also Vipond, 2000, pp. 64–86). These apparently neutral decisions are implicated in the practices of racism and sexism, as they have the effect of eliminating good journalism on particular issues and on particular kinds of people. When Aboriginal issues are of interest to the media, they are often unidimensionally presented. Goulding, a white journalist, writes:

> Racism in the media begins subtly. . . . When a violent incident occurs in [a predominantly Aboriginal] one of these areas, editors and news directors . . . make a basic evaluation: is it news? . . . In Saskatoon, if someone is beaten in an alley in Riversdale or Pleasant Hill, it isn't news; if a similar incident happens in upper-middle-class Silverwood Heights or Lakeview, it is. (2001, p. 213)

The implication is that "bad things only happen to people who deserve them" (2001, p. 213).

Yet the media is also a vehicle for free speech, a right in democratic societies, and explicitly a constitutional right of citizens in Canada. It informs citizens about "news" and about diverse experiences and opinions, and did much to bring the matter of Neil Stonechild's death to the attention of the public and of political elites.

While racism is most violently experienced by Aboriginal people, it also maims the humanity and civility of those who perpetuate it, deny it or ignore it. Racism injures the capacity of the body politic to work collaboratively towards common visions. It disables a common citizenship in a collective political project. In other words, the social cohesion that could sustain all of us is dependent on confronting and eliminating racism from Canada's social fabric.

This will be no easy task. Racism is the legitimating ideology of colonialism. Over decades, the racist assumptions that legitimate our politico-social order have been dignified by intellectuals, by policy and by politics, until they have become part of what many understand as common sense. In families, in schools and in popular culture, racism is reproduced intergenerationally and unconsciously by good people. This culture of white racism operates in ways that appear to be benign, unintentional, passive or unknowing. It can only operate thus because of its very normativeness and because of the conventional consensus on the suspect nature of Aboriginal people.

Racism is supported by myths embedded in our political culture, such as variations on the theme that "we" trace our origins to brave, tenacious ancestors who came from elsewhere to create this good society. These myths ignore the reality of colonial occupation of Aboriginal lands and the displacement and subordination of Aboriginal peoples, all through official policies. Racism exists in the faith so many have in the myth of liberalism—that, ultimately, we are all autonomous agents who choose the conditions of our lives. This myth is tied to a lack of appreciation of how, to paraphrase Karl Marx, if we act as agents, it is in contexts, and in conditions, that are not of our choosing. Racism exists because of the conflation of the circumstances of peoples' lives with their aspirations about their lives—as though Aboriginal people "choose" statistically probable lives of immiseration. Above all, the myths of the dominant society ignore the reality that the social context and economic wealth for the settler community is based on "white privilege," the tool kit of positive assumptions and advantages that Aboriginal citizens do not share.

The effects of racism may be found in the negative Aboriginal socio-economic measures, such as dramatic differences in life expectancies, education levels, workforce participation rates, infant mortality rates, rates of access to healthy, sufficient water and sewage infrastructure and housing, and in high rates of social pathologies. These social pathologies disturb many whites, but too few appreciate these phenomena in a political context. The miserable statistics are seldom accompanied by political and theoretical analysis that might explain how certain communities come to be systemically liable to particular kinds of misery. And seldom are governments reminded by white citizens that their policies dictate the lack of public money for changing these conditions; that is, there is little awareness, concern or solidarity expressed in politically significant ways by those who benefit from race privilege with those who are oppressed by it. Intriguingly, Irlbacher-Fox (2005) points out that these markers of marginalization are used in Canadian political arguments, both for greater indigenous autonomy and for renewed colonization, through "new partnerships" based on definition by the colonial government (pp. 10, 14).

In his "final comments" section in the Stonechild Inquiry, Mr. Justice Wright wrote: "As I reviewed the evidence in this Inquiry, I was reminded, again and again, of the chasm that separates Aboriginal and non-Aboriginal people in this city and province. *Our two communities do not know each other and do not seem to want to*" (2004, p. 208, emphasis added). He was troubled by the fact that "the Saskatoon Police Service's submissions regarding the improvements to the Service did not contain any reference at all to attempts to improve the Service's interaction with Aboriginals and other racial groups" (2004, p. 210). Apparently, then, the police force did not think it had a race/ism problem that needed to be fixed. The Stonechild matter was interpreted as an incident, decontextualized from the political and institutional culture of racism and the specifics of colonialism in Saskatchewan. Particular individuals could be faulted, but the system remained uninterrogated. Wright, whose report was in so many ways illuminative of the depth and pervasiveness of racism in the Saskatoon Police force, was unable to grapple with its systemic and structural nature, and he concluded with the erroneous implication that the "chasm" is created by both communities, and is a matter of misunderstanding and of cultural differences rather than systemic power relations with historical origins and contemporary practices. In concluding thus, he invoked comforting myths of cultural difference to explain systemic racism—the myths of inalterable and incommensurate cultural essences that are mutually incomprehensible. While cultures assuredly have differences, some profound, these differences do not create the racism that leads to practices like "Starlight Tours."

Retreat to cultural essentialism avoids the more difficult questions about privilege, dominance and subordination that are intrinsic to colonial relationships. Cultural difference has become a form of code for a less explicit racism, according to Teun van Dijk (1993). He considers this to be the "neutral facade of what is usually meant: cultural incompatibility, if not white/Western superiority." In other words, this is still racism, but one that pretends to respect other cultures, to be non-judgmental and non-responsible. In popular discourse and in contemporary ideology, it means replacing the notion of "race" with that of "ethnicity" (pp. 160–62).

Wright departed from the context for the institutional racism that led to the deaths of the frozen men by calling for greater "understanding" between the two communities. This suggests that the problem of racism is caused by misunderstandings, rather than by the disproportionate power and malice held by those in the dominant community, who also benefit from the subordinated status of Aboriginal people. Stonechild et al. did not die because of a misunderstanding. Indeed, on the same page that Wright turned to culturalist explanations, he also cited evidence from witnesses demonstrating the awareness and fear of white racism with which Aboriginal people live (2004, p. 209). Yet he seemed unable to analyze clearly the discrete notions of culture and racism, nor could he distinguish between them. Cultural awareness activities, such as having police officers participate in a smudge ceremony, are a good start, but on their own they will not bring about a shift in racist practices or institutions.

Racism in Canada is the malaise of colonialism. The continued structural racism sustains the "toxic gulf " between Aboriginal and settler communities that Wright identified but misunderstood, and its remedy will be found in positive strategies for decolonization. Wright misunderstood the toxic gulf because he saw it as personal and relational and as being equally the responsibility of the dominant and Aboriginal communities. He did not conceptualize it as a logical consequence of the processes of colonialism. His even-handed condemnation of it, then, places an unfair portion of the blame on Aboriginal communities for the racism initiated by the dominant community's elites. This is not to suggest that there is no racism in Aboriginal communities—there is. But I argue that institutional racism on the order demonstrated by *Stonechild* is emblematic of relations of dominance and subordination, and that the reactionary racism in Aboriginal communities is just that, not the legitimating ideology of dominance.[11] Destabilizing institutional and structural racism requires grappling

---

11.   Teun van Dijk (1993) writes: "Essential for racism is a relation of group power or dominance. (It is not) personal or individual, but social, cultural, political, or economic. . . . Given the definition of racism as a form of dominance, reverse racism or black racism in white-dominated societies are theoretically excluded in our framework" (p. 21).

with the relations of dominance and, consequently, with the race-coded privileges that accrue especially to white Canadians. White privilege is sustained by what Bonita Lawrence calls "[t]he intensely white supremacist nature of Canadian society, where power and privilege are organized along lines of skin colour" (2004, p. 175). The chasm is about unequal power relations, not moral equivalence.

Racism's roots are embedded in the history of colonialism. Recognizing this deep background of racism as problematic, and then eliminating it, requires more than simply the goodwill of well-intentioned white people and the superficial recognition of Aboriginal cultural practices. It requires the systematic dismantling of colonialism. This, in turn, depends on political leadership that confronts the past, takes responsibility for it in politically meaningful ways and leads us all into new relationships that will not be like the old, and will not always be uncontroversial. It means requiring institutions, like justice and education systems and police forces, to learn and to change. It means land claims settlements, resource sharing, a shift in political culture and power sharing in social, political and economic institutions. It means hearing harsh truths from those who have had to swallow racism to date. It means a diminishment of power on the part of those who have always assumed that their merit and goodness, rather than their race (and gender) privilege, are the reasons they enjoy the lion's share of social goods.

Colonization corrupts the colonizers and the colonized (Memmi, 1965, pp. 89, 151). Yet the descendants of the settlers, Canadians, can also refuse to be a part of this system by, as Memmi suggests, "either withdrawing physically from those conditions or remaining to fight and change them" (1965, p. 19). The problematic of motivating the privileged to join this struggle is considerable, for not only must they become aware of their privilege and work through all of the tensions that attend that awareness, but they must also commit to a new order in which this privilege is gone.

But a post-colonial Canada must have a place for the former holders of privilege. Unlike the British in India, the Belgians in Congo, and other instances of "elsewhere" decolonization, Canadians are a settler society. The solution of withdrawing from the colony is not available to the vast majority of non-Aboriginal Canadians. Time has done its work of erasing boundaries and options, and creating rootedness and community. We must, in all our diversity and much hybridity (Said, 1994), find ways to live together, to "bear with" each other in our stranger-hood (Hansen, 2004) and also in our commonalities. No collective public can be manufactured without some collective stake in a transformed future; no decolonization is probable in Canada without a beneficial future, both for the colonized and for those who are privileged by whiteness. And no profound transformation can occur without systemic, institutional, constitutional and, above all, cultural shifts.

Transforming any foundational intergenerational process is dicey. However, governments have on occasion taken the coercive apparatus and financing capacity of the state via government and have initiated new directions in public policy, in acts of political will. This is what governments must do: provide a combination of ethical and pragmatic leadership in setting the conditions for and parameters of the Good Society for all of those to whom they are responsible. In the case of systemic, institutional and cultural racism, this is a challenge, as those who must take the lead on this are also those who, overwhelmingly, benefit from the relations of dominance and subordination that are the *raison d'être* of racism.

There is some modest, albeit marginal, movement in these areas, as the following examples suggest. The government of Saskatchewan, responding to the *Stonechild* inquiry and, in particular, to how the province deals with police complaints from Aboriginal people, has created a new and strengthened Public Complaints Commission, which includes a First Nations and a Métis member.[12]

Universities are beginning to create some meaningful space for critical, anti-racist, anti-sexist scholarship of the kind that can challenge relations, theories and practices of oppression. On December 1, 2004, the Law Foundation of Saskatchewan announced a $750,000 donation to establish the Law Foundation of Saskatchewan Chair in Police Studies. One of its objectives is to "address the concerns of the aboriginal community and recruit more aboriginal people into policing" (Cataldo, 2004). It is to be hoped that this process will be transformative for police education, not merely co-optive or integrative of Aboriginal recruits. Some law schools have an indigenous, and indigenous black, component. At the University of Regina, a Canada Research Chair in Social Justice and Anti-Oppressive Education is vested in the Faculty of Education.[13] At the University of Manitoba, two Canada Research Chairs (CRC) on Canadian Aboriginal issues are being appointed in the Faculty of Arts, while a similar CRC has just been appointed at the University of Northern British Columbia. Native Studies departments exist at several universities (although indigenous critiques are not often mainstreamed in the "regular" disciplines) (Green, 2002). Initiatives like this will lead to shifts in knowledge production, and in the preparation of cohorts of students obtaining elite education. They, in turn, will help shift the consciousness of civil society.

There are also some historical models of courageous political leadership in the service of positive social transformation. One example may be found in the Yukon government of Tony Penikett in the 1980s and early 1990s. Penikett's government built enough support in white society, through popular education, for subsequent implementation of the Yukon Umbrella Final Agreement, which

12.   CBC Radio One. 2006. "Province launches new police complaints body." March 22. http://www.cbc.ca/sask/story/complaints-commission060314.html.

13.   This chair was eliminated in July 2009, following a reduction of research funding in social sciences on the part the federal government.

serves as the basis for the self-government and resource-sharing agreements of the 14 Yukon First Nations. Penikett simultaneously built more cordial and equitable relations with Indian politicians. The result is a better model in Yukon, but it wasn't easy, it wasn't fast and it took vision, commitment and leadership. It took the courage to adopt a principled political position that could become a political liability. Another model can be found in the history of the Woodrow Lloyd government in Saskatchewan, which stared down a doctors' strike in bringing in medicare in 1962. Again, this required political leadership and courage in the face of opposition and consequences. Now, the Douglas-Lloyd initiative is a core component of Canadian citizenship and political culture.

Will the dominant society, the settler community, support the expensive and difficult transformation of a racist colonial order to one that is genuinely post-colonial? It should, for principled ethical reasons. It must, because of enlightened self-interest. Our communities are beginning to fracture from the stresses of racism. As Joel Olson (2002) argues, "instability is also an opportunity to expand democracy if whites can be convinced that short-term racial privileges are not worth their long-term costs" (p. 329).

Marginalization and racism breed social pathologies, one example of which is the growing incidence of Aboriginal gangs now attracting media attention. CBC Radio in Saskatchewan ran a week-long (March 21–25, 2005) series on the phenomenon. The CBC[14] reported: "According to a recent report by Criminal Intelligence Service Saskatchewan, a coalition of police agencies, Saskatchewan now has the largest number of aboriginal street gang members per capita in Canada. . . . The province needs to put more resources into dealing with gangs. If nothing is done, some communities will eventually be completely controlled by gangs" (CBC, 2005b). The CBC also broadcast a story on Aboriginal teenage girls in custody at the Paul Dojack Youth Facility.[15]

> Some say they see gang activity as part of a struggle against white society, and they're willing to do what it takes to be part of that struggle. . . . One of the aboriginal teens said gang members see themselves fighting a war against a white power structure. "It's kind of like Indians against white people," she said. . . . Last week, a coalition of Saskatchewan police agencies released a report indicating the province now has more than 1,300 gang members—the most young people per capita involved in street gangs of all the provinces. . . . Police chiefs from across Saskatchewan are hoping the province will create a strategy to reduce gang activity. (CBC, 2005a)

---

14.   CBC Radio Saskatchewan, 2005. "They're young and often aboriginal—and they say they're waging a war." Morning Edition. http://sask.cbc.ca/regional/servlet/View? filename_fave1030522 (March 21, 2005).

15.   CBC Radio Saskatchewan, 2005. "Girls in gangs: disturbing reports from the inside." March 21. http://sask.cbc.ca/regional/servlet/View?filename_gangs-girls050321 (accessed March 22, 2005).

Gangs are, without exception, involved in criminal activity, including prostitution and drugs. Yet the Aboriginal gangs have fused identity and resistance with the sordid side of gang life to create a form of loyalty against the oppressor and in favour of the gang. The wilder speculations suggest this is a race war, and it is troubling that the CBC focused on the racialized nature of the gangs in opposition to white society. "Should white people be afraid?" morning show host Sheila Coles asked, and thus directed her primarily white listeners to the question of fear of the Other. Yet little attention was paid to the context that sustains the violent and oppositional cultures of gangs. One gets the sense that if white Saskatchewan could but guarantee its own security the gangs could run amok. That is, there is much concern for "our" security, but no great political push to eliminate the complex and intransigent conditions, including economic and political commitment to ending race privilege and oppression, the conditions that breed gangs.

Saskatchewan, with its burgeoning population of young Aboriginals, should be concerned: there will either be a culture of redress, sharing and commitment to a common future, or there will be alternatives, forms of resistance and alienation, like gangs. As the CBC's Rosalie Woloski (2005) reported,

> A prominent Saskatoon lawyer says native youth are growing increasingly more militant. Donald Worme told a conference on human rights yesterday that the problem is systemic racism that continues to plague Canadian society. "If there isn't any change, I mean fundamental change, radical change, we'll be 50 per cent of the population in this province in short order. If we don't have that then we need to make a decision about whether we want to live in a society that has compounds and ghettos, nothing in between."

But the apparent ethos that "we" must control "them" lest they hurt "us" is precisely the ethos in which the gangs have emerged, and which must be transformed.

2005 was Saskatchewan's (and Alberta's) centennial year. The province celebrated, complete with a visit from the Queen. A significant amount of public money and energy went into this birthday party. The myths continue, even as Aboriginal people are encouraged to participate, providing the illusion of inclusion and diversity to a society that largely excludes Aboriginal peoples and voices. The myths of social harmony and a tradition of co-operation are true for some, less true for others. Colonialism is not named, much less confronted and dismantled. Solutions proposed for Aboriginal problems amount to suggestions for inclusion into the dominant processes and paradigms, while the dominant population is not expected to change at all. Thus, the patterns of the past and present are likely to extend into the future, while white Saskatchewan insists it is not racist and that it wishes the best in its relationship with

Aboriginal peoples. The future of Saskatchewan depends on cohorts of Aboriginal children, most still unborn. Saskatchewan is an early warning system for the reality of racism across Canada.

Acknowledgments:

Thanks to Frances Abele, Carleton University, who commented on an earlier iteration of this paper, to the two anonymous reviewers of this article for the *Canadian Journal of Political Science / Revue canadienne de science politique* who provided helpful suggestions, and to Donna Grant and Anne James for their careful proofreading of this chapter. The focus and analysis remain the responsibility of the author.

REFERENCES

Adam, B. A. (2005, November 1). Stonechild family sues for $30M. Regina *Leader-Post,* A1.

Buydens, N. (2005, January). The Melfort rape and children's rights: Why R v. Edmondson matters to all Canadian kids. Canadian Centre for Policy Alternatives-Saskatchewan. *Saskatchewan Notes, 4*(1), 1–4.

Canadian Broadcasting Corporation (CBC). (2005a). Girls in gangs: Disturbing reports from the inside. Retrieved March 21, 2005 from http://sask.cbc.ca/regional/servlet/View?filename_gangs-girls050321

CBC. (2005b). Morning Edition. They're young and often aboriginal—and they say they're waging a war. Retrieved March 21, 2005, from http://sask.cbc.ca/regional/servlet/View?filename_fave1030522

CBC. (2005c). Radio One. Re Saskatoon Police Service appeal of Dan Wiks' one-day suspension. October 31.

CBC. (2005d). Radio One. Re Hartwig and Senger appeals for their jobs with the Saskatoon Police Service. November 1.

CBC. (2006). Radio One. Re Federation of Saskatchewan Indian Nations honouring outgoing Saskatoon Police Chief Russell Sabo. March 14.

Cataldo, S. (2004). $750,000 donation to fund chair in police studies. University Relations, University of Regina communication. December 1, 2004.

Cesaire, A. (1972). *Discourse on colonialism.* New York and London: Monthly Review Press.

Comeau, L. (2004, February 25). The purpose of education in European colonies: Mid-19th to early 20th century. Unpublished paper presented to SIDRU (Saskatchewan Instructional Development & Research Unit), University of Regina.

Coolican, L. (2001, October 16). Family wants look at accused. Regina *Leader-Post,* pp. A1, A2.

Dickerson, M., & Flanagan, T. (1999). *An introduction to government and politics: A conceptual approach* (5th ed.). Toronto: ITP Nelson.

Fourhorns, C. (2005). Education for Indians: The colonial experiment on Piapot's kids." *Canadian Dimension, 39*(3), 42–44.

Goodale, R. (2003). Speaking notes for The Honourable Ralph Goodale, P.C., M.P., November 8th, 2003. Retrieved May 25, 2004 from http://www.ralphgoodale.ca/Speeches/speech-ReginaAffordable Housing.html

Goulding, W. (2001). *Just another Indian: A serial killer and Canada's indifference.* Calgary: Fifth House Limited.

Goulding, W. (2004). Reconnecting with Human Rights. Notes for an address by Warren Goulding, Friday, December 10, 2004, Regina, Saskatchewan. Unpublished, on file with the author.

Government of Saskatchewan. (2005). Retrieved May 22, 2005, from http://www.sask2005.ca/; http://www.cyr.gov.sk.ca/ saskatchewans_centennial.html; http://www.gov.sk.ca/govinfo/news/premier_speech. html?0085 Premier's speech.

Green, J. (2002). Transforming at the margins of the academy. In E. Hannah, L. Paul & S. Vethamany-Globus (Eds.), *Women in the Canadian academic tundra: Challenging the chill* (pp. 85–91). Kingston and Montreal: McGill-Queen's University Press.

Green, J. (2005). Self-determination, citizenship, and federalism: Indigenous and Canadian palimpsest." In M. Murphy (Ed.), *State of the Federation: Reconfiguring Aboriginal-State Relations* (pp. 329–352). Institute of Intergovernmental Relations, School of Policy Studies, Queen's University. Kingston and Montreal: McGill-Queen's University Press.

Haight, L. (2005, October 8). "Wiks going back to work." Regina *Leader-Post.*

Hansen, P. (2004). Hannah Arendt and bearing with strangers. *Contemporary Political Theory, 3*(1), 3–22.

Harding, K. (2004, November 13). Two police officers fired in Stonechild case. Toronto *Globe and Mail*, p. A6.

Irlbacher-Fox, S. (2005, June). Practical implications of philosophical approaches within Canada's aboriginal policy. Unpublished paper presented to the Canadian Political Science Association, University of Western Ontario, London, Ontario.

Jaccoud, M., & Brassard, R. (2003). The marginalization of aboriginal women in Montreal. In D. Newhouse & E. Peters (Eds.), *Not strangers in these parts: Urban Aboriginal peoples* (pp. 131–145). Ottawa: Policy Research Initiative.

Kuokkanen, R. (2005, June). The responsibility of the academy: A call for doing homework. Unpublished paper presented to the Canadian Political Science Association, University of Western Ontario, London, Ontario.

Lawrence, B. (2004). *"Real" Indians and others: Mixed-blood urban native peoples and indigenous nationhood.* Vancouver: UBC Press.

Memmi, A. (1965). *The colonizer and the colonized.* Boston: Beacon Press.

Olson, J. (2002). Whiteness and the participation-inclusion dilemma. *Political Theory, 30*(3), 384–409.

Prober, R. (2003). What no child should endure: *R. v. Edmonston, Kindrat and Brown. Beyond Borders Newsletter, 3*(Fall), 1–2.

Razack, S. (1998). *Looking white people in the eye: Gender, race, and culture in courtrooms and classrooms.* Toronto: University of Toronto Press.

Razack, S. (2002). Gendered racial violence and spatialized justice: The murder of Pamela George. In S. Razack (Ed.), *Race, space, and the law: Unmapping a white settler society* (pp. 121–156). Toronto: Between The Lines.

Said, E. (1994). *Culture and imperialism.* New York: Vintage Books.

Saskatchewan Labour, Status of Women Office. (2003). A profile of Aboriginal women in Saskatchewan. Unpublished, on file with the author.

Smith, L. T. (1999). *Decolonizing methodologies: Research and indigenous peoples.* London and New York: Zed Books.

Statistics Canada. (2003). Aboriginal peoples survey: Well-being of the non-reserve Aboriginal population. *The Daily,* September 24, 2003. Retrieved May 9, 2006, from www.statcan.ca/Daily/English/ 030924d030924b.htm

van Dijk, T. (1993). *Elite discourse and racism.* Newbury Park: Sage.

Vipond, M. (2000). *The mass media in Canada* (3rd ed.). Toronto: James Lorimer and Company Ltd.

Warick, J. (2006, March 15). Saskatoon police chief to be honoured. Regina *Leader-Post,* p. A7.

Woloski, R. (2005). Re Donald Worme and systemic racism. *CBC Radio One,* Saskatoon, June 21, 2005. Script on file with the author.

Wright, D. H., Mr. Justice. (2004). *Report of the Commission of Inquiry Into Matters Relating to the Death of Neil Stonechild.* Regina: Government of Saskatchewan.

CHAPTER 10

"I THOUGHT POCAHONTAS WAS A MOVIE": USING CRITICAL DISCOURSE ANALYSIS TO UNDERSTAND RACE AND SEX AS SOCIAL CONSTRUCTS

James McNinch

PART A: INTRODUCTION

This paper examines trial transcripts from the 2003 cases of the 2001 sexual assault of a 12-year-old Aboriginal child by three twenty-something men of Saskatchewan white settler stock. I suggest that a "cross-cultural" sexual assault case compels us to question the illusion of objectivity embedded in legal culture and to interrogate coercive functions of the law. Inspired by a "social constructionist conception of law as hegemonic discourse that can be deconstructed," Chunn and Lacombe (2000, p. 2) argue that the law is not an impartial instrument but a gendering practice. It is now commonplace to see gender as historically and culturally situated and actively constructed in social settings. Many have shown how hegemonic masculinity (unidimensional, inherent and static) works to create power relations against the "Other" (Mac an Ghaill, 1994; Martino & Meyenn, 2001; Martino & Pallotta-Chiarolli, 2003; Messerschmidt, 2000, 1997). A critical discourse analysis of the trial transcripts provides insights into how gender, race, sex and class are linguistically and textually mediated processes rather than pre-discursive identities. Norman Fairclough's approach (2006, 1993, 1989) to critical discourse analysis, which explores relationships between the structures of texts and agents of texts, provides a method for revealing how linguistic ways of being ("speech acts") are forms of social power. By attending to discourse, I argue, we might better understand how white privilege, as a sexual and racial construct, is normalized in the everyday in Saskatchewan. In this sense, critical discourse analysis is an act of ideological interpretation. In this chapter, therefore, the reader will see where I have italicized extracts from the court transcripts in order to trouble commonplace assumptions and to highlight the signification of received meaning. The implication for all of us is to recognize that if such discourse does not change, then social change is not possible.

The story so far

On September 30, 2001, three white men from the town of Tisdale, Saskatchewan, were accused of sexually assaulting a 12-year-old Saulteaux girl from the Yellow Quill First Nation. At the time, this reserve was known for having what was called "the worst water in Canada," while nearby Tisdale still advertises itself as the land of "sparkling waters" and the land of "rape and honey." In a previous article on this topic (McNinch, 2008) I use Pierre Bourdieu's sociological constructs of masculine domination (1993, 2001) and Lacan's view of patriarchy (1977).[1] I que(e)ry heterosexual discourse at the private, social and public level in light of my own prairie whiteness, my own queerness and my role as an educator. In so doing, my purpose previously, as here, is to illustrate the poisoning of the social and cultural environment by white homosocial racism and "the prison of masculinity," as James Baldwin called it more than fifty years ago.

This case reveals that there are at least four "frames" for better understanding white privilege: (1) the history of colonization and immigration in this country, (2) the homosociality of male heterosexuality, (3) embodied and vicarious linguistic interpretations of "reality," and (4) the social and cultural practice of the law itself. In que(e)rying the trial transcripts through critical discourse analysis, this chapter focuses on the last two frames identified.

Summary of the argument for the defence

In the two sexual assault trials in 2003, the Tisdale "boys" (as these men in their twenties were repeatedly referred to by the trial judge) deflected blame away from themselves in four revealing and contradictory ways.[2] First, the defence painted the men as ordinary youth; their profile was a presumed strong, and

---

1.   That paper was inspired by the epic work of William Pinar on race and violence (2001), built on Eve Kosofsky Sedgwick's understanding of homosociality (1985), and extended the work of Sherene Razack on race, space and the law (2002, 1998). I interrogated this Tisdale group sexual assault as the ultimate act of white heterosexual privilege, compared it to the gang killing that same autumn of gay man Aaron Webster in Vancouver (Janoff, 2005) and saw in both events signs of internalized homoerotic panic that offer insights into how white masculinity is built on race, sex, class and gender on the Canadian landscape (Cf. Janoff, 2005; McNinch, 2008; Pronger, 2002, 1990).

2.   Ironically, and revealingly, while these twenty-something men were referred to as boys, the 12-year-old female was referred to formally as "Ms."

hence "healthy," heterosexuality. Their interaction with the girl (a 12-year-old weighing 95 pounds) was considered a normative way of performing gender. Second, the defence insisted that, in carrying the baggage of a troubled family life, the girl not only welcomed sexual advances, but was, in fact, the sexual aggressor. Although she was never referred to as an "Indian" in the transcripts, this is how she would have been "othered" by her assailants. Neither was she called a First Nations child, but only "Ms. Caslain" (my pseudonym for her). Thirdly, the defendants played dumb: a conspiracy of silence became a disingenuous code of honour among friends. Jeffrey Kindrat refused to testify, and Jeffrey Brown retracted or contradicted much of what he had initially said to police. After his own trial and (very light) sentencing, Dean Edmondson flatly denied any knowledge of the actions of his two buddies. Finally, and most ironically, the accused insisted there could not have been anal or vaginal penetration because between the three of them they could not sustain an erection (R. v. Brown & Kindrat, 2003, p. 619). Three flaccid penises are tendered as proof of a limp innocence because female penetration is the standard by which the exercise of manhood is proven in our society. Lack of an erection or ejaculate preserves the phallic status quo. In this context, a limp penis is code for the shame, humiliation and anxiety inherent in the hysteric and homoerotic position of white heterosexual privilege symbolized and embodied in the act of sexual assault.

Such is the discursive and signifying power of these events and the revelatory impact of their reification to the symbolic that our encounters with them allow us an insight into and critique of fundamental ontologies of whiteness and privilege, and of gender and race; that is what this paper proposes to do.

Where do we go from here? What questions need we ask?

In their exploration of police brutality in the Rodney King affair, critical race theorists Crenshaw and Peller (1993) write that "at stake at each axis of conflict is a contest over whose narrative structure will prevail in the interpretation of events in the social world" (p. 283). We first must ask how, at this particular axis of conflict, did these three men and this one girl embody and then relate and transcribe the experience. Secondly, we need to ask how the court officials (lawyers, judge and jury engaged in determining guilt or innocence) vicariously experienced the "incident" through their own linguistic filters. How did all of the players, both first and second hand, "make sense of" and construct the events of the evening of the sexual assault? An elliptical approximation of that embodied reality percolates from the transcripts of the trial proceedings. It is clear, however, that we are very much in a topsy-turvy, through-the-looking-glass, Alice-in-Wonderland world. Here we see white privilege, embodied in the Tisdale "boys" and the Melfort courtroom, as a racial and cultural construct literally and figuratively up against the mostly invisible and mostly silenced "Other," embodied in the person of Melissa Caslain.

The legacy of white settler privilege

The construct of white privilege extends back at least as far as the so-called Age of Reason. "[W]hite racial thinking has constituted a social and natural continuity in which whiteness is not only privileged, but part of the discourse of an ostensibly transparent and timeless vehicle of logic" (DiPiero, 2002, p. 98).[3] In small town Saskatchewan this vehicle of logic thrives illogically, as this critical discourse analysis of the trial transcripts will show.

Native Studies, eco-feminism and critical race theory have shown how both women and the land have been exploited by patriarchy. Conquest is both literal and metaphorical (Amnesty International, 2004; Nelson, 1998; Phillips, 2004; Razack, 2002). The historical reality of the dependence of Europeans on the generosity of North America's First Peoples is also well-documented, despite being excluded from our collective national memory. On Canada's prairie, because of trade in furs and buffalo, distinct Métis peoples flourished through intermarriage as a result of just such mutual interdependence. Unfortunately, this truly multicultural history has been twisted into myths of the white man who has "gone Indian," and of the Indians "offering their women" and thereby acknowledging their people's inferiority (in the eyes of the white man). Official histories and such myths continue to play themselves out today along a race and culture divide where we see un/clearly what is un/consciously privileged in our white settler society.

PART B: PORTRAITS OF THE "BOYS" AND POSITIONALITY OF THE PLAYERS

Jeffrey Brown

At the time of his arrest Jeffrey Brown was 25 years old, weighed 220 pounds and was five feet nine inches tall. He was working at Lesel Welding with his buddy and fellow assailant, Dean Edmondson. He had lived in Tisdale all his life, completing grade 11 and then taking some welding courses. He claims to have consumed two dozen of the 54 beer purchased on the evening of the assault because "My grandmother passed away that day" (R. v. Edmondson, p. 418). Ironically, in describing Melissa, Brown says, "She couldn't talk real good" (p. 419). In an exchange with one of the lawyers, Edmondson describes his friendship with Brown in this way:

---

3.   In the hierarchical calibrations of the Great Chain of Being, God is in heaven and all is right with the world because it has been ordered naturally. Angels form the apex, followed by kings and priests, all the way down the pecking order to the animals, trees and rocks. Just above them (as I saw once vividly painted on the altar in the nineteenth-century Mission church in Lac La Biche in northern Alberta) stand the indigenous peoples of the "new" world. It is this unconscious metahistory that makes the friendly homogeneity of a place like Tisdale so "normal" and so privileged.

EDMONDSON: [We've been] friends, for about 10 years.

LAWYER: And do the two of you do anything together?

E: Well, yeah?

L: What?

E: [we're] buddies, so I don't know, fishing—

L: Okay.

E: I guess we worked together . . . the past year and a half, I guess
(R v. Brown & Kindrat, p. 11).

This lack of expressiveness is a typical code of homosocial connections ("hey, we're just guys, eh"). There isn't really much here, in part because it emanates from the witness stand, and yet this imprecise inarticulation is never challenged by the lawyers or the court in the way that Melissa's halting and hesitant testimony is challenged (See below: "Please you must speak up, Melissa, we can't hear you." R. v. Edmondson, p. 89). In other words, inarticulate heterosexual maleness is acceptable and normative—we expect, accept and thereby privilege it. Alternately, because heterosexual maleness is both normative and privileged, whatever is done under this identification will also be considered understandable, even if it is inarticulate and understood as "just the way they talk."

Dean Edmondson

The arresting officer commented regarding 27-year-old Dean Edmondson: "He was co-operative and he was matter of factly answering my questions. . . . He wasn't being ignorant or . . . abrasive or anything. He was co-operative and pleasant" (R. v. Edmondson, p. 23). This "pleasantness" marks whiteness because it formulates a privileged kind of discourse: of being an insider, that is, "one of us." An RCMP officer taking a statement from Edmondson recounts, "it was my opinion that, quite frankly, that he wasn't gonna be held. He was known to *me*. He's known in *the community*. He lives in *the community*" [italics added] (R. v. Edmondson, p. 88).

This "community" of Tisdale is exclusively white; it is definitely not Melissa's community. In fact, "town" specifically excludes the Yellow Quill Reserve through the privileged assumption that there is only *one* community. "Had the decision been mine . . . I would've released him," continues the interrogating officer (R. v. Edmondson, p. 89). Similarly, in his opening statement to the jury, defence lawyer Hugh Harradence emphasizes: "it is the basis of the Canadian criminal justice system that an individual like you or I [*sic*] or Mr. Edmondson is entitled to be judged by his peers" (R. v. Edmondson, p. 21). What he means is people like himself, that is, white people, not people of Melissa's community. It does not go unnoticed by the press that the jury is all white. Judge Kovatch concludes later: "Mr. Edmondson is a mature, intelligent individual who should, within reason and after consulting counsel, be capable of determining what is in his own best interest" (R. v. Edmondson, p. 747). Such a summary description of a man just found guilty of a sexual assault—as a free agent and a reasonable and autonomous male—leaves little doubt about how power is manifested both in and out of the courtroom in Saskatchewan.

Jeffrey Kindrat

At the time of the "incident," Jeffrey Kindrat was 20 years old and working for a contractor re-roofing a farmhouse. The arresting officer and Kindrat talked about Kindrat's plan to travel to Ireland to work. The officer comments, "He was very polite and co-operative. I didn't handcuff or anything. Didn't think there was a need" (R. v. Brown & Kindrat, pp. 18–19).

Another RCMP officer asked to comment on Kindrat's "reputation in the Tisdale community for honesty and integrity" responds to Melfort defence lawyer Stuart Eisner: "It's good. He's . . . involved in the community, slow-pitch. Just recently we've played against each other, very polite. He's involved heavily in the curling in the winter, same thing" (R. v. Brown & Kindrat, p. 215).

Although Kindrat refused to testify on his own behalf, his lawyer called several of his former schoolteachers and coaches to the stand to vouch for his "honesty, integrity, and *morality*" [italics added] (R. v. Brown & Kindrat, p. 640). We learn that Kindrat was his class valedictorian. One of his former teachers testified: "He has always been a leader in school. He's caring. He comes from an excellent family, and also from a community that cares about—about their young people" (R. v. Brown & Kindrat, p. 643). Even if we make allowance for the influence of peer pressure and Pilsner, the story about being privileged here is a white one: Kindrat "comes from a community that cares about their young," implicitly, but also directly, in contrast to Melissa's reserve and the "tragic" background the defence is so keen to highlight.

The axis of conflict

In this "axis of conflict" on this "lonely country road," as the press called it (Canadian Press, 2003), we can interpret what the assailants and the complainant say they experienced by applying Linda Mulvey's concept of "the gaze" (1988, 1989). This concept suggests that what we see is determined by the lens set before us and by who determines what this lens should be. In this case, the accused present themselves, through their stories, as passive and unexceptional, as victims of a situation rather than as aggressors. Through the discourse of the trial, I argue, we see clearly whose story, whose race and whose socio-economic status is privileged.

"That's all I seen"

"Once we hit the highway" says Edmondson, "we *probably* would have opened a beer." The three men bought 18 Pilsner and consumed them on the way to the town of Chelan. They bought another 12 or 18 Pilsner in Chelan, where they found Melissa sitting on the steps and offered her a ride as they left. In

Mistatim (another small town) they bought another box of beer and "polished them off" on the ride with Melissa (Edmondson, R. v. Brown & Kindrat, 2003, p. 412, p. 449).

> CROWN: And during that time the truck is being driven, what are you doing?
> EDMONDSON: Drinking beer—
> C: And?
> E: Driving, listening to music
> C: Drinking beer and—
> E: Talking on and off in there. (Edmondson, R. v. Brown & Kindrat, p. 425)

On the witness stand, describing his contact with Melissa after they stopped the truck, Edmondson says:

> [I] can't look around the corner. . . . Well, I was kissing and—she was kissing me. Well, her face *would be* [italics added: why hypothetical?] in my face, so my vision was fairly blocked, so all I seen was him [Brown] come up behind her. . . . That's all I seen. (Edmondson, R. v. Brown & Kindrat, p. 434–435)

In his written statement, however, Edmondson said:

> They had sex with her too, I think, and then she started *passing out on us* [italics added: assailants as victims] so we get her dressed and put her back in the truck and started driving. (R. v. Edmondson, 2003, p. 30)

Under interrogation by the Crown, Edmondson says:

> EDMONDSON: Well, I'd been drinking but still movin' around. . . . Well, I undid my pants and pulled my penis out, I guess, and tried to, but it was—wasn't erect enough.
> CROWN: Why?
> E: So I put it back.
> C: Sorry, why wasn't it erect?
> E: I don't know. (R. v. Brown & Kindrat, pp. 440, 447)

"We thought we were doing her a favour"

Upon arrest Jeffrey Brown flatly denies any sex occurred. The RCMP officer asks, "Why do you think she would say you and your buddies sexually assaulted her?" His reply: "Honest to God, I have no clue. We thought we were doing her a favour by giving her a ride" (R. v. Brown & Kindrat, p. 195).

Under oath, Brown later says:

And this went on for a minute or two [Dean and Melissa "hugging and kiss-ing" on the hood of the truck] and then me and Jeff Kindrat *exited* [italics added: a strange formality, why not "left" or "got out of"?] the truck and went to the front of the truck and then the two of us started to—she wanted to, she said, to make love to all of us and . . . we were behind her . . . and then we put her back in the truck. (R. v. Brown & Kindrat, 2003, p. 421–423)

The Crown catches Brown in a departure from his lawyer-prepped script:

CROWN: Okay. So you were trying to get erect.
BROWN: Trying to.
C:. . . . What were you trying to do? Just tell us.
B: Trying to *have*—make love to her. (R. v. Brown & Kindrat, 2003, pp. 424–425)

One version of the truth lies behind the linguistic change in direction. "Trying to have sex" is what Brown almost says, but then he halts in mid-sentence and veers to "trying to make love to her," a highly inappropriate phrase in light of a sexual assault charge.

Kindrat noted in his written statement to the police: "It was Jeff Brown that pulled her out of the truck when she was puking" (R. v. Brown & Kindrat , 2003, pp. 67–68). None of "the boys," however, could remember how Melissa's clothes came off, or who dressed her afterwards or who offered her the beer to drink in the first place.

"So I undid my pants and I, I tried"
In his statement to the RCMP, Jeffrey Kindrat claims:

They [Edmondson and Melissa] were having sex out front of the truck and then Jeff Brown went, he was behind her, I was up front watching. . . . He [Brown] had his pants pulled down. . . . He pulled away and then she was like, more, more, so I undid my pants and I, I tried, but I don't know, I couldn't get it up. (R. v. Brown & Kindrat, 2003, p. 112)

The RCMP officer asks:

OFFICER: Were you able to penetrate her either anally or vaginally?
KINDRAT: Like I don't know. . . . I, yea, I tried, but I don't know if I did or not.
O: You didn't ejaculate then?
K: No. (R. v. Brown & Kindrat, 2003, p. 112)

"That's gross"
Melissa remembers the beginning of events quite differently: "these guys came out of the bar [in Chelan] and . . . one of them saying, 'I thought Pocahontas was

a movie'" (R. v. Edmondson, 2003, p. 54). In context, the comment may well have been intended as a compliment, and even received by the girl as such. Nonetheless, it stereotypes racial difference and, like a sleazy pickup line, defines power relations.

> He [Edmondson] asked me if I needed a ride, and I . . . thought to myself, this is the only way that I'm going to get out of here, and it's dark and so I said okay. And I got in. . . . They started going and I remember them saying that I could trust them. . . . [They were] way older than me. (R. v. Edmondson, 2003, pp. 57–59)

> At the bar in Mistatim he [Brown] said he wanted me to come in the bar naked. He'd make sure everyone would give me money, but I kept saying no, because that's gross. (R. v. Edmondston, 2003, p. 78)

PART C: BUILDING A DEFENCE FOR THE ACCUSED

These introductory sketches are meant to illustrate how, even though the three white men were the ones on trial, these accused men still operated from positions of considerable power in comparison to the vulnerability of the victim. The testimony in the courtroom continues to consolidate this power and helps us better to understand how white privilege is revealed in legal tactics designed to consolidate portraits of innocence. In the following section, through an analysis of the language used by the police, the lawyers, the witnesses and the judge himself, we can see how the incident is constructed at second hand. The "gaze" in these instances is constructed through white heterosexual privilege, as the discourse analysis of the transcripts illustrates. Specific strategies, although often contradictory, include: (a) depicting excessive drinking as a norm in preparation for sex, (b) assuming sex is a "right" and nothing to be ashamed of, as well as a matter of (c) luck and a payoff for (d) the natural "horniness" of healthy young white men who believe everyone "wants it." Other tactics include: (e) taking an ironic stance to distance oneself from the actual events, (f) feigning embarrassment, (g) feigning blindness, and, finally, (h) claiming to be an innocent bystander.

a) VLTs and a paralyzer and 2 Pil = "no grief"
The bartender in Chelan, the small town where the men first stopped, is called by the defence to remember that Edmondson ordered a paralyzer, and his friends each had a Pilsner. "Three young men dressed casually, were polite and didn't give me any grief. And, after they received their drinks, they went over to the VLT gaming machines and were playing over there . . . and then they bought a box of beer off-sale [12 or 18 bottles]" (R. v. Edmondson, pp. 65–67).

b) No shame = no guilt

Stuart Eisner, Kindrat's lawyer, in cross-examination of Gary Pierce, the father of Melissa's friend, at whose house the boys "delivered" Melissa, establishes: "So we're on common ground that these [boys] . . . the three people that came up in this truck with Melissa did nothing whatsoever to attempt to hide their identity from you or anyone else who happened to be there" (R. v. Brown & Kindrat, p. 582).

The judge finds this significant and adds when he later speaks directly to the jury:

> One further thing you might want to consider is whether the conduct of Mr. Edmondson, or indeed *the three of the boys,* in *delivering* [emphasis added: like a package of damaged goods?] Ms. Caslain to the Pierce residence was consistent with what you'd expect to find from an individual who, who thought they just had been involved in sexual activity with someone that they knew was under 14, or is it indeed more consistent with how one would act in a circumstance where they were maybe embarrassed at being involved with a young lady but not believing they'd been involved with someone who was under 14. *I just throw that out for what it's worth.* [italics added: don't think for a moment that I'm trying to influence you?]. (R. v. Edmondson, pp. 628–629)

Quite apart from changing the identity of the 12-year-old child to a "young lady," the judge's language focuses on ensuring that the jury understands "the embarrassment of the boys" rather than the situation the child finds herself in.

c) "Get lucky"

When the homosocial ejaculates into the homoerotic, as I am suggesting, it does so on a foundation of misogyny and racism. Alcohol is the lubricant for sexual initiation, and such "liquid bravery" encourages the three friends to talk about sex and leads eventually to sex itself, if they "get lucky," as a defence lawyer put it in cross-examining Edmondson. "And so whether that person was standing there, trying to get hard, so that . . . maybe he could *get lucky and get a turn* [italics added: it's okay to share?], you don't know . . ." (R. v. Brown & Kindrat, 2003, p. 623).

d) Be horny

"The idea that you might bump into some female company—well, I'm not saying that it wouldn't be something that you might appreciate," suggests Brown's defence lawyer, Mark Brayford (R. v. Brown & Kindrat, p. 605). We are able to see here racial and sexual violence as the discourse of "social processes that are created . . . by people in their daily lives and social interactions" (Winans, 2005,

p. 30). What is being privileged or "appreciated" here is "healthy sexuality," that it is considered normal for young men to be in a continual state of arousal at the possibility of sexual encounters.

e) Be ironic

Edmondson, in claiming that Melissa was the sexual aggressor, describes her climbing into his lap while he is trying to drive. Brown's lawyer quips, "Okay, you don't like to kiss and drive?" and Edmondson retorts, "Well, it makes it difficult" (R. v. Brown & Kindrat, 2003, p. 600). In this ironic hetero-banter we clearly hear the privilege of power: mutuality between lawyer and defendant is presumed on the grounds of white heterosexuality. The irony and familiarity predicates the stance of the accused: He's not worried; he can even joke on the witness stand.

f) Be embarrassed

The defence presented the "boys" as solid citizens, from "good" families, "respectable" members of the community, "normal" and conventional (R. v. Edmondson, Sentencing, pp. 16–17; R. v. Brown & Kindrat, pp. 215, 336, 640–43). Dubinsky and Givertz (1999) illustrate how in nineteenth-century Canada the legal system and the popular press labelled sexual offenders as "brutes, fiends and animals" and placed them outside the realm of "normal" Victorian manliness. "These men no longer reflected the relations of a masculine heterosexual order" (p. 68). Conversely, our Tisdale "white boys" are not monsters; they are conceived to be ordinary people in unfortunate, compromising and "embarrassing" circumstances, as one RCMP officer said in encouraging Edmondson to make a statement: "You're not comfortable, you're probably a bit embarrassed, ya' know, and I'm damn sure this isn't the way you were brought up" (R. v. Edmondson, p. 151).

g) Shut your eyes—"just like in the movies"

Defence lawyer Brayford, to ensure that Edmondson's gaze on his two accomplices is blinkered, spent considerable time insisting that "just like in the movies, when people are being intimate, it's just not *normal* to keep your eyes open." "Yea. I guess so," Edmondson replies (R. v. Brown & Kindrat, pp. 620–621). Brayford then suggests Edmondson "couldn't care less" what his buddies were doing, whether their pants were down, or whether they were touching themselves or Melissa from behind, even though only Melissa's petite ninety-five-pound body separated the three two-hundred-pound men from each other. This strident defence of heterosexuality rests, like unwritten locker-room protocol, on the assumption that straight guys don't look at other guys, or aren't supposed to be caught doing so (Pronger, 2002, 1990). In other words, a cultural trait of white heterosexual identity becomes a "legitimate" excuse for not testifying.

h) Be an innocent bystander

Judge Kovatch adds, in discussing the case with the Crown prosecutors, "If he [Brown] was masturbating or attempting to make himself erect, and *I'm just throwing those out almost as speculation* [italics added: again, interfering by imposing his gaze?], it would not amount to sexual assault. So we really don't know what, if anything, Mr. Brown did outside the truck" (R. v. Brown & Kindrat, 2003, p. 768). Kovatch's interpretation of the law pertaining to sexual assault is that touching must occur in order for the integrity of the complainant to be violated; such a stance, as the Crown pointed out, is not supported by precedents set by sexual assault case law.

PART D: THE LOGIC OF THE LAW— MELISSA IN WONDERLAND

In this section, I draw attention to an array of assumptions, strategies and attitudes that are embedded in the conduct of the courtroom itself. Everyone is implicated in the "Melissa in Wonderland" logic of the law: the judge, the Crown, the lawyers for the defence, the three accused and the witnesses. The court scene in Lewis Carroll's *Alice in Wonderland* is an apt metaphor for the "topsy-turvy" discourse in this real court of law. As I will show later, only Melissa, the victim, is not complicit. Her difference, her other-ness from the normative behaviour of the court, prevents her from playing the same game as her interrogators.

Appropriately, and quite logically, Judge Kovatch tells the jury: "You should always remember . . . that the only memory of the evidence that counts in this case is yours and not mine" (R. v. Edmondson, 2003 p. 195). Linguistically, however, the jury's memory here can be seen as a metaphor for our collective memory—or, rather, collective amnesia—of race relations in this province. In summary, then, the next section outlines twenty trial tactics that can be seen to reify white heterosexual privilege: Proof, doubt and certainty become conflated in the minds of the jurors (a). An arbitrary distinction is made between morality and legality that, in turn, denies the moral views on which laws are based (b). Lawyers for the defendants make dubious distinctions between truth and reality (c). The intent of the accused is given as much weight in determining guilt as the question of the victim's consent (d). The judge repeatedly overlooks contradictions in how one can be both "an innocent bystander" and an active participant in a crime (e). While the assault involves three men, and two of the men are tried within the same trial, the court insists that each man must, before the law, remain an individual (f). Similarly, the court privileges the idea that "common sense" trumps both intention and knowledge (g). Police officers, attempting to encourage a complete statement, bond with the accused by blaming the victim (h). In addition, by laying claim to disinterest and impartiality, the court can overlook potential conflicts of interest (i).

Permeating these machinations, both conscious and unconscious, both naïve and manipulative, is the overall tone of a white courtroom. The transcripts illustrate how a civil and legal space created by and for "us," complete with the privileges we white and middle class assume we deserve (j), has been sullied and imposed upon because a dirty little "secret" was made public (k, l). "Playing by the rules" means privileging the printed word (m) and using words and ranges of discourse as weapons (n, o, p). Finally, in sentencing, we see how alcohol is considered a legitimate excuse for wrongdoing (q), how fear of retribution is racialized (r), how the Protestant work ethic is privileged at law (s) and how white space and hence whiteness itself is privileged (t).

a) Proof, doubt and certainty

"Our concept of justice is based on innocence until proven guilty," Judge Kovatch reminds us. "It is not enough for you to believe that Mr. Edmondson is probably or likely guilty. In those circumstances, you must find him not guilty because Crown counsel would've failed to satisfy you of his guilt beyond a reasonable doubt" (R. v. Edmondson, 2003, p. 196). But then Kovatch adds, "You should also remember, however, that it is nearly impossible to prove anything with absolute certainty" (R. v. Edmondson, 2003, p. 197). But in his charge to the jury he later says, "The standard of proof beyond a reasonable doubt falls much closer to absolute certainty than to proof on a balance of probabilities" (p. 64). What must jurors make of this? What should we, the public, make of this in light of the racial tension inherent in this case?

b) Separating morality and legality

Three times in addressing the jury in the trial of Edmondson and twice in the summation in the trial of Brown and Kindrat, Judge Kovatch reminds the jury:

> I told you this is a court of law, not a court of morals. You may believe that it is morally unacceptable for a person of Dean Edmondson's age to engage in sexual activity with a person he believes to be 14 or 15 years of age. You must not judge the actions of Dean Edmondson or, for that matter, the actions of the complainant, according to your own moral standard. (R. v. Edmondson, 2003, p. 46)

Clearly, separating morality from the law, even though laws are premised on morals and community standards, is a privilege of those who, through the powers invested in their office, control the construction of the gaze.

c) Separating truth from reality

Lawyer Mark Brayford, defending Jeffrey Brown's dissembling on the witness stand, suggests, "Even if the Crown was correct in their [*sic*] suggestion that my client's statement isn't candid, that's not a substitute for evidence; that just because you say something that's not true, doesn't mean that the opposite is true" (R. v. Brown & Kindrat, 2003, p. 698). We can, at the very least, begin here to understand how "truth" is a linguistic construction based on positionality. At most, perhaps, we can understand that the laws of the land are intended to protect not everyone, but only certain "clients" who can, with the assistance of an adept lawyer, wiggle through the logic of the law.

d) Consent and intent: can one be honest but not reasonable?
On the important issue of consent, Judge Kovatch says to the jury:

> The boys or either of them must honestly believe that Ms. Caslain voluntarily agreed to participate in the sexual activity. The boys' belief must be honest, but it does not have to be reasonable. The reasonableness of the belief, however, may be an important factor for you to consider in deciding whether they actually had the belief that they claim. (R. v. Brown & Kindrat, 2003, p. 781)

Pointing out that in other sexual assault cases involving minors, where the issue of taking reasonable steps to ascertain age is paramount, the Crown notes that differences in age and education between the victim and the assailants (dubbed differences in "sophistication" by the Crown) are crucial in determining whether so-called "reasonable" steps were taken. For example, the older the assailants and the younger the victim, the greater such care must be. But blinkered by social constraints, even the Crown is unable to go far enough: it does not address paramount race/culture differences that mediate the borders of behaviour, looks, attitudes and assumptions that are crossed when the white town "boys," who are men, encourage a First Nations "woman," who is a child, to engage in sex.

e) Overlook contradictions
Responding to the jury's question about aiding and abetting or standing by and doing nothing while a crime is being committed, Judge Kovatch says, "just being there does not make a person guilty as an aider of any or every crime someone else commits in the person's presence. Sometimes people are in the wrong place at the wrong time" (R. v. Brown & Kindrat, 2003, p. 74). Again, in his charge to the jury the judge says, "I should emphasize: aiding requires something more than just standing by and watching someone commit an offence" (p. 789). He says this even though he has just read the jury the appropriate section [2191] of the Criminal Code, which states, "*Everyone* is a party to an offence who: (a) actually commits it or (b) does, *or omits to do, anything* [italics added], for the purpose of aiding a person to commit it" (p. 783). White privilege, particularly white male privilege, apparently allows for this flagrant contradiction, a contradiction borne by society's acquiescence to the "rule of law," which conveniently forgets that the discourse of law in theory and practice is a matter of interpretation.

f) Remain an individual

Through the transcripts of the trials, we are also reminded that, although this was a group sexual assault, and although Brown and Kindrat are both on trial at the same time, they are treated under the law as separate individuals whose statements and testimonies are regarded as prejudicial to everyone but themselves. In other words, whatever they say about each other cannot be used against the other, only themselves. Such legal emphasis on individuality is another crucial element of white privilege embedded in our social construct. This "through-the-looking-glass" doublethink first separates morality and law and then trumps the rights of an individual man over the collective activities of a group of men who together engage in sexual activity with one child.

g) Invoke common sense

Over and above this, in Judge Kovatch's logic, the concept of "common sense" trumps both intention and knowledge:

> You may find it difficult to decide whether Brown and [or] Kindrat knew or intended that his actions would aid Edmondson to commit the offence of sexual assault. *This is because intention and knowledge are matters of the mind* [italics added]. We cannot see inside other people's minds. In deciding what Brown and Kindrat knew or intended, *use your common sense to infer* [italics added] from all the evidence you have heard what they knew or intended to do. (R. v. Brown & Kindrat, p. 790)

In critical discourse analysis and critical race theory, just the opposite is true: we learn to distrust common sense because, like notions of race and sex, it is embedded in received knowledge that is often prescriptive, restrictive and oppressive (Kumashiro, 2004; Wadham, 2002).

h) Bond by blaming the victim

Over the course of the two sexual assault trials, we see further examples of normative masculine heterosexual privilege in the daily exchanges between court officials and witnesses. For example, in interrogating the three "boys" and encouraging them to make statements, the RCMP readily admit under examination by the defense lawyer Hugh Harradence that they deliberately imply bail is forthcoming; they "downplay the significance of the offence and . . . blame the victim" and dismiss the advice and role of lawyers who caution against talking to the police just "to make their [the lawyers'] job easier" (R. v. Edmondson, 2003, pp. 105–108).

In taking Edmondson's statement, Constable Shepherd talks about "the way girls dress these days" and "lapses in judgment being excusable" because "when you're in a jam . . . your history and what you think comes into play" (R. v. Edmondson, 2003, pp. 106–108, 110, 129, 151). This kind of faux male bonding talk stems from the familiarity and narrowness of small towns. Further, it is premised on the similarity between the accused and the interrogator: they are both white heterosexual men of the same social class who presume to understand each other's sexuality. For example, Constable Shepherd says, "*I may be married but I'm not dead*" [italics added] (p. 107), suggesting that this "commonsensical" understanding of sexual impulse can be used as a ruse to encourage the individual under arrest to make a confession. Such an intimate and complicit understanding of being able to "play on the same side" in terms of understanding sexual formation and motivation is, semiotically, a form of empathetic discourse. The familiarity and uses of this discourse offer us, I would suggest, deep insights into the culture and politics of racial and sexual violence embedded and embodied in the formation of white heterosexual masculinity.

i) Be on the same side—but claim impartiality

As the trial of Brown and Kindrat proceeds, one of the jurors admits that he knows Brown and had worked with him "five or six—quite a few years ago." Judge Kovatch comments:

> [This] wasn't brought to our attention at the time we were selecting a jury. I've discussed that with all counsel involved. *None of us* [italics added: 2 Crown and 2 defence lawyers and the judge, all middle-aged white men] have any particular concerns about that, but I do thank you for bringing it to our attention. Okay. (R. v. Brown & Kindrat, p. 216)

What seems to be articulated here is an assumption that white men of privilege and power (and common sense) can presume impartiality and need not worry themselves about a conflict of interest in a case like this. Furthermore, in the context of this case, I suggest we hear a privileged sense of "us (white guys) versus them (Indians)."

j) Make accommodations for "us"

Another subtext not directly stated, although discursively available through the transcripts, is the notion that the whole incident is an imposition forced on us, an imposition that inconveniences "us," that is, white society. A dirty little secret, essentially a private matter between three white males and a First Nations female, became a public affair because Melissa told. This is clearly seen in extemporaneous conversations occurring during the two trials about making accommodations for the jurors and the court officials. There are many examples.

The judge says to the all-white jury in the Edmondson trial, "And for any of you who happen to be smokers, we'll certainly make arrangements to accommodate that" (R. v. Edmondson, 2003, p. 198). A dark and contrasting irony here is that the RCMP took a cigarette butt discarded by Melissa's stepfather outside the courthouse to run a DNA test and found a match with the semen found on her underpants. Everyone is not "free" to smoke in this context.

Similarly, Judge Kovatch expresses concern for members of the jury "travelling from places like Hudson Bay and Preeceville" and driving two hours to and from court. "That's it for the day here, ladies and gentlemen. Have a nice weekend. We'll return please, ten o'clock, Monday morning" (R. v. Brown & Kindrat, p. 588). Again, several values associated with patriarchy are privileged in the following quote from the judge:

> . . . my distinct preference would be to have the jury out of here in very good time . . . because some of them are driving several hours and the young lady, in particular, has a young family at home. (R. v. Edmondson, p. 359)

k) Feel imposed upon

At the trial of Brown and Kindrat, Crown Prosecutor Parker, in examining the (white) owner of the bar in the town of Mistatim says, "And you never thought that sale [of beer] would lead to this?" Parker suggests it is uncanny that such an apparently simple transaction would lead to two trials for sexual assault. The judge interjects, however, suggesting that the owner could not have predicted the sale of beer would lead to "repeated trips to Melfort?" and the owner answers, "Right" (R. v. Brown & Kindrat, p. 338). Again the court turns the assault trial into an imposition on the privilege of a white entrepreneur who has better things to do and a woman who wouldn't serve them because it was past closing time, but who did sell "the boys" (as she, too, referred to them) off-sale beer and sent them on their way. It was hunting season and Melissa is fair game for a gangbang, but the owner of the bar says defensively, "They came in a clump and they left in a clump and I didn't know which boy was which" (R. v. Brown & Kindrat, p. 341).

It is not only the language of the court that signals cultural, class and racial divides; the signals are also found in the details of the lives that are privileged. The court system and the homes of most of the lawyers are based in urban centres at least two hours' drive away, such as Saskatoon, and not in small towns like Melfort, the site of the trials. Defence counsel Eisner says, "*we* [italics added] wanted to leave early Friday" (R. v. Brown & Kindrat, p. 400). And defence counsel Brayford says on another day, "for personal reasons I don't want to sit tomorrow afternoon . . . *I would really like to get back* [emphasis added: back to normal?] to go to a graduation, kind of a little concert tomorrow afternoon" (R. v. Brown & Kindrat, p. 529). And Crown Prosecutor Parker adds that he has a boy in grade 6 and there is an end of school year ceremony that he, too, would like to attend. The priorities of the officers of the court take precedence over those of the complainant and the three accused.

l) Don't waste our time

Melissa speaks haltingly and very softly; the amplification system is anti-quated; the court has trouble hearing her, and a frustrated Crown prosecutor, Parker, attempting to build a case against the accused men, says "So could you just answer the question please, *in fairness to all the people who are here and waiting*" [emphasis added] (R. v. Brown & Kindrat, p. 395). The ironic impli-cation is that, in spite of much deference, Melissa is still being unreasonable and uncooperative.

m) Play by the rules

Another example of this unconscious but presumed sense of privilege arises when, at the sentencing of Dean Edmondson, 53 individual "letters from var-ious members of the community, including his family members" are submitted by the defence to demonstrate "that his family and friends are all supportive of him, supportive of his character, supportive of his honesty, supportive of his . . . life in the community" (R. v. Edmondson, p. 789). Embedded in these let-ters is the idea that you "can have your cake and eat it, too," that is, you can commit a crime of sexual assault and be found guilty of it, but still somehow "deserve" leniency because your family and community support you. This is a culture that privileges a particular kind of family-value literacy. Letter writing "proves" identity; as a young, white, male heterosexual, you are deemed to be an individual of worth.

In stark contrast to this are the confessed literacy levels of Melissa's family. Her stepfather yells out from the back of the court that he can't read. Her mother says, "but like I can read, but I don't understand things very good." These comments are provoked by the lawyers for Brown and Kindrat insinuat-ing that the family filed a "suit [that] made claim for money against these three [accused] men" (R. v. Brown & Kindrat, p. 325–326). Ironically, however, it turns out that it was the lawyer who approached the family about filing a lawsuit, a lawyer not from the First Nations community, but a white lawyer whose priv-ileged position allows him easy access to the distress of others.

n) Don't be intimidated

Contrast Edmondson's letters of support with the time Melissa's supporters staged a demonstration outside the courthouse as the Edmondson trial was winding down. Complete with Aboriginal drummers and singers, such support is interpreted by the court as a form of harassment and intimidation, a political and public response, as opposed to a personal or private and, hence, a more appropriate response. Defence counsel Hugh Harradence, referring to the protest outside the court, says, "I believe that was just a coincidence and I do not believe that anyone would . . . try to affect the outcome of a trial by having a demonstration. They must have been doing something else." Calling the demonstration a "spectacle," counsel for Kindrat is quoted as being "confounded" as to how "the acts of his client could be [construed as] racially motivated. Nothing can be further from the truth" (Canadian Press, 2003). Such dissembling may be common for lawyers in and around courthouses, but it is also indicative of a larger force operating in the narratives of white privilege. Thomas DiPiero (2002) calls this force "believing is seeing" (p. 99). I would suggest that this is precisely how cultural and socio-economic differences are racialized here in Saskatchewan. At one point, Harradence says, "If I have to raise my voice over the din outside I will" (R. v. Edmondson, Final Arguments, p. 36), and in his instructions to the jury, Judge Kovatch adds: "We will not be influenced by public opinion or demonstrations or ceremonies of one kind or another that may take place outside the courtroom" (R. v. Edmondson, Summation, p. 48).

o) Use words as weapons

Perhaps nowhere but in a courtroom or a classroom do we see so clearly how formal education defines class and culture and how this definition splits along a racial line. White lawyers are able to use their words as weapons to create a racial divide. Condescension masked as honeyed politeness is evident in the words of Kindrat's lawyer as he addresses Melissa's mother using an antiquated Victorian trope: "Mrs. Caslain, my name is Stuart Eisner. *I won't impose on you long*" (italics added, R. v. Brown & Kindrat, p. 313). Then Edmondson's lawyer says to Melissa's mother, "I take it Ma'am, on other occasions prior to September 30, 2001, when Melissa had ran [*sic*] away, you had phoned the police for assistance in locating her." In light of the fact that she is unlikely to ever have been addressed as "Ma'am" before, Melissa's mother simply says, "What does that mean?" (R. v. Brown & Kindrat, p. 310). Later, defence lawyer Mark Brayford's cross-examination of Melissa's mother is insulting and demeaning: "And I take it the reason that you reported [the car gone] to the police as a theft was—is just an indication of your inability to deal with her [Melissa] without the police's help?" Again, Mrs. Caslain responds, "What's that supposed to mean?" But Brayford won't be stopped. "So that's why you wanted the criminal justice to help to try and provide appropriate discipline, not because you wanted her punished." And Melissa's mother can only reply, "I don't know" (R. v. Brown & Kindrat, p. 323).

p) Use a range of discourses

Behind the public and obviously theatrical forum of the court, out of earshot of the jury, the public and the media, when the lawyers and the judge get together to discuss procedure, their language becomes suddenly much more intimate and colloquial. We overhear how revealing the conversation of privileged insiders is:

> Gentlemen, I've tried to put together in very rough form a draft decision tree, which has caused me no end of problems, but I'd appreciate if you'd

take a quick look at that and *we'll see if we're on all fours here,* [italics added] if you want something like that put to the jury, if it's even correct. (R. v. Brown & Kindrat, p. 716)

Similarly, while deliberating about sentencing, the judge says, "like we've got a 12 year old girl with three guys with her pants off outside of a vehicle in the country" (R. v. Edmondson, p. 779). Now we are talking.

Sometimes this lower register slips through into the courtroom. In cross-examining the owner of the home where the men dropped off Melissa, Harradence says crudely, "so you phoned the police wanting someone *to take her off your hands*" [italics added] (R. v. Brown & Kindrat, p. 587). During the Edmondson trial, Harradence uses slang that demeans the medical witness and the complainant: "Ma'am, I understand that you—it was your observation that this *girl had—had some alcohol on board* [italics added] (R. v. Edmondson, p. 37). Such a lack of sensitivity to the difference between the formal and informal language of the court is in itself an acknowledgement of "owning" the space.

q) Excuse the boys their booze

Saskatchewan's culture of white male privilege also excuses alcohol and privileges the normative ideal of heterosexual sexuality. Both concepts serve to trivialize the crime in question. Against all legal precedent, the judge comments, "I think it's a significant factor from a sentencing perspective whether or not there was penetration in some form" (R. v. Edmondson, p. 796). He also says, in sentencing Edmondson, "I am *satisfied* [italics added: satisfied because lack of penetration constitutes a "legitimate out"?] that alcohol played a very significant role in the offence" (R. v. Edmondson, Sentencing, p. 16). In Lacanian terms, the Phallus (symbolically, the Court) has to protect and excuse the Penis (the "little pricks"), as I have referred to the Tisdale "boys" elsewhere (McNinch, 2008).

r) Acknowledge racialized fear

Behind white privilege we see signs of panic in the pleas for mercy when Edmondson's lawyer argues that jail time is inappropriate for his client. "He is petrified of going to jail. He—it keeps him up at night" (R v. Edmondson, p. 782):

> I say with the greatest of respect and the greatest of candour, to send this accused to any kind of jail facility in Saskatchewan could, at the very least, is going to make this accused's life extremely difficult if not endangered, and, I ask myself to what end? (R. v. Edmondson, p. 791)

Without daring to or having to spell it out specifically, the lawyer is identifying a racialized fear: 70 percent of the male prison population in Saskatchewan is Aboriginal, and Edmondson knows what some of those men would do to someone who assaults a 12-year-old Aboriginal girl. In this sense, the justice system can be seen to be protecting the white assailant rather than the Aboriginal complainant.

s) Privilege the Protestant work ethic

The rationale for a conditional sentence for Dean Edmondson (two years to be served and monitored in his home community) also reveals the values that white patriarchy privileges—values grounded in white settler identity and culture. This rationale includes the testimony that Edmondson is "steadily employed" and has "a very supportive family," as well as the 53 letters of support that confirm "that he's not a risk in the community" (R. v. Edmondson, Sentencing, pp. 16–17). Judge Kovatch privileges the Protestant work ethic to save Edmondson from the "natural" justice that would be meted out in prison:

> . . . like the whole purpose of it [house arrest] is, or part of the purpose of it, is to encourage Mr. Edmondson to maintain his employment. I'm assuming that the supervisor will exempt him from his home for purposes of his employment. (R. v. Edmondson, Sentencing, p. 26)

This is the way the culture of whiteness becomes racialized—not in itself, but in an unstated but implied comparison to and fear of the "Other." This privileging of a white man working off his sexual crime contrasts starkly to a backdrop of devastatingly high unemployment figures for Aboriginal peoples in this province, especially on reserves. Indeed, Edmondson's sentence, complete with 200 hours of community service, can be seen to bolster the concept of a white citizenship grounded in productivity, in contrast, *sotto voce,* to the stereotype of the "lazy" Indian seeking a handout.

t) Privileging white space and, hence, whiteness itself

The defence lawyers remind the judge that this girl was picked up on the steps of a bar, not a school. When he is speaking *in camera* with the lawyers, Judge Kovatch comes closest to exposing the nature of the race and culture divide in this province:

> [If] this was a young girl going from volley-ball practise after school or something and hopped into the car with three guys, it would be a *wickedly different situation* [italics added], in my estimation. Like I think the complainant's background here is obviously a significant factor, at least from my perspective. (R. v. Edmondson, p. 784)

It is revealing to note that the judge has never called Melissa "a young girl" in front of the jury, only "Ms." Demonizing Melissa's "otherness" in this instance is effected by the language of the court, not by the defendants.

PART E: CONCLUSION

These 20 discursive strategies outlined in some detail above depend entirely on there being an outside "other" who "the boys" most avowedly are not. What they offer instead is a flawed white masculinity that is, nevertheless, dominant and excusable, no matter how it is performed. It is the necessity and disavowal of the "other" that makes "sense" of these defensive strategies.

No wonder that the Native Women's Association of Canada (NWAC) intervened several times in this case in 2004 to protest in the strongest terms the outcomes of both trials. Making more than three dozen salient points grounded in legal precedents and constitutional rulings, Mary Eberts, counsel for NWAC, concluded:

> While all women are vulnerable to sexual assault, certain women are more vulnerable because they suffer additional types of discrimination on the basis of, among other things, race, age, disability, or economic status. Sexual assault is an abuse of power, and women who have, or are perceived to have, diminished social status by reason of, for example, race, sexual orientation, disability or poverty are more likely to be victims. Thus, sexual assault is often another incident of oppression along a continuum of disempowering and dehumanizing experiences. (Eberts, 2004)

Melissa in her own defence: "I'm not stupid"

Although the testimony of Melissa is often laboured and difficult, despite the Crown calming and encouraging her—"That was just the wind, Melissa" (R. v. Brown & Kindrat, p. 352)—and gently asking her to explain what happened in her own words, a kind of horrible pall of shame and embarrassment hangs over the transcripts. The very courtroom and the processes of law serve to insult the complainant herself, if only because she must accuse and identify the assailants (Cf. Eribon, 2004). Melissa is often yawning or distracted and can refer only to "my private parts." "I remember waking up with those guys doing stuff to me. . . . I don't like talking about stuff like that," she whispers. "It makes me uncomfortable. . . . It hurts seeing [my] clothes. It reminds me of that day" (R. v. Edmondson, pp. 68–72). She covers her eyes, but eventually identifies Edmondson as "the guy in the box in the white shirt and tie." With a lot of encouragement she finally says, "They were sexually touching me . . . but I can't say it. It makes me feel stupid." Eventually she spells it out on a piece of paper. They were touching her with "their penus [*sic*]" (R. v. Edmondson, pp. 88–91).

At this point Edmondson's lawyer jumps up and says, "Did anyone hear that last answer other than the last words, 'she thinks she's stupid'" (p. 89). The judge ignores Harradence's remark but reminds the jury please to indicate if they can't hear the testimony. Then Harradence says, "I am sorry, My Lord, I was unable to hear, I shouldn't have phrased it that way" (p. 89).

When it is Harradence's turn to cross-examine Melissa, he says to her, "Many people were making suggestions to you as to what happened to you." The exchange continues:

MELISSA: They weren't telling me what to say—
HARRADENCE: No, I
M: because I know what happened. I'm not stupid.
H: Sorry?
M: I said I know what happened.
H: You said something else?
M: And I'm not stupid.
H: I'm not suggesting that at all, Melissa, not for a second. (R. v. Edmondson, May 21, 2003, p. 14)

Melissa is able to prove her point again later in the cross-examination. Harradence says, "I take it, Melissa, that if you had have thought that you were in any difficulty, you certainly would have asked Mrs. Hill [the bar operator] to use the phone?" Melissa replies, "Yeah, but . . . how would I know that they were going to do that?" (R. v. Edmondson, May 21, 2003, p. 55).

Sexual assault as a trope of colonialism

The charge of the "complainant," Melissa, lamenting her fate, is a potent metaphor for all colonized people at the hands of white settlers. In strictly legal terms, for these three men and this one girl, the Crown must prove: first, that Edmondson, Brown and Kindrat intentionally applied force to Melissa; second, that Melissa did not consent to the force that Edmondson, Brown and Kindrat applied; and, third, that neither Edmondson nor Brown nor Kindrat knew that Melissa Caslain did not consent to the force that they intentionally applied.

If we consider this in its historical, cultural and racial context, the Crown, that is, the Queen's representative, must "prove" that white settlers intentionally applied force to colonized peoples, that the colonized peoples did not consent to the force that the white settlers intentionally applied and that those white settlers knew that the indigenous population did not consent to the force that they intentionally applied. When it is put like this, how else can we comprehend this "private" act of these white "boys" but as a symbol of the ongoing processes of colonization of this country?

Of course, one "official" version of our history is that no force was ever applied and that First Nations people signed treaties of their own accord. But the question of justice cannot be predicated on the past, and, in fact, history proves to be a poor predictor of the outcome of the appeal trials that were eventually held in 2007. Both Brown and Kindrat were again found not guilty. The appeal trials were delayed for more than a year because Jeffrey Brown was involved in a near-fatal motorcycle crash involving alcohol, the rear end of a truck and a high-speed chase by police in May 2006.

Despite this sexual assault being called "so highly unusual" by Judge Kovatch (R. v. Edmondson, Sentencing, p. 17), it must be regarded, unfortunately, as part of the normative structures of our schools, our courts and our society, part of the everyday structures and discourses that are grounded and reified in white privilege. It is not abstract concepts, like poverty or culture or race, that marginalize or oppress us. Rather, as discourse analysis shows, it is in the very ways we embody and enact our being and how we use language both consciously and unconsciously to construct identity that we push other people to the margins and attempt to keep them there. If such discourse does not change, then social equity is not possible because identities as they are lived out will remain static and stuck in the past. The discourse analysis of these court proceedings has argued that we are compelled to bridge these gaps created by our colonial past if our society is ever going to be a place for the Melissa Caslains of this world as much as it is for the Tisdale "boys."

REFERENCES

Amnesty International (2004). *Stolen sisters: discrimination and violence against indigenous women in Canada.* Retrieved June 3, 2005, from <http://www.amnesty.ca/campaigns/sisters_overview.php>

Baldwin, J. (1985). *The price of the ticket: Collected non-fiction, 1948–1985.* New York: St. Martins.

Bourdieu, P. (2001). *Masculine domination.* (R. Nice, Trans.). Stanford CA: Stanford University Press.

Bourdieu, P. (1993). *Sociology in question.* (R. Nice, Trans.). London: Sage.

Canadian Press. (2003, May 30). Sask. man guilty of raping pre-teen native girl. Retrieved March 4, 2005, from <http://www.ctv.ca/servlet/ArticleNews/story/CTVNews/1054327854361_210?s_name>

Crenshaw, K., & Peller, G. (1993). Reel time/Real justice. In R. Gooding-Williams (Ed.), *Reading Rodney King, reading urban uprising* (pp. 56–70). New York: Routledge.

Chunn, D. E., & Lacombe D. (Eds.). (2000). *Law as a gendering practice.* Don Mills ON: Oxford University Press.

DiPiero, T. (2002). *White men aren't.* Durham NC: Duke University Press.

Dubinsky, K., & Givertz, A. (1999). 'It was only a matter of passion': Masculinity and sexual danger. In K. McPherson, C. Morgan, and N. Forestell (Eds.), *Gendered pasts: Historical essays in femininity and masculinity in Canada* (pp. 65–79). Toronto: University of Toronto Press.

Eberts, M. (2004). Factum for the Intervener. Native Women's Association of Canada. November 19, 2004. Retrieved October 14, 2005, from www.nwac-hq.org/Edmondson NWAC.pdf

Eribon, D. (2004). *Insult and the making of the gay self.* (M. Lucey, Trans.). London: Duke University Press.

Fairclough, N. (2006). *Language and globalization.* London; New York: Routledge.

Fairclough, N. (1993). *Discourse and social change.* Oxford: Polity Press.

Fairclough, N. (1989). *Language and power.* London; New York: Longman.

Janoff, D.V. (2005). *Pink blood: Homophobic violence in Canada.* Toronto: University of Toronto Press.

Kumashiro, K. K. (2004). *Against common sense: Teaching and learning toward social justice.* New York: Routledge & Falmer.

Lacan, J. (1977). *Écrits.* (A. Sheridan, Trans.). New York: Norton.

Mac an Ghaill, M. (1994). *The making of men: Masculinities, sexualities and schooling.* Buckingham: Open University Press.

Martino, W., & Pallotta-Chiarolli, M. (Eds.). (2003). *So what's a boy? Addressing issues of masculinity and schooling.* Maidenhead UK: Open University Press.

Martino, W., & Meyenn, B. (Eds.). (2001). *What about the boys: Issues of masculinity in schools.* Buckingham UK: Open University Press.

McNinch, J. (2008). Queer eye on straight youth: Homoerotics and racial violence in the narrative discourse of white settler masculinity. *Journal of LGBT Youth, 5*(2), 87–108.

Messerschmidt, J. W. (2000). *Nine lives: Adolescent masculinities, the body, and violence.* Boulder, CO: Westview Press.

Messerschmidt, J. W. (1997). *Crime as structure action: Gender, race, class, and crime in the making.* Thousand Oaks, CA: Sage Publications.

Mulvey, L. (1989). *Visual and other pleasures.* Bloomington: University of Indiana Press.

Mulvey, L. (1988). Visual pleasure and narrative cinema. In C. Penley (Ed.), *Feminism and film theory* (pp. 57–68). New York: Routledge.

Nelson, D. D. (1998). *National manhood: Capitalist citizenship and the imagined fraternity of white men.* Durham NC: Duke University Press.

Pinar, W. F. (2001). *The gender of racial politics and violence in America: Lynching, prison rape, and the crisis of masculinity.* New York: Peter Lang.

Phillips, B. (2004). The rape of mother earth in 17th century English poetry: An ecofeminist interpretation. *Atlantis, 26*(1), 49–60.

Pronger, B. (2002). *Body fascism: Salvation in the technology of physical fitness.* Toronto: University of Toronto Press.

Pronger, B. (1990). *The arena of masculinity.* Toronto: Summerhill Press.

Razack, S. H. (2002). Gendered racial violence and spatialized justice: The murder of Pamela George. In S.H. Razack (Ed.), *Race, space and the law: Unmapping a white settler society* (pp. 121–156). Toronto: Between the Lines Press.

Razack, S. H. (1998). *Looking white people in the eye: Gender, race, and culture in courtrooms and classrooms.* Toronto: University of Toronto Press.

Regina v. Edmondson. (2003). Transcript of proceedings at trial (6 volumes). Court of Queen's Bench for Saskatchewan (Melfort), 1358/02. CA# 673 & 703.

Regina v. Brown & Kindrat. (2003). Transcript of proceedings at trial (3 volumes). Court of Queen's Bench for Saskatchewan (Melfort), 1357. CA# 687.

Sedgwick, E. K. (1985). *Between men: English literature and male homosocial desire.* New York: Columbia University Press.

Wadham, B. (2002). What does the white man want? White masculinities and Aboriginal reconciliation. In S. Pearce and V. Muller (Eds.), *Manning the next millennium: Studies in masculinities* (pp. 215–223). Bentley Australia: Black Swan Press.

Winans, A. (2005). Local pedagogies and race: Interrogating white safety in the rural classroom. *College English, 67*(3), 253–273.

CONTRIBUTORS

Frédéric Dupré obtained a master's degree in anthropology from Laval University (1998) and is currently a PH.D. candidate at the University of Regina, Saskatchewan, where he holds the position of research coordinator of the *Institut français*. For his research, Dupré examines the University of Regina as a case study of the integration of national minority units into higher educational institutions. His unique position as both a researcher and paid staff affords Dupré crucial insight into his areas of study, as well as presenting ethical and ethnographical challenges.

Joyce Green is professor of political science at the University of Regina. Her research interests focus both on Aboriginal-settler relations and the possibility of decolonization in Canada and on a transformative ecology of relationship with place, epitomized by many traditional Aboriginal conceptions of land and place. She is the editor of *Making Space for Indigenous Feminism* (Fernwood and Zed Books, 2008) and the author of "Self-determination, Citizenship, and Federalism: Indigenous and Canadian Palimpsest," in *Reconfiguring Aboriginal-State Relations* (Michael Murphy, Ed.), Institute of Intergovernmental Relations, School of Policy Studies, Queen's University, 2005.

Donna Jeffery is associate professor in the School of Social Work at the University of Victoria, Canada. Her research focuses on professional education and knowledge production. She holds a SSHRC grant, with Jennifer J. Nelson, examining professional helping encounters.

James McNinch is the Dean of the Faculty of Education at the University of Regina. He is the co-editor of and contributing author to *I Could Not Speak My Heart: Education and Social Justice for Gay and Lesbian Youth* (Canadian Plains Research Center, 2004). Current research interests include Aboriginal youth who self-identify as Two-Spirit. He serves on the steering committee responsible for bringing *Camp fYrefly*, a summer camp for sexual minority/gender variant youth, to Saskatchewan.

Jennifer J. Nelson is co-founder of Cardinal Consultants, which provides research services in healthcare, law, education and social sciences to professional and government agencies. She is assistant professor in the Department of Public Health Sciences, University of Toronto, where she holds a SSHRC grant examining professional helping encounters.

Alison Sammel teaches at the School of Education and Professional Studies at Griffith University on the Gold Coast of Australia and researches in the fields of postmodern science education and diversity pedagogies.

Carol Schick is associate professor at the Faculty of Education at the University of Regina. She is involved in anti-oppressive education in teacher preparation programs and uses feminist, critical race theories and whiteness studies to live and work through tensions of post-colonial education at all levels of schooling as found on the Canadian prairies.

Andrea Smith is assistant professor of media/cultural studies at University of California Riverside. She is the author of *Native Americans and the Christian Right: The Gendered Politics of Unlikely Alliances* (Duke, 2008) and *Conquest: Sexual Violence and American Indian Genocide* (South End Press, 2005). Through Incite!, she is also editor of *The Revolution Will Not Be Funded: Beyond the Non-Profit Industrial Complex* (South End Press, 2007). Smith is a co-founder of Incite! Women of Color Against Violence and the Boarding School Healing Project.

Andrea Sterzuk holds a PH.D. in second language education from McGill University and is an assistant professor of language and literacies education in the Faculty of Education at the University of Regina. Her research interests include minority language education, multiliteracies, educator language bias and education in post-colonial contexts.

INDEX

A

Aaronson, D., 29; *Childhood bilingualism: Aspects of linguistic, cognitive, and social development,* 13

Abd-Khalick, F., 54, 62

Abele, Frances, 147

Abell, S.K., 50, 62

Abelson, J., 31

Aboriginal education, 39–40, 43, 114, 117. *see also* First Nations education; residential schools

Aboriginal Education Program Advisory Committee, 114

Aboriginal gangs, xx, 145–46

Aboriginal lands: claim settlements of, 143; colonial occupation of, 140

Aboriginal languages and education: The Canadian experience, 12

Aboriginal men: as ejected from white urban society, 138

Aboriginal peoples, 33, 113, 117, 132, 134, 141, 146–47; and colonization, 101; cultural practices of, 121; and health, 101, 136; high unemployment of, 171; marginalization of, 136; and media, 136; and police service, 129, 131, 137; and poverty, 113; and racism, 135, 140, 142; subordination of, 140, 142; and universities, 136. *see also* First Nations peoples; indigenous peoples

Aboriginal treaties, 38, 173; rights of, 33, 38–39

Aboriginal women: as missing, 139; and prostitution, 138

About face, 88

Abrums, M.E., 22, 29

academy. *see* universities

Achieving scientific literacy: From purposes to practices, 63

Action Plan 2000–2005, 114

Activist scholarship: Antiracism, feminism, and social change, 79

Adair, c.e., 31

Adam, B.A., 130, 147

Against common sense: Teaching and learning toward social justice, 78, 175

ageism: and science education, 49, 55

Aguirre, J.M., 50, 62

Ahenakew, Chief, 39

Ahmed, Sara, 65–67, 76–77, 99, 124–25; *The cultural politics of emotion,* 126; *Strange encounters: Embodied others in postcoloniality,* 78, 106

Al-Krenawi, A.: *Multicultural social work in Canada: Working with diverse ethno-racial communities,* 32, 110

Allen, David, 20, 25, 29, 71, 78

Althusser, Louis, 82; *Lenin and philosophy and other essays,* 88

Altman, R., 21, 94; *Waking up/fighting back: The politics of breast cancer,* 29, 106

American Indian English, 12

American Indian Movement, 86

Amnesty International Canada (AIC), 2, 154; *Stolen sisters: discrimination and violence against indigenous women in Canada,* 174; *Without discrimination: The fundamental right of all Canadians to human rights protection,* 11

Ananeh-Firempong, O., 29, 106

Anderson, Brenda, Dr., 139

Anderson, D., 12

Anderson, E., 110

Anderson, J.M.: *Cross-cultural caring: A handbook for health professionals in Western Canada,* 110

Angela Davis: An autobiography, 88

Anti-discrimination committee concludes consideration of Canada's reports on compliance with international convention, 12

anti-oppressive pedagogies, 112, 115–116, 119, 121, 125

anti-oppressive practice (AOP), 100

anti-racist pedagogy, 111–12, 119, 123

Anti-racist science teaching, 63–64

Anti-racist social work: A challenge for white practitioners and educators, 107

anti-violence movement, 80, 87

Arena of masculinity, The, 175

Arnason, J., 64

Art of critical pedagogy: Possibilities for moving from theory to practice in urban schools, The, xxi

As one who serves: The making of the University of Regina, 47

Association of Canadian Colleges and Universities, 40

Association of Métis and Non-Status Indians of Saskatchewan, 40

Asti, J., 95; *A spiritual journey through breast cancer: Strength for today, hope for tomorrow,* 106

autobiography, critical, 77

The body of this book is set in ADOBE CASLON. The Englishman William Caslon punchcut many roman, italic, and non-Latin typefaces from 1720 until his death in 1766. At that time most types were being imported to England from Dutch sources, so Caslon was influenced by the characteristics of Dutch types. He did, however, achieve a level of craft that enabled his recognition as the first great English punchcutter. Caslon's roman became so popular that it was known as the script of kings, although on the other side of the political spectrum (and the ocean), the Americans used it for their Declaration of Independence in 1776. The original Caslon specimen sheets and punches have long provided a fertile source for the range of types bearing his name.

Carol Twombly designed this Caslon revival for Adobe in 1990, after studying Caslon's own specimen sheets from the mid-eighteenth century. This elegant version is quite true to the source, and has been optimized for the demands of digital design and printing. *Adobe Caslon™* makes an excellent text font and includes just about everything needed by the discriminating typographer: small caps, oldstyle figures, swash letters, alternates, ligatures, expert characters, central European characters, and a plethora of period ornaments.

The titles and accents in the book are set in SWISS 721. It was designed in 1982 by Bitstream Inc., and is a variation of Helvetica.